Lecture Notes in Computer Science   9701

Commenced Publication in 1973
Founding and Former Series Editors:
Gerhard Goos, Juris Hartmanis, and Jan van Leeuwen

More information about this series at http://www.springer.com/series/7411

Rémi Badonnel · Robert Koch
Aiko Pras · Martin Drašar
Burkhard Stiller (Eds.)

Management and Security in the Age of Hyperconnectivity

10th IFIP WG 6.6 International Conference
on Autonomous Infrastructure, Management, and Security, AIMS 2016
Munich, Germany, June 20–23, 2016
Proceedings

 Springer

Editors
Rémi Badonnel
LORIA - Inria
Vandoeuvre-lès-Nancy
France

Martin Drašar
Masaryk University
Brno
Czech Republic

Robert Koch
Universität der Bundeswehr
Neubiberg
Germany

Burkhard Stiller
University of Zürich
Zürich
Switzerland

Aiko Pras
University of Twente
Enschede
The Netherlands

ISSN 0302-9743   ISSN 1611-3349   (electronic)
Lecture Notes in Computer Science
ISBN 978-3-319-39813-6   ISBN 978-3-319-39814-3   (eBook)
DOI 10.1007/978-3-319-39814-3

Library of Congress Control Number: 2016939999

LNCS Sublibrary: SL5 – Computer Communication Networks and Telecommunications

Printed on acid-free paper

This Springer imprint is published by Springer Nature
The registered company is Springer International Publishing AG Switzerland

Preface

The International Conference on Autonomous Infrastructure, Management, and Security (AIMS 2016) is a single-track event integrating regular conference paper sessions, tutorials, keynotes, and a PhD student workshop into a highly interactive event. Within the network and service management community, AIMS is focused on PhD students and young researchers. One of the key goals of AIMS is to provide early-stage researchers with constructive feedback by senior scientists and give them the possibility to grow in the research community by means of targeted lab sessions on technical and educational aspects of their research activity. This focus on early-stage researchers is immediately observable in the program, featuring a high number of educational sessions and PhD sessions, where young PhD students present their research.

AIMS 2016 — which took place during June 20–23, 2016, in Neubiberg, Germany, and was hosted by the Universität der Bundeswehr München — was the tenth edition of a conference series on management and security aspects of distributed and autonomous systems. It followed the established tradition of an unusually vivid and interactive conference series, after successful events in Ghent, Belgium in 2015, Brno, Czech Republic in 2014, Barcelona, Spain in 2013, Luxembourg, Luxembourg in 2012, Nancy, France in 2011, Zürich, Switzerland in 2010, Enschede, The Netherlands in 2009, Bremen, Germany in 2008, and Oslo, Norway in 2007.

AIMS 2016 focused on management and security in the age of hyperconnectivity. New paradigms, smart and fully distributed algorithms, and large-scale virtualization are investigated to design scalable and resilient frameworks able to deal with more complex, more dynamic and hyperconnected environments. This theme was addressed in the technical program with papers related to monitoring, configuration, and security in areas from cloud infrastructures to the Internet-of-Things. AIMS 2016 was organized as a 4-day program to encourage the interaction with and the active participation of the audience. The program consisted of technical sessions for the main track and PhD sessions, interleaved with research keynotes, an educational panel, and lab sessions.

The lab sessions offered hands-on experience in network and service management topics and they were organized in on-site labs preceded by short tutorial-style teaching sessions. The first lab session addressed big data analysis for the Domain Name System (DNS), explaining how tracking DNS changes based on measurements may provide valuable information about the evolution of the Internet. The other lab sessions were centered on traffic mining for flow-based forensic and network troubleshooting, using Tranalyzer, a lightweight flow generator and packet analyzer designed for practitioners and researchers. In line with its educational mission, this year the conference also included an educational panel, which was chaired by Daphné Tuncer and Marinos Charalambides (University College London, UK) on "Experiences with MOOCs and Flipped Classrooms." Additionally, AIMS 2016 featured two research keynotes: one on "Today's Cyber Security Threats and Challenges for Telco Providers" by Bernd

Eßer (Telekom CDC, Germany) and one on "Cyber Resilience of Complex Interdependent Infrastructures" by Tobias Kiesling (IABG, Germany).

The technical program consisted of two sessions — covering the topics of autonomic and smart management, and security attacks and defenses — and included seven full papers, which were selected after a thorough reviewing process out of a total of 22 submissions. Each paper received at least three independent reviews. Three papers were also selected for presentation as short papers.

The AIMS PhD workshop is a venue for doctoral students to present and discuss their research ideas, and more importantly to obtain valuable feedback from the AIMS audience about their planned PhD research work. This year, the workshop was structured into two technical sessions covering the management of future networks and security management. All PhD papers included in this volume describe the current state of these investigations, including their clear research problem statements, proposed approaches, and an outline of results achieved so far. A total of nine PhD papers were presented and discussed. These papers were selected after a separate review process out of 21 submissions, while all PhD papers received at least three independent reviews.

The present volume of the *Lecture Notes in Computer Science* series includes all papers presented at AIMS 2016 as defined within the overall final program. It demonstrates again the European scope of this conference series, since most of the accepted papers originate from European research groups. Also, AIMS 2016 proved true to its defined DNA of a conference with a strong educational goal, as indicated by the number of submissions attracted by the PhD Workshop.

The editors would like to thank the many people who helped to make AIMS 2016 such a high-quality and successful event. Firstly, many thanks are extended to all authors who submitted their contributions to AIMS 2016, and to the lab session speakers, namely, Anna Sperotto, Mattijs Jonker, Christian Dietz, Stefan Burschka, and Benoît Dupasquier, and the keynote speakers Bernd Eßer and Tobias Kiesling. The great review work performed by the members of both the AIMS Technical Program Committee and the PhD Student Workshop Committee as well as additional reviewers is highly acknowledged. Thanks are also addressed to Volker Eiseler and Lars Stiemert for setting up and organizing the lab sessions. Additionally, many thanks to the local organizers for handling all the logistics and hosting the AIMS 2016 event.

Finally, the editors would like to express their thanks to Springer, especially Anna Kramer, for the smooth cooperation in finalizing these proceedings. Additionally, special thanks go to the AIMS 2016 supporters, Universität der Bundeswehr München, ITIS, and the European FP7 NoE FLAMINGO under Grant No. 318488.

April 2016

Rémi Badonnel
Robert Koch
Martin Drašar
Aiko Pras

Organization

General Chair AIMS 2016

Gabi Dreo Rodosek   Universität der Bundeswehr München, Germany

Technical Program Committee Co-chairs

Rémi Badonnel   LORIA - Inria, France
Robert Koch   Universität der Bundeswehr München, Germany

PhD Student Workshop Co-chairs

Martin Drašar   Masaryk University, Czech Republic
Aiko Pras   University of Twente, The Netherlands

Labs Co-chairs

Volker Eiseler   Universität der Bundeswehr München, Germany
Lars Stiemert   Universität der Bundeswehr München, Germany

Publications Chair

Burkhard Stiller   University of Zürich, Switzerland

Local Chair

Volker Eiseler   Universität der Bundeswehr München, Germany

AIMS Steering Committee

Guillaume Doyen   Troyes University of Technology, France
Anna Sperotto   University of Twente, The Netherlands
Pavel Čeleda   Masaryk University, Czech Republic
Filip De Turck   Ghent University - iMinds, Belgium
Aiko Pras   University of Twente, The Netherlands
Burkhard Stiller   University of Zürich, Switzerland

Technical Program Committee

Alexander Clemm   Cisco Systems, USA
Alexander Keller   IBM Global Technology Services, USA

Alva L. Couch   Tufts University, USA
Anandha Gopalan   Imperial College London, UK
Anna Sperotto   University of Twente, The Netherlands
Bruno Quoitin   Université de Mons, Belgium
Burkhard Stiller   University of Zürich, Switzerland
Clarissa Marquezan   Huawei Technologies, Germany
Daniele Sgandurra   Imperial College London, UK
Daphné Tuncer   University College of London, UK
David Hausheer   Technical University Darmstadt, Germany
Filip De Turck   Ghent University - iMinds, Belgium
Guillaume Doyen   Troyes University of Technology, France
Henning Sanneck   Nokia Networks, Germany
Isabelle Chrisment   TELECOM Nancy, Université de Lorraine, France
Jan Kořenek   Brno University of Technology, Czech Republic
Jérôme François   Inria Nancy Grand Est, France
Jürgen Schönwälder   Jacobs University Bremen, Germany
Kurt Tutschku   Blekinge Institute of Technology, Sweden
Lisandro Zambenedetti   UFRGS, Brazil
  Granville
Marinos Charalambides   University College London, UK
Martin Barrère   Imperial College London, UK
Martin Drašar   Masaryk University, Czech Republic
Martin Žádník   Brno University of Technology, Czech Republic
Mauro Tortonesi   University of Ferrara, Italy
Michael Menth   University of Tübingen, Germany
Michele Nogueira   Universidade Federal do Parana, Brazil
Michelle Sibilla   Paul Sabatier University, France
Paulo Simoes   University of Coimbra, Portugal
Philippe Owezarski   LAAS-CNRS, France
Piotr Chołda   AGH University of Science and Technology, Poland
Ramin Sadre   Université Catholique de Louvain, Belgium
Rashid Mijumbi   Waterford Institute of Technology, Ireland
Ricardo Schmidt   University of Twente, The Netherlands
Roberto Riggio   CREATE-NET, Italy
Shingo Ata   Osaka City University, Japan
Steven Latré   University of Antwerp - iMinds, Belgium
Thomas Bocek   University of Zürich, Switzerland
Thomas Schaaf   University of Munich (LMU), Germany

PhD Student Workshop Committee

Pavel Čeleda   Masaryk University, Czech Republic
Idilio Drago   Politecnico di Torino, Italy
Gabi Dreo Rodosek   Universität der Bundeswehr München, Germany
Gunnar Karlsson   KTH, Sweden
Abdelkader Lahmadi   University of Lorraine, France

Guy Leduc	University of Liege, Belgium
Emil Lupu	Imperial College London, UK
Edmundo Monteiro	University of Coimbra, Portugal
Corinna Schmitt	University of Zürich, Switzerland
Burkhard Stiller	University of Zürich, Switzerland
Sofie Verbrugge	Ghent University - IMEC - IBBT, Belgium
Jan Vykopal	Masaryk University, Czech Republic

Additional Reviewers

Detailed reviews for papers submitted to AIMS 2016 were performed by the Technical Program Committee as well as the PhD Student Workshop Committee as stated and additionally by the following reviewers:

Filipe Caldeira, Florian Heimgärtner, Michael Höfling, Christian Koch, Muhammad Naseer-ul-Islam, Leonhard Nobach, Luis Rosa

Keynotes and Panel

Keynote 1
Today's Cyber Security Threats
and Challenges for Telco Providers

Bernd Eßer

Telekom Cyber Defense Center (CDC), Deutsche Telekom, Bonn, Germany
EsserB@telekom.de

Abstract. This keynote focuses on the threat landscape and its evolution as seen from a Tier-1 operator's perspective. This includes the development of threats that affect mainly consumers, such as botnets, as well as threats that address primarily organizations.

So called Advanced Persistent Threats (APT) are analyzed in the way offenders usually pursue such attacks. Strategic and operational options to detect and remediate such attacks are discussed. This keynote closes with thoughts on possible future roles of telcos in this threat context.

Keynote 2
Cyber Resilience of Complex Interdependent Infrastructures

Tobias Kiesling

Industrieanlagen Betriebsgesellschaft mbH, IABG, Ottobrunn, Germany
kiesling@iabg.de

Abstract. Most of the critical infrastructures that we utilize in our daily life are quite complex and interdependent on one another. This poses a huge challenge to our understanding with respect to major risks connected to those infrastructures. This is especially true when considering the imminent threat of potential cyber attacks that are generally seen as possible already in our current time.

What we need is a more thorough understanding of cyber-related risks that can guide the implementation of measures to secure the resilience of critical infrastructures. One example for a vulnerable infrastructure is the air traffic system at large, which is an attractive target for cyber attacks due to its importance and prominence. The current system is already vulnerable and the advent of more automation and pervasion of standard IT in the wake of future approaches leads to ever more complex and interconnected systems with an increasing attack surface.

To cope with this situation, we need to follow a resilience-oriented view and utilize suitable methods and tools to achieve understanding of the consequences in potential cyber threat situations. This keynote introduces the notion of cyber operational resilience and shows how this can be applied to the air transport infrastructure as an example of other complex interdependent systems.

Educational Panel
Experiences with MOOCs and Flipped Classrooms

Daphné Tuncer, Marinos Charalambides

University College London, UK
d.tuncer@ee.ucl.ac.uk, marinos.charalambides@ucl.ac.uk

Abstract. Massive Open Online Courses (MOOC) are open access and scalable online higher education courses. MOOCs have been gaining increasing popularity in recent years mainly due to their extended outreach and lack of entry requirements as well as tuition fees. Given their initial success and the interest from the higher education community, they have the potential of becoming an essential part of the education system.

However, due to their online nature they do not follow the traditional teaching paradigm that requires classroom presence and involves direct interaction with the lecturer. In addition, MOOCs can be developed through various platforms and can have different formats. These factors can influence the student learning experience and the future uptake of such courses.

This panel will mainly consist of PhD researchers, that have followed at least one MOOC, who will discuss their personal experience and expectations, and share their insights with the audience. The panel will be structured in three parts. First, the panelists will present their views based on a short questionnaire that will be provided prior to the event. Second, the moderators will ask questions concerning, course integration, interaction with other students/instructor, MOOC format, course customization, and grading systems. Finally, an open discussion with the audience will conclude the panel. The overall objective is to collect valuable feedback of the panelists and potentially the audience, which can be used to suggest changes in current practices and make learning more effective.

Lab Sessions

Lab Session 1
The Internet of Names: Big Data Analysis for DNS

Anna Sperotto[1], Mattijs Jonker[1], Christian Dietz[2]

[1]University of Twente, The Netherlands
[2]Universität der Bundeswehr München, Germany
a.sperotto@utwente.nl, m.jonker@utwente.nl, christian.
dietz@unibw.de

Abstract. The Domain Name System (DNS) is part of the core infrastructure of the Internet. Tracking changes in the DNS, therefore, provide valuable information about the evolution of the Internet. Think about adoption of protocols (e.g., IPv6 and DNSSEC) and applications (e.g., cloud e-mail providers), distribution of content (Web domains), and network security (e.g., botnets).

Since February 2015, the University of Twente, SURFnet, and SIDN run a largescale active measurement of the DNS, which cover the domain names in the .com, .net, and .org zones. Since February 2016, the .nl zone has also been added. In total, our measurement currently queries over 50 % of the DNS name space on a daily basis. The measurement results are stored in an Hadoop cluster for later analysis [1].

The goal of this hands-on tutorial is to familiarize the participants with DNS, DNS measurements, and possible research application. The session will start with a general introduction to the measurement including a few example use cases. Then, we will briefly introduce the participants to a virtualized lab environment, in which they can experiment with the data themselves. The remainder of the session is then spent "hackathon"-style, in groups, each of which will present their experiences and possible findings from the data at the end of the session in a short presentation. The lab environment will contain real data for the Alexa Top 1 Million domains.

Reference

1. van Rijswijk-Deij, R., Jonker, M., Sperotto, A., Pras, A.: The internet of names: a DNS big dataset. In: SIGCOMM 2015 Poster Paper, ACM, London, UK, August 17–21 (2015)

Lab Sessions 2 and 3
Traffic Mining (TM) using Brain
and Tranalyzer

Stefan Burschka, Benoît Dupasquier

RUAG, Switzerland

stefan.burschka@ruag.com, benoit.dupasquier@ruag.com

Abstract. Tranalyzer is a lightweight flow generator and packet analyzer designed for practitioners and researchers [1]. Special value is set to simplicity, performance, and scalability. It extends netflow functionality and supports the analysis in processing ultra large packet dumps. It supports the drill down process to the very flow of interest, which can be analyzed in depth by tcpdump or wireshark. It provides support for assessing and generating key parameters and statistics from IP traces either being live-captured from ethernet interfaces or pcap files, in the context of flow forensics and network troubleshooting.

These lab sessions are literally defined by the title, Traffic Mining (TM) using your brain and Tranalyzer. Participants will do a hands-on job of analysists trying to find anomalies in real IP traffic.

After a short introduction to the most important IP protocols and header features, they will get familiar with Tranalyzer's main concepts, such as configuration and compilation operations, most important plugins including configuration constants, flows and global reports, and how to write their own plugins in C. They will experiment it in groups or alone on several pcaps traffic captures through different practical exercises. They might get stuck in a foxhole and have to learn how to dig themselves out. Nothing is like it initially seems, or maybe it is. It is addressed to everybody who is willing to learn further about IP traffic and the way of flow based traffic mining.

Reference

1. Opensource Version of Tranalyzer2-0.5.8 http://sourceforge.net/projects/tranalyzer/

Contents

PhD Student Workshop — Security Management

Short Papers — Methods for Management and Security

Autonomic and Smart Management

Network Element Stability Aware Method for Verifying Configuration Changes in Mobile Communication Networks

Janne Ali-Tolppa[1(✉)] and Tsvetko Tsvetkov[2(✉)]

[1] Nokia Bell Labs, Munich, Germany
janne.ali-tolppa@nokia.com
[2] Department of Computer Science,
Technische Universität München, Munich, Germany
tsvetko.tsvetkov@in.tum.de

Abstract. Automatic Configuration Management (CM) parameter change assessment, the so-called Self-Organizing Network (SON) verification, is an important enabler for stable and high-quality modern SONs. However, it also presents a new set of challenges. While improving network stability and resolving unexpected conflicts caused by parallel configuration changes, the SON verification can also make the network optimization less dynamic. This flexibility can be desirable, especially when the network is in an unstable state. One such example is Network Element (NE) commissioning, after which it may be preferable for the SON functions to explore the configuration space more freely in order to find the optimal configuration. On the other hand, at some point in time, the NE has to converge to a stable configuration.

To address these challenges, we introduce in this paper the concept of Network Element Virtual Temperature (NEVT), which indicates the state of stability of a NE, and propose how it can be utilized to optimize the verification process. This approach is evaluated in a simulated environment and compared to other verification mechanisms. The results show that the proposed method allows the network to better react to changes without sacrificing on its stability.

1 Introduction

The Self-Organizing Network (SON) concept is a key enabler for managing the complex modern networks. It covers the tasks of self-configuration, self-optimization and self-healing [8]. A SON-enabled network is managed by a set of autonomous SON functions performing specific network management tasks. The functions are designed as control loops, which monitor Performance Management (PM) and Fault Management (FM) data, and based on their goals configure the Configuration Management (CM) parameters. For example, the Coverage and Capacity Optimization (CCO) function has been developed to optimize the coverage within a cell by changing the antenna tilt or the transmission power.

© IFIP International Federation for Information Processing 2016
R. Badonnel et al. (Eds.): AIMS 2016, LNCS 9701, pp. 3–15, 2016.
DOI: 10.1007/978-3-319-39814-3_1

However, in a complex system the functions may have unexpected side-effects. Especially, when several SON function instances and human operators are operating independently in parallel. For this reason, policy-based pre-action coordination is applied to avoid known conflicts between SON function instances [3,12]. Such conflicts may include, for example, two SON function instances changing the same CM parameters (lost update problem) or one function influencing the input data of another (race condition), causing it to base its decisions on invalid data. However, pre-action coordination can only prevent potential conflicts that are known beforehand. As a consequence, the concept of SON verification has been developed [5,7,17]. It automatically verifies the impact of configuration changes and, in case a degradation is detected, returns the network to the last known stable configuration by performing a rollback of the changes.

The verification process introduces its own challenges too, however. While it makes the network more stable by quickly rectifying degradations, it can also make the system less dynamic by preventing optimization paths that may lead to a minor transient decrease in performance. A related concrete problem is the configuration of the verification observation window length. If it is too short, the verification mechanism may try to rollback short, transient performance degradations, and therefore generate false positive undo requests. On the other hand, if the observation window is configured long, it makes the verification cycle slower, increases the number of parallel and potentially conflicting verification operations and makes determining the CM change causing a degradation more difficult.

In this paper, we propose an approach that mitigates these issues. We introduce the concept of Network Element Virtual Temperature (NEVT), which indicates the state of stability of a Network Element (NE). The NEs with high NEVT are considered unstable and therefore, for example, more likely to accept optimization steps that lead to minor transient degradations. Similarly, as the NEs becomes more stable, i.e. there are no further changes in the NE as the time passes, NEVT "cools down" and the NE becomes less likely to accept major changes. Utilizing the NEVT, the verification process can give the SON functions the necessary freedom when needed, but ensure that the optimization will converge to a stable, well-performing configuration.

2   The Verification Process

The purpose of the SON verification is to automatically verify CM changes done in the network, either by SON functions or human operators, and in case a degradation is detected, return the network back to a stable configuration by performing a rollback, also known as an undo operation. The automatic verification process operates in three phases: (1) it divides the network into verification areas according to the CM changes, (2) observes each area during the so-called *observation window* and (3) in case a degradation is detected, marks the changes for an undo that are most likely responsible for it.

Composition of Verification Areas. A verification area consists of the recon-figured cell, also called the *target cell*, and a set of cells impacted by the CM change(s), also referred to as the *target extension set* [16]. The extension set is often based on the neighbor relations of the target cell. Furthermore, if we have SON function activities in the network, we may define the verification area as the combined impact areas [2] of the SON functions that are verified in a given verification operation. We may also enlarge a verification area based on its loca-tion [6], e.g., more cells are added if they are part of known trouble spots or dense traffic.

Observation Window. After the verification area has been determined, the verification process monitors the performance of the area after the CM changes have been applied. It does this by monitoring the set of Key Performance Indi-cators (KPIs) selected to be used in verification. The assessment of the KPIs is usually done by profiling [9] the network behavior, which requires analyzing the network performance indicators and specifying how the network should typically behave and how it has behaved before and after the changes.

Generating CM Undo Requests. At the end of the observation window the verification process calculates a *verification score* for the verified changes. This score can be compared to an *acceptance threshold*. If the score is higher than the threshold, the changes are accepted, otherwise the process attempts to return the degraded verification areas to a known previous stable configu-ration by performing an automatic CM undo [17]. It determines, which CM changes have an overlapping impact areas with the verification area, and can thus have contributed to the degradation, and creates an undo request for them. Several methods have been developed to optimize the selection of undo areas and requests [15].

3   Challenges

Many SON functions require not only one step, but several, during which they observe whether they have moved closer towards achieving their goal. In the process, the functions may induce a transient performance decrease in the net-work. For instance, the CCO function monitors the impact of its last deployed antenna tilt or transmission power changes, and adjusts them if required [8]. The same applies also to the combined, and often unpredicted, effects of several independent SON function instances running in parallel. They might introduce a transient degradation, to which the functions react and adapt to a more optimal configuration.

This poses a problem to the SON verification. Namely, how long should the verification observation window be? If the observation window is made too short, there is a risk that the true impact of the CM changes is not yet visible in the network. Changes are rolled back, although they are just transient and the SON

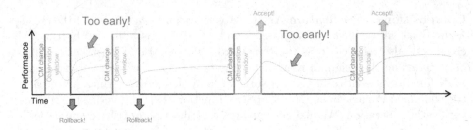

Fig. 1. The problem of choosing the correct observation window length

functions would adapt to the situation in the upcoming rounds. In the same manner, the opposite may happen and changes are accepted before the negative impacts show in the monitored KPI. Figure 1 depicts this problem.

On the other hand, a long observation window is not desirable, because it means a longer verification cycle, which can block other SON functions from executing. Also, the longer observation window, the more difficult it becomes to find out which changes have actually caused a degradation, especially if there are several parallel changes made by more than one SON function instances. Yet one more problem with a long observation window is that as it makes the verification process longer, it increases the number of parallel verification operations, which can lead to conflicts between them [15]. This can be problematic, especially in more complex networks.

The CM scoring method proposed in [10] answers these questions partly. It introduces a mechanism that assesses the changes made by SON functions over a certain period of time and categorizes their behavior by assigning them to a certain zone. For example, changes leading to a drop in performance are assigned to a so-called red zone. The difficulty, however, is choosing the correct length of the required time period. Once again we would like to keep the observation window as short as possible, but if it is too short, the scoring mechanism does not work anymore.

4   Concept

To address the problems stated in Sect. 3, we propose a method to incorporate NE stability awareness into SON functions, especially in the SON verification. We introduce the concept of Network Element Virtual Temperature (NEVT), which indicates the state of stability of a NE. In the following, we are going to explain the concept in detail and describe how the NEVT can be used to improve SON verification.

4.1   Network Element Virtual Temperature

The Network Element Virtual Temperature (NEVT), similar to the temperature concept in simulated annealing [14], shall be understood as an indicator of the stability of a NE, in particular of a cell. A NE becomes "hotter" after operations such as commissioning, SON function activity, or manual reconfiguration. Another example is when NE software is upgraded, which inserts new heat into the NE to indicate the reduced stability of its state. The resulting NEVT value depends on the event that has occurred in the network, i.e., a certain type of changes results in a much higher increase of the temperature than others. However, if there are no changes in the NE, it will cool down over time according to its *cooling factor* to indicate increased stability. A less stable NE with a high NEVT value is more likely to accept intermediate optimization steps that lead to somewhat reduced performance, in order to reach improved performance in the future. In contrast, a NE with a low NEVT value should retain its stability and is less likely to accept transient degraded optimization steps.

A change in a cell may not only affect the cell itself, but can also have an impact on its neighboring cells. For example, if a CCO function tilts an antenna up, this may not only influence the cell, where the tilt change was made, but also the neighboring cells may start experiencing higher interference. Therefore, the NEVT is transfered to the neighboring cells, analogous to heat conduction in physics. The amount of heat conducted to the neighboring cells depends on the selected *conduction factor*.

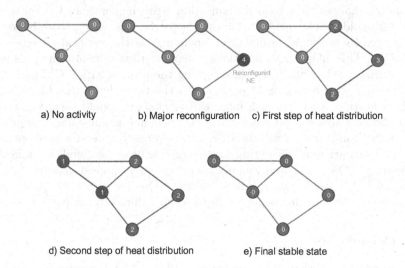

a) No activity   b) Major reconfiguration   c) First step of heat distribution

d) Second step of heat distribution   e) Final stable state

Fig. 2. Example of distributing NEVT ϵ [0; 4] in the network

These three concepts, i.e., heat introduction, cooling factor and conduction factor, define the temperature of each NE over time. In Fig. 2 we have outlined an example, where a new NE is introduced into an existing network resulting in introduction of a new, "hot" NE, heat conduction and subsequent cooling down.

4.2 Application of NEVT in SON Verification

The SON verification function can use the NE stability indication, the NEVT, in several different ways:

- Choose to completely omit hot verification areas
- Select the observation window length based on the NEVT
- Accept changes causing minor degradations if the NE is hot.

Firstly, if the verification function is heavily loaded, i.e., there are several, perhaps overlapping verification operations running, it may opt to completely omit hot verification areas to reduce the number of potential verification conflicts. Since the NEs in the verification area are unstable, also the verification decision would be unreliable and it might be better to let the SON functionality to continue optimizing the area.

Secondly, SON verification may adapt the observation window length according to the NEVT. For more unstable NEs, a longer observation window is used, in order to let them better stabilize after each change before making a verification decision. Likewise, for more stable NEs, a shorter window can be used.

Thirdly, the verification may accept changes leading to minor degradations, in case the verification area has a high NEVT value. The verification process accepts all changes that have a verification score higher than the set acceptance threshold, but it may in addition accept changes with a score below the threshold with a certain probability depending on the verification score and the NEVT. This allows SON functions to explore the configuration space more freely, without SON verification interrupting the process with a CM undo, and thus "escaping" potential local optima. On the other hand, the likelihood of SON verification accepting such intermediate changes should become lower, as the verification area cools down. Analogous to simulated annealing, this ensures that the NE configuration will stabilize and converge to at least a local optimum solution. Contrary to offline optimization solutions based on simulated annealing [4], however, SON verification can always accept only minor degradations, since it operates in a live network, where sufficient Quality of Service (QoS) must always be ensured. In this paper we focus on this third alternative.

4.3 Components

The architecture consists of two components: (1) a NEVT aggregator and (2) a NEVT parser, as shown in Fig. 3.

The NEVT aggregator consists of three sub-components. The first one is an event monitor that is responsible for monitoring the events occurring on the NE. Typical events are the change of CM parameters, software upgrades, etc. The second component, the NEVT calculator, computes the temperature. The third component is the NEVT distributor. It is the connection point, used to exchange NEVT values between the NEVT aggregators of neighboring NEs. Its task is to generate (send) and receive NEVT forward messages.

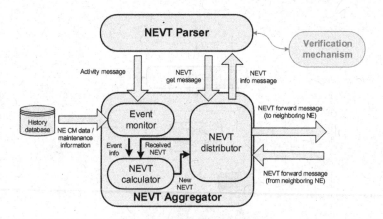

Fig. 3. Input, output, and components of the concept

Upon receiving a NEVT forward message, a NEVT distributor delegates the received information to the NEVT calculator. It uses the information to update the temperature of the NE.

The second main component, the NEVT parser, is the connection point to the verification mechanism [16] or any other network anomaly analyzer. First of all, it allows the verification mechanism to read the current NEVT. It can be also provide aggregated NEVT values for the current verification area.

Secondly, it gives a verification mechanism the ability to inform the NEVT aggregator about its planned undo activities. For example, if it requires a certain period of time to resolve verification collisions, an aggregator may artificially keep the temperature at a high level, indicating that the NEs have not stabilized.

4.4 Message Flow

An example of the message flow in a heterogeneous mobile network is given in Fig. 4.

1. A SON function triggers major CM changes within the fifth generation of mobile communications (5G) network.
2. The responsible NEVT aggregator computes the temperature.
3. The same NEVT aggregator distributes the computed values to the neighboring NE, including those being part of the fourth generation (4G) network, by generating NEVT forward messages. The corresponding NEVT aggregators receive the message and adapt the temperature respectively. The receiving NEVT aggregators dynamically configure the temperature, based on the temperature of the sending entity, as well as the conductivity factor.
4. When the verification mechanism is triggered, it requests the temperature of the verification area from the NEVT parser.
5. The parser collects the NEVTs of the NEs by issuing a NEVT get message. The corresponding aggregators reply with an NEVT info message.

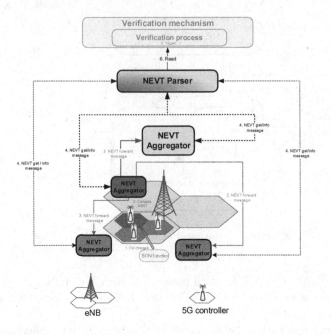

Fig. 4. Message flow

6. Based on the gathered information the verification mechanism is able to assess the change and decide whether or not it can be accepted.

4.5   Design of NEVT Aggregator

Let us define NEVT as $\chi \in [0, 100]$ and that the NEVT of a cell c at Granularity Period (GP) t is given by the function $\tau_t(c)$. An operation performed on a cell c, for example a major re-configuration, can increase the χ_c to indicate a reduced state of stability, i.e., $\tau_{t+1}(c) = \tau_t(c) + \delta$, where δ is the added heat. Note that δ must be scaled so that $\tau_{t+1}(c) \in [0, 100]$.

NEVT is also *conducted* to the neighboring cells. To simplify the model and to reduce the need for signaling, the NEVT conduction is done only when NEVT is added in the system. Let us denote the set of all cells as Σ. When δ of NEVT is added to a cell $c \in \Sigma$, the NEVT conducted to each neighbor of c is given by

$$\tau_{t+1}(c_n) = \tau_t(c_n) + K(\tau_t(c) + \delta - \tau_t(c_n)), \forall c_n \in N, \tag{1}$$

where $N \subset \Sigma$ is the set of cells neighboring c and $K \in [0, 1]$ is the NEVT conductivity factor.

Additionally, on each GP each cell cools down according to the *cooling factor*. That is, for each cell $c \in \Sigma$, $\tau_{t+1}(c) = F\tau_t(c)$, where $F \in [0, 1]$ is the cooling factor.

4.6 Design of NEVT Parser

For implementing the improved verification mechanism, we need the NEVT Parser to calculate the NEVT of a verification area. For this purpose, let us denote the set of all cells as Σ and the set of all verification areas as V. Furthermore, let us define an extraction function f_e that returns the cells of a verification area, i.e., $f_e \colon V \to \mathcal{P}(\Sigma) \setminus \{\varnothing\}$. Now the aggregated NEVT of a verification area $v \in V$ at a time t can be defined as

$$T(v) = \frac{1}{|f_e(v)|} \sum_{i=1}^{|f_e(v)|} \tau_t(c)_i, \tag{2}$$

where $\tau_t(c)$ is the NEVT of a cell $c \in f_e(v)$ as given by the NEVT Aggregator.

4.7 Enhanced Verification Process

In order to compute an anomaly score for verification, we define for each cell an anomaly vector $\mathbf{a} = (a_1, a_2, \ldots, a_n)$ that is an element of $\mathbb{R}^n$. Each element $a_k \in \mathbb{R}, k \in [1, n]$ represents the deviation of a KPI from the expected value, also known as the *KPI anomaly level*. The value of n equals $|K|$, where K is the set of KPIs that are selected to determine the cell performance.

To calculate the anomaly vector, the expected behavior is learned in a training phase, during which we collect samples $p_1 \ldots p_t$ for each given KPI, where t marks a training period. Then, we measure the current value of the KPI, denoted as p_{t+1}. The collected data, i.e., $p_1 \ldots p_t, p_{t+1}$, is normalized by computing the z-score of each data point. The KPI anomaly level is the z-score of p_{t+1}. The z-score itself represents the distance between the given point and the sample mean in units of the standard deviation. It is negative, when the raw score is below the mean, and positive when above. In addition, the anomaly level is normalized so that a positive level value means better than average performance and negative level worse than average. For example, for a success KPI, such as Handover Success Rate (HOSR), we can use the z-score as such. However, for a failure KPI, such as Radio Link Failure (RLF), we use the negative z-score.

The verification is done for a verification area consisting of one or more cells. In order to calculate the verification score for the area, we collect the anomaly vectors of each cell in the verification area into a verification area anomaly matrix $\mathbf{A}$, where each column represents a cell and each row a KPI. Next, we aggregate all elements a_{jk} of the matrix $\mathbf{A}$ into one single z-score that represents the overall verification area performance. The aggregation function $\varphi(\mathbf{A})$ calculates it by taking the arithmetic average of all a_{jk}, as defined in Eq. 3.

$$\varphi(\mathbf{A}) = \frac{1}{mn} \sum_{j=1}^{m} \sum_{k=1}^{n} a_{jk}, \tag{3}$$

where m is the number of cells in the verification area.

Now, following the proposal in [13] for simulated annealing, we can define an *acceptance function* $\psi(v, \mathbf{A}) \in [0, 1]$ that defines the probability of the verification process accepting a change, which is resulting in an anomaly matrix $\mathbf{A}$ in verification area $v \in V$, as

$$\psi(v, \mathbf{A}) = \begin{cases} 1, & \text{if } \varphi(\mathbf{A}) \geq \epsilon \\ 0, & \text{if } \varphi(\mathbf{A}) < \epsilon \text{ and } T(v) = 0 \\ e^{\dfrac{-c(\epsilon - \varphi(\mathbf{A}))}{T(v)}}, & \text{otherwise,} \end{cases} \tag{4}$$

where ϵ is the acceptance threshold and c is a scaling factor.

For example, by setting $\epsilon = 0$, all changes having a positive verification score will always be accepted and changes with negative score will have a probability of acceptance depending on the verification score and the NEVT of the verification area.

5 Evaluation

In this section we present the results of our experimental case study with the presented NE stability aware verification method. We also give an overview of the used simulation system.

5.1 Environment

To evaluate the behavior of SON coordination and verification concepts, we have developed the SON Simulation System (S3), as presented in [15].

The simulator models a Long Term Evolution (LTE) macro cell network based on simulated mobile users and radio propagation models [11]. The simulated network consists of 32 cells spread over an area of $50\,\text{km}^2$. Furthermore, 1500 uniformly distributed mobile users follow a random walk mobility model and use the network. The PM data calculated based on the radio simulation is collected in rounds corresponding to approximately $100\,\text{min}$ in real time, i.e. GPs, and forwarded to the SON functions.

For all simulation test runs, we employ two optimization functions: Mobility Robustness Optimization (MRO) and CCO, and the verification function. The CCO function adapts the antenna tilt and transmission power and the MRO changes the Cell Individual Offset (CIO) parameters. An instance of each of the two functions is running for each cell in the network.

5.2 Setup and Scenario

Each simulation round consists of 21 GPs. In the tested scenario, a disturbance is introduced after the 4th GP by turning one of the cells off. CCO and MRO adapt to this change and the verification function keeps monitoring their changes. During the 13th GP the cell is turned on again. When the cell is turned on and

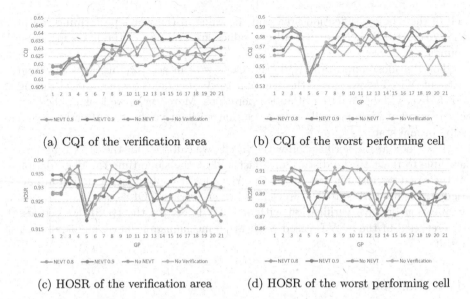

(a) CQI of the verification area   (b) CQI of the worst performing cell

(c) HOSR of the verification area   (d) HOSR of the worst performing cell

Fig. 5. Comparison of different verification strategies

off, the NEVT calculator adds a fixed amount of 80 units of NEVT in the reconfigured cell.

The scenario is repeated by using four different configurations:

1. verification with NEVT, cooling factor 0.8
2. verification with NEVT, cooling factor 0.9
3. verification without NEVT, i.e., rejecting all changes with verification score below the acceptance threshold
4. no verification.

Furthermore, NEVT conductivity factor is set to 0.8 and the verification acceptance function scaling factor to equal the maximum NEVT value of 100. Verification area is the target cell and its neighboring cells. A short observation window of only one GP was selected. Each scenario in each configuration is simulated 5 times and values for each GP averaged over the simulations. The followed KPIs are the Channel Quality Indicator (CQI) and the Handover Success Rate (HOSR), which are also used in the verification process. The CQI is computed as the harmonic mean over the channel efficiency [1].

5.3   Simulation Results

The simulation results show that the SON verification with the NEVT is able to adapt better to the disturbances while ensuring the stability of the system. Figure 5 shows the results. It depicts the CQI and HOSR values of the cell that was shutdown and its neighbors. Both the average value of the KPI of every cell in the whole verification area and the value of the worst performing cell in the area are shown. Note that all the values are averages of the five simulation rounds.

For the most important KPI, the CQI, we can see that using verification without NEVT slows down the reaction to the degradation introduced during GP 5 due to higher number of undo operations. Moreover, if we look at the CQI of the worst performing cell, we can see that without verification it ends up in a sub-optimal state.

If we look at the verification with NEVT, we can see that the SON functions are able to react to the disturbance fast and at the same time the degradation of the worst performing cell is avoided. With lower cooling factor of 0.9, in particular, the network stabilizes in clearly better average CQI values than without verification or with verification without NEVT. As for the HOSR we see less differences, but the NEVT-based verification mechanism achieves slightly better results.

6   Conclusion

The Self-Organizing Network (SON) verification is an important enabler of modern SONs. While it improves the stability of the network, verification can also make it less flexible, which can be undesirable in certain circumstances. For example, after commissioning a new Network Element (NE), it can be preferable to let the SON functions configure the Configuration Management (CM) parameters more freely to better adapt to the environment.

In this paper, we proposed the concept of Network Element Virtual Temperature (NEVT), which indicates the state of stability of a NE. Major reconfigurations of a NE increase its NEVT to indicate reduced stability. Over time, if there are no further reconfigurations, the NEVT decreases according to the *cooling factor* as the NE becomes more stable. NEVT is *conducted* to the neighboring NEs to indicate that they should also adapt to the changes. Utilizing the concept of NEVT, we introduced a NE stability aware verification process. In the process, all CM changes that exceed a set threshold for the verification score are accepted. However, also CM changes that do not exceed the threshold have a certain probability of being accepted, depending on the verification score and the NEVT of the NE.

Our evaluation, based on radio environment and subscriber simulation, shows that the NEVT-based verification allows the network to react and adapt to major changes faster. At the same time it avoids the degradations that occurred, when no verification was used. Distribution of NEVT to neighboring NEs enables the whole subnetwork to react to changes in one NE and the "cooling down" of NEVT ensures that the network stabilizes to an optimal configuration.

Future work includes studying the application of NEVT to other Network Management (NM) use cases.

References

1. 3GPP: Evolved Universal Terrestrial Radio Access (E-UTRA); Physical layer procedures. Technical specification 36.213 v12.1.0, 3rd Generation Partnership Project (3GPP), March 2014
2. Bandh, T.: Coordination of autonomic function execution in Self-Organizing Networks. Ph.D. thesis, Technische Universität München, April 2013
3. Bandh, T., Romeikat, R., Sanneck, H.: Policy-based coordination and management of SON functions. In: 12th IFIP/IEEE International Symposium on Integrated Network Management (IM 2011) Work, pp. 827–840. IEEE, Dublin, May 2011
4. Berger, S., Fehske, A., Zanier, P., Viering, I., Fettweis, G.: Comparing online and offline SON solutions for concurrent capacity and coverage optimization. In: Proceedings of the Vehicular Technology Conference (VTC Fall), Vancouver, Canada, September 2014
5. Ciocarlie, G.F., Connolly, C., Cheng, C.-C., Lindqvist, U., Nováczki, S., Sanneck, H., Naseer-ul-Islam, M.: Anomaly detection and diagnosis for automatic radio network verification. In: Agüero, R., Zinner, T., Goleva, R., Timm-Giel, A., Tran-Gia, P. (eds.) MONAMI 2014. LNICST, vol. 141, pp. 163–176. Springer, Heidelberg (2015)
6. Ericsson: Transparent Network-Performance Verification For LTE Rollouts. White Paper, 284 23–3179 Uen, Sep 2012
7. Gajic, B., Nováczki, S., Mwanje, S.: An improved anomaly detection in mobile networks by using incremental time-aware clustering. In: IFIP/IEEE Workshop on Cognitive Network and Service Management (CogMan 2015), Ottawa, Canada, May 2015
8. Hämäläinen, S., Sanneck, H., Sartori, C. (eds.): LTE Self-Organising Networks (SON): Network Management Automation for Operational Efficiency. Wiley, Chichester (2011)
9. Nováczki, S.: An improved anomaly detection and diagnosis framework for mobile network operators. In: 9th International Conference on Design of Reliable Communication Networks (DRCN 2013), March 2013
10. Liu, Z., et al.: A scoring method for the verification of configuration changes in self-organizing networks. In: Agüero, R., et al. (eds.) MONAMI 2015. LNICST, vol. 158, pp. 3–15. Springer, Heidelberg (2015). doi:10.1007/978-3-319-26925-2_1
11. NSN: Self-Organizing Network (SON): Introducing the Nokia Siemens Networks SON Suite - an efficient, future-proof platform for SON. White Paper, Oct 2009
12. Romeikat, R., Sanneck, H., Bandh, T.: Efficient, dynamic coordination of request batches in C-SON systems. In: IEEE Vehicular Technology Conference (VTC Spring 2013), Dresden, Germany, June 2013
13. Kirkpatrick, S., Gelatt, C.D., Vecchi, M.P.: Optimization by simulated annealing. Sci. New Series 220, 671–680 (1983)
14. Szu, H., Hartley, R.: Fast simulated annealing. Phy. Lett. A. 122, 157–162 (1987)
15. Tsvetkov, T., Sanneck, H., Carle, G.: A graph coloring approach for scheduling undo actions in self-organizing networks. In: IEEE IM, Ottawa, Canada, May 2015
16. Tsvetkov, T., Frenzel, C., Sanneck, H., Carle, G.: A constraint optimization-based resolution of verification collisions in self-organizing networks. In: IEEE Global Communications Conference (GlobeCom 2015), San Diego, CA, USA, Dec 2015
17. Tsvetkov, T., Nováczki, S., Sanneck, H., Carle, G.: A configuration management assessment method for SON verification. In: International Workshop on Self-Organizing Networks (IWSON 2014), Barcelona, Spain, Aug 2014

A Framework for Publish/Subscribe Protocol Transitions in Mobile Crowds

Björn Richerzhagen[✉], Alexander Wagener, Nils Richerzhagen,
Rhaban Hark, and Ralf Steinmetz

Multimedia Communications Lab (KOM), Technische Universität Darmstadt,
Darmstadt, Germany
{bjorn.richerzhagen,alexander.wagener,nils.richerzhagen,
rhaban.hark,ralf.steinmetz}@kom.tu-darmstadt.de

Abstract. The increasing number of sensor-equipped mobile devices enables new applications for communication within crowds of people. Ranging from monitoring services that provide insights into the crowd's behavior to fully fledged messaging applications for end users, all such applications require communication protocols that are tailored to the characteristics of a mobile ad hoc network (MANET). A common communication scheme for such dynamic networks is the publish/subscribe (pub/sub) paradigm, that offers temporal and spatial decoupling. However, pub/sub protocols for MANETs are designed and evaluated under very restricted conditions regarding the expected mobility, number of users, application workload, and application requirements, targeting rather specific scenarios. In reality, such conditions are subject to change, especially considering people's behavior during crowded events. In this work, we propose a framework that enables dynamic transitions between different pub/sub protocols based on the currently monitored conditions or caused by an external trigger. We analyze the behavior during transitions and the overhead introduced by our framework through extensive simulations. By using simple pub/sub protocols and switching between them based on the observed conditions, we are able to maintain good service quality at reasonable overhead, thereby enabling applications to operate in dynamic conditions representative of mobile crowds.

1   Introduction

The trend towards mobile devices and their continuously increasing capabilities in terms of processing power, sensors, and communication interfaces motivates a range of applications for communication in crowds. Application objectives range from crowd sensing and monitoring, e.g., to detect critical densities of people, to messaging and infotainment [12,15]. Often, these applications are tailored towards a specific type of crowd (e.g., visitors of a music festival, or first responders [2,16]), where central infrastructure might be overloaded, too costly, or not available at all. In addition, user-generated content is often only relevant in vicinity of its creator [10], a property that can be exploited to increase system

© IFIP International Federation for Information Processing 2016
R. Badonnel et al. (Eds.): AIMS 2016, LNCS 9701, pp. 16–29, 2016.
DOI: 10.1007/978-3-319-39814-3_2

performance and scalability [11,31]. Therefore, direct ad hoc communication is used to replace – or at least augment [23] – the communication via a central infrastructure. Consequently, a plethora of pub/sub systems for MANETs have been proposed in recent years, ranging from simple approaches based on notification or subscription flooding to more complex overlays that maintain distribution trees. Each approach focuses on a particular optimization target such as increasing robustness [19], providing low latency communication [20], or achieving a high resilience towards mobility [1]. Furthermore, each approach is able to deliver the desired performance only within bounded environmental conditions specific to the scenario it was initially designed for.

In this work we propose a framework that is able to dynamically exchange the utilized pub/sub protocol for a crowd of people, based on status information gathered within the system or based on extrinsic triggers. This allows us to adjust the performance vs. cost characteristics of the system based on the current conditions and application requirements, while at the same time relying on rather simple pub/sub protocols with well-known properties. Extending the concept of transitions and their corresponding lifecycles as proposed in [9], our framework addresses challenges related to the state transfer as well as message translation during the execution of a transition. We argue that existing protocols can be integrated easily, as they only need to provide access to stored subcriptions through a basic and easily extendable subscription model. By relaying network operations – e.g., sending and receiving of messages – as well as interaction with the application through simple proxy interfaces, transitions between protocols are executed transparent to the application.

Based on a simulative evaluation of a prototype of our proposed framework we quantify the performance benefits as well as the additional overhead introduced by executing transitions between two basic pub/sub protocols. The simulation setup is derived from real-world measurements of people's behavior during a large-scale music festival [8], thereby providing valuable insights into protocol performance in a realistic setting. Our findings reveal that transitions executed by our framework enable the system to adapt to changing conditions, while at the same time keeping the control overhead reasonably low. The system is able to maintain the desired performance characteristics and ensure delivery of notifications during and after the execution of a transition. The evaluation results further indicate the need for efficient bootstrapping mechanisms to improve the benefit of – especially short-lived – transitions. Overall, the execution of transitions between basic pub/sub protocols is a promising approach to tackle the challenge of communication in mobile crowds under dynamic conditions.

The remainder of this paper is structured as follows: In Sect. 2 we describe and discuss our proposed framework for transitions between pub/sub protocols in mobile crowds. We evaluate the framwork in a simulative setup derived from real-world crowdsourced measurements of people movement during a large-scale music festival and present the results in Sect. 3. After discussing relevant related work in Sect. 4, we conclude the paper and discuss future research directions in Sect. 5.

2   A Transition-Enabled Pub/Sub Framework

Figure 1 provides an overview of the entities of the transition-enabled pub/sub framework and their interactions. At the core of the framework, a number of pub/sub protocols are provided. Proper activation and termination of protocols during transitions is assured by the *lifecycle management*. Instead of directly interacting with the respective pub/sub protocol, applications publish, subscribe, and unsubscribe through an *interaction proxy*. To this end, the proxy takes care of relaying the respective method calls to the currently active pub/sub protocol. Additionally, it handles callbacks and notifications triggered by the pub/sub protocol upon reception of a notification and forwards the notification to the application for further processing. The methods provided by the proxy follow the proposal for a common pub/sub application programming interface, as defined in [21]. This ensures that transitions between protocols are transparent to the application – no modification of application code is required.

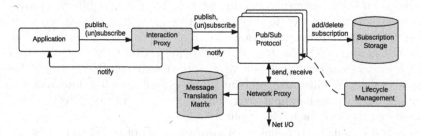

Fig. 1. Overview of the entities and their interactions in the proposed framework.

The currently active pub/sub protocol stores its subscriptions – local subscriptions originating from the application, as well as subscriptions managed on behalf of other nodes – in the provided *subscription storage*. To this end, a uniform abstraction for subscriptions is required. This abstraction is provided by the interaction proxy and further discussed in Sect. 2.2. To enable communication among nodes in the system, each pub/sub protocol sends and receives messages through a common *network proxy* provided by the framework. The network proxy relays incoming messages to the currently active pub/sub protocol. During protocol transitions, some nodes may receive messages originating from a different protocol than their currently active one. Rather than simply discarding these messages, the network proxy attempts to resolve basic information and translate it into a form that can be processed by the currently active pub/sub protocol. This (optional) functionality is implemented on a per-protocol basis by adding the respective transformation functions to the *message translation matrix*. In the following section, the process of a transition within our framework is discussed in detail.

2.1 Execution of Transitions

The process of a transition itself is shown in Fig. 2. For simplicity, we assume that there exists a logically centralized coordinator. For most scenarios, this assumption is reasonable, as applications usually report their data to some kind of sink infrastructure, e.g., the coordination unit of an emergency response team. In cases involving multiple coordinators, distributed consensus protocols [18] could be used to agree on a transition. The coordinator starts a transition in consequence to a trigger event. Such an event can be the outcome of monitored state (e.g., a sharp decrease in system performance, or sudden increase in people movement), or based on an external trigger. Based on the target pub/sub protocol, a transition strategy is selected and the decision is disseminated to all mobile nodes. Dissemination can either be performed by the pub/sub protocol itself (in this case, the framework registers as a subscriber to the respective event type) or via an out-of-band dissemination protocol.

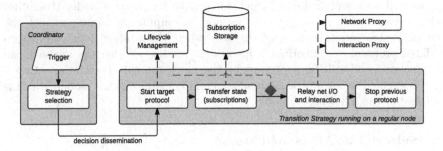

Fig. 2. Control flow and execution steps for a transition.

Once the decision arrives at a mobile node, the respective transition strategy is executed. Each strategy consists of four basic steps: (i) start the new protocol through the lifecycle manager, (ii) transfer state to the new protocol, relying on the subscription storage, (iii) relay application and network interaction to the new protocol by utilizing the respective proxies, and (iv) terminate the previously running protocol. Before actually relaying all interaction to the new protocol, the strategy needs to wait until the lifecycle manager signals successful startup of the new protocol, as discussed in [9]. Depending on the protocol, startup might involve the formation of a topology and, as a consequence thereof, some message exchange unrelated to the application payload. The network proxy allows such communication during the startup and shutdown phase of a protocol, thereby ensuring the functionality of bootstrap mechanisms and a graceful shutdown. Once the new protocol is ready, all further interaction is relayed through the new protocol and the old one is terminated.

Without any additional information about the pub/sub protocols involved in a transition, the framework is already able to execute a transition by only relying on the common abstraction of the subscription storage as well as the interaction proxy. However, such a transition would involve unsubscribing with the old protocol and then re-subscribing for all locally stored subscriptions afterwards, introducing significant overhead. Therefore, state transfer can be refined on a per-protocol basis, leading to more evolved transition strategies. If, for example, the target protocol and the currently active protocol have a notion of brokers (e.g., some nodes in the mobile network act as message brokers serving other nodes that act solely as clients), one can bootstrap the new protocol by assigning the role of a broker to the nodes that already previously acted as brokers. Thereby, state does not need to be redistributed during startup, but instead only as a consequence of the default maintenance mechanisms of the new protocol. This strategy significantly reduces the overhead caused by a transition.

As our framework is used for communication within a crowd of people, we demand the whole network to execute transitions. In a MANET, partitions might occur and decisions might not reach all affected nodes, potentially leading to protocol misbehavior once partitions merge. To this end, the network proxy piggybacks an identifier of the currently active protocol, the transition strategy, as well as a simple logical clock to messages sent by a node. If another node receives such a message, but does not yet employ the same protocol, the appropriate transition is executed. In cases where the sending node employs an outdated protocol, the identifier helps in determining whether the message can be translated and still be processed by the new protocol. Translation of messages is enabled as all protocols deploy a common subscription model, which is discussed in the following section.

2.2 Subscription Model and Storage

As our framework utilizes a common storage for subscriptions, all pub/sub protocols need to use or extend our basic subscription model. To this end, we deploy an attribute-based subscription scheme that supports dynamic types, as illustrated in Fig. 3. In addition to an arbitrary number of types and attributes, each subscription may carry one string-typed attribute denoting a topic. In this way, the resulting subscriptions can be processed by attribute-based and simple channel- or topic-based pub/sub protocols. Subscriptions (and notifications) are built by the application, relying on factory methods provided by the interaction proxy. Therefore, applications do not depend on subscription schemes introduced by the individual protocols.

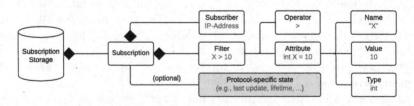

Fig. 3. Subscription model within the proposed framework.

To enable protocol-independent management of subscriptions, the respective objects that are used to compose a subscription (e.g., filters and attributes) are created through factory methods provided by the interaction proxy. Therefore, if an existing pub/sub protocol needs to extend the basic subscription model, it can simply extend the respective factory method to include additional, protocol-specific state within a subscription. The same model and factory concept is also used by applications for the creation of notifications. If nodes act as brokers within the current protocol (i.e., they manage subscriptions on behalf of other nodes), the subscribers are also attached to the respective subscription. In the basic model, only an IP address is required for each subscriber.

2.3   Integrating Existing Pub/Sub Protocols

One goal of our framework is to keep the required modifications of existing protocols as simple as possible. To ensure basic interoperabilit one needs to (i) provide an adapter for the interaction proxy and the network proxy, (ii) utilize the subscription storage, and (iii) implement the basic lifecycle methods. While the current network proxy requires some modifications (the use of a custom socket), a future version of the framework could intercept[1] calls to the respective methods. As a basic lifecycle handling is already part of most protocols, and our subscription model is fairly generic, (ii) and (iii) do not pose significant challenges and only require minor changes.

To enhance system performance during a transition, one may provide a custom transition strategy for the respective protocol. As discussed in Sect. 2.1, a strategy might include more complex state exchange mechanisms to reduce messaging overhead. Usually, the resulting state exchange mechanisms depend on specific combinations of source and target protocol. If a matching state exchange mechanism is provided for the current transition, it is executed automatically by our framework. In addition to that, protocols might also provide custom entries to the message translation matrix. The matrix simply consists of descriptions of messages used by a protocol and pointers to some common data fields within those messages, like subscriptions or notifications. In this way, incoming messages of the wrong protocol type can be interpreted by the currently running protocol to some extent.

We aim to support simple integration of existing pub/sub protocols into the transition-enabled framework by requiring only minor modifications. However, the framework allows protocol designers to provide more elaborate transition strategies tailored towards the peculiarities of the specific protocols.

3   Prototype and Evaluation

We implemented a Java-based prototype of the proposed framework on top of the Simonstrator-Platform [24] to enable both simulative, and prototypical performance studies. Goal of the evaluation is to verify the concept of transitions

---

[1] We are currently extending the prototype to rely on Java Reflections for this purpose.

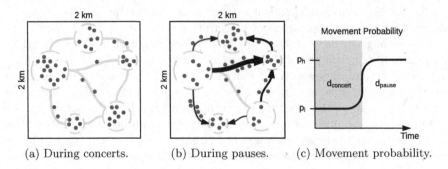

(a) During concerts.   (b) During pauses.   (c) Movement probability.

Fig. 4. Illustration of the evaluation scenario, derived from crowdsourced movement profiles of visitors of a music festival [8].

in pub/sub systems for crowd communication as a viable solution to react to environmental changes in a flexible and generic way. Therefore, we model a scaled-down scenario based on real-world crowdsourced measurements of people movement during a music festival [8], as illustrated in Fig. 4. The scenario can roughly be categorized into two phases with respect to movement characteristics: a relatively static phase during concerts (c.f. Fig. 4a), and an active phase where the crowd moves to different stages or enters and leaves the festival area (c.f. Fig. 4b). Stages and other relevant points of interest (e.g., food booths) are modeled as attraction areas, allowing us to rely on a modified version of the SLAW movement model [14,30]. In our evaluation scenario, we vary the probability that a node selects a new attraction area and starts moving towards it, mimicking real-world behavior during and after a concert (c.f. Fig. 4c).

The evaluation was conducted by means of simulation on the Simonstrator-Platform [24], relying on the overlay simulator PeerfactSim. KOM [29] and the NS-3 802.11 g underlay model [26]. We simulated 400 nodes on a $2000\,m \times 2000\,m$ area, with a publication rate of 1 publication per second and a fan-out of $1 : 20$, meaing each publication had 20 interested subscribers. Two hours of operation are simulated: (i) during the first 30 min all nodes join; (ii) after 40 min, the workload phase starts and subscriptions, as well as publications, are issued; (iii) performance and cost metrics are measured between minute 60 and 100; (iv) the workload is applied until the end of the simulation. Each run was repeated five times with different random seeds, and the plots show the average over these five runs. The scenario starts with a concert phase lasting until minute 70. During this concert phase, the probability of a node to start moving to a new attraction area is set to $p_l = 0.05$. Two minutes before the end of the concert, this probability starts to increase linearly, until it reaches $p_h = 0.7$ at minute 72, leading to a noticeable number of nodes moving around in-between attraction areas. The probability is reduced back to $p_l = 0.05$ around minute 80, when the next concert starts. This cycle is repeated once more around minute 90.

For the evaluation, two basic pub/sub protocols are integrated into the framework: (i) an approach using notification flooding through a gossiping mechanism

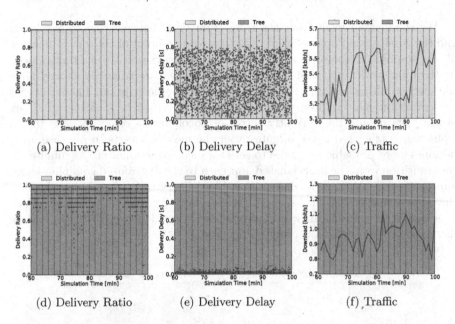

Fig. 5. Performance in terms of delivery ratio and delay, and cost in terms of traffic for static deployment of the distributed (a–c) and the tree-based (d–f) pub/sub protocol in the dynamic scenario.

(termed *distributed* in the following), and (ii) a broker-based approach, where a subset of the nodes is elected as brokers that maintain subscriptions on behalf of the remaining nodes. In the broker-based approach, notifications are sent along a delivery tree formed by the broker nodes, thereby reducing the traffic. To understand the behavior of both protocols in our dynamic scenario, we evaluated them within our framework without triggering any transitions. The resulting performance and cost characteristics over time are shown in Fig. 5.

The gossip-based approach is robust enough to maintain a delivery ratio of one over the whole duration of the simulation (c.f. Fig. 5a). However, due to the utilization of a gossiping mechanism, event delivery can take up to one second (c.f. Fig. 5b), and the resulting traffic is five times higher than for the broker-based approach that forms a delivery tree (c.f. Fig. 5c and f). While delivery ratio and delay remain constant even during phases of high mobility, a slight increase in average traffic (c.f. Fig. 5c) can be observed. For the broker-based approach, the formation of delivery trees in the dynamic scenario leads to an average delivery ratio of 0.9 in the more static phases of the scenario (c.f. Fig. 5d). However, the ratio falls to an average 0.8 with significantly worse performance for a fraction of the nodes during phases with higher mobility. This is the result of failures in the delivery tree, caused by brokers that move out of range of each other. Until the failure is detected and repaired, the performance suffers. As long as the delivery tree remains functional, the broker-based approach achieves significantly better delivery delays (c.f. Fig. 5e) and consumes less traffic than the gossip-based approach.

We conduct an evaluation featuring transitions between the broker-based and the gossip-based approach in order to provide a proof-of-concept evaluation of our proposed framework, as well as for an estimation of the cost introduced by the framework to control transitions. Transitions are triggered shortly after the user-mobility changes, according to the scenario description. The results for the transition-enabled framework are shown in Fig. 6. The background colors of the plots denote the currently active protocol. It can easily be seen that a transition is triggered a few minutes after the mobility starts to increase, as it becomes more probable for nodes to select a new attraction area. At minute 72, the transition from the broker-based approach to the distributed gossiping-based approach takes place. As a consequence, the delivery ratio directly increases, as the more robust protocol is used (c.f. Fig. 6a). However, this transition also leads to a significant increase in variation of the delivery delay (c.f. Fig. 6b) and an increased overall traffic consumption (c.f. Fig. 7a).

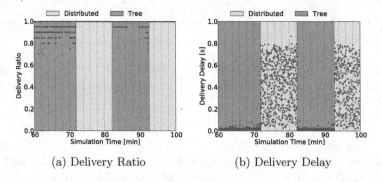

(a) Delivery Ratio   (b) Delivery Delay

Fig. 6. Transitions between the broker-based and the distributed, gossip-based protocol occur at minutes 72, 82, and 92. The performance characteristics of the system change accordingly.

As the gossip-based protocol relies on notification flooding, nodes only need to filter based on their own, locally stored subscriptions. Therefore, there is no need for state transfer when initializing the protocol. This becomes apparent from the sharp transition of the traffic at minute 72, as shown in Fig. 7a. In contrast to that, the transition back to the broker-based approach at minute 82 requires some initial bootstrapping and, thus, causes higher traffic, as brokers have to be elected. Due to the scale of the x-axis, one might get the impression of a discrete switch between pub/sub protocols. A zoomed-in version of the first transition, shown in Fig. 7b, reveals that it takes up to 180 ms in our setting until the last node executes the transition. As shown in our evaluation, the framework successfully executes transitions between two different pub/sub protocols during runtime. The performance of the overall system remains stable during and after transitions. Our proposed approach, thus, is able to adapt to the dynamics of the considered scenario by switching between protocols, as initially motivated.

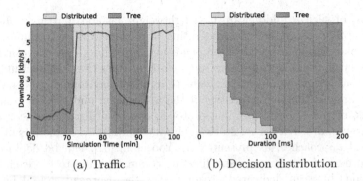

(a) Traffic   (b) Decision distribution

Fig. 7. Bootstrapping the tree-based protocol consumes more traffic directly after the transition at minute 82. A zoomed-in version of the transition at minute 82 shows how the decision spreads in the network.

4   Related Work

There exists a number of reconfigurable and adaptive pub/sub middleware concepts for fixed [6,13] and mobile networks [27,28]. As our work specifically targets mobile crowds, we focus on the latter and additionally discuss related, self-adaptive pub/sub protocols.

Sivaharan et al. propose GREEN [27], a component-based middleware for Internet-scale pub/sub, inspired by REDS [6]. In contrast to REDS, the authors specifically aim at integrating local MANET regions into the overall pub/sub system. To this end, mobile devices using the middleware can be configured to act as gateways for nearby devices. The device-to-device communication is then handled via a range of configurable protocols that can be integrated into GREEN. However, the authors do not evaluate or discuss the implications of dynamic reconfigurations on mobile networks and solely consider a protocol based on notification-flooding, thereby obviating the need for any state transfer or maintenance mechanism. With our framework, the pub/sub middleware can be extended to actually react to environmental changes and dynamics by executing protocol transitions on the fly.

Sørensen et al. propose a middleware for context-aware applications on mobile networks [28]. While focusing explicitly on providing a higher level programming abstraction to pervasive applications, the proposed middleware also includes a communication substrate that provides pub/sub capabilities. The authors base their pub/sub substrate on the design of the MANET pub/sub protocol STEAM [17]. Unfortunately, no performance figures are given, and adaptability to changing dynamics is not evaluated. According to a recent survey of middleware approaches for pervasive applications by Raychoudhury et al. [22], event-based communication is a key building block for all kinds of middleware solutions. Therefore, we believe that our framework poses a valuable foundation for middleware concepts, such as [28]. Instead of proposing a new middleware concept as in [3,28], we aim at providing a core functionality as a potential component of such a middleware in a lightweight fashion, putting a focus on reconfigurability. Therefore, by integrating our framework as communication substrate as envisioned by Sørensen et al. and providing higher-level pub/sub functionality on top, one can realize mobile applications that can acutally adapt their local ad hoc communication means to dynamic environmental conditions.

Depending on the characteristics of the application and the environmental conditions, more elaborate pub/sub protocols can be utilized and incorporated into our framework. For rather static environments but large amounts of nodes, hierarchical approaches, as presented by Yoo et al. [32], can be deployed. By relying on fixed delivery trees, and limiting communication to the exchange of subscriptions between dedicated broker nodes, the overhead caused by flooding of notifications can be avoided. However, such a structured approach suffers from node mobility. To this end, a semi-structured, density-based approach has been presented by Friedmann et al. [7]. Here, routing between brokers relies on a gradient-based scheme, making it more robust against broker movement. Additionally, the election of brokers requires only very limited knowledge – the density of the two-hop neighborhood – and, thus, can be performed without adding significant overhead. To address high mobility, or frequent connection failures, completely topology-less approaches have been proposed. Extending flooding-based concepts, approaches such as [19] utilize gossip-based communication protocols to limit the amount of redundant data transmissions.

Within our proposed framework, one can leverage the benefits of these different approaches by switching between pub/sub protocols at runtime and choosing the protocol that best fits the current conditions. At the same time, application developers just utilize a simple and well-known pub/sub interface, as all functionality of our proposed framework remains transparent to the application.

5   Discussion and Conclusion

A number of interesting application concepts rely on direct ad hoc communication in crowds of people, where cellular infrastructure might be unavailable or simply overloaded. The performance of the utilized communication protocol, however, can vary significantly depending on the dynamics of the considered scenario. In this work, we propose a framework that is able to switch between different pub/sub protocols for mobile networks at runtime. To this end, the framework provides a basic abstraction for subscriptions, as well as mechanisms for state transfer and interaction with the network and the application, allowing to easily integrate new protocols. Based on real-world measurements of a music festival, we derive a representative workload for a communication system in such an environment, and use it to evaluate a prototype of our proposed framework including two basic pub/sub protocols. In contrast to a static configuration of the protocols, our framework is able to maintain the desired performance vs. cost characteristics even in the face of dynamic changes of network conditions by executing transitions between the different protocols.

Our framework can work as a wrapper for existing pub/sub middleware, as the application interface relies on default pub/sub methods (c.f. [21]) defined by the interaction proxy. To trigger transitions, the pub/sub system itself can be utilized: in such a case, the lifecycle management simply acts as a subscriber to a well-defined control channel. It is beyond the scope of this work to provide means to accurately monitor the network state as a foundation for transition execution – however, we are currently integrating an adaptive monitoring system that is targeted towards similar scenarios [25].

We are currently in the process of integrating a wider range of more complex pub/sub protocols into our framework, especially looking into protocols that support location-based or context-based publish/subscribe semantics. These protocols offer richer subscription semantics, enabling more sophisticated filtering of relevant notifications. One interesting application for the proposed framework is switching between direct delivery of notifications and delay-tolerant protocols [4,5]. Here, our framework could help in preserving energy by disabling the direct communication interfaces opportunistically, as consequence of a protocol transition, if applications do not require instant delivery for certain types of events. However, this would require centralized coordination via a cellular interface, as previously explored in [23]. The prototype of the framework is available online as part of the Simonstrator platform [24].

Acknowledgments. This work has been funded by the German Research Foundation (DFG) as part of projects B1, C2 and C3 within the Collaborative Research Centre (CRC) 1053 – MAKI. Ralf Steinmetz has been partially supported by a Chair of Excellence from University Carlos III, Madrid, Spain. The authors would like to thank Sophie Schönherr for her valuable contributions.

References

1. Anceaume, E., Datta, A.K., Gradinariu, M., Simon, G.: Publish/subscribe scheme for mobile networks. In: Proceedings of the POMC (2002)
2. Baldini, G., Karanasios, S., Allen, D., Vergari, F.: Survey of wireless communication technologies for public safety. IEEE Commun. Surv. Tutorials **16**(2), 961–987 (2014)
3. Batista, T.V., Joolia, A., Coulson, G.: Managing dynamic reconfiguration in component-based systems. In: Morrison, R., Oquendo, F. (eds.) EWSA 2005. LNCS, vol. 3527, pp. 1–17. Springer, Heidelberg (2005)
4. Boldrini, C., Conti, M., Passarella, A.: Design and performance evaluation of contentplace, a social-aware data dissemination system for opportunistic networks. Comput. Netw. **54**(4), 589–604 (2010)
5. Costa, P., Mascolo, C., Musolesi, M., Picco, G.P.: Socially-aware routing for publish-subscribe in delay-tolerant mobile ad hoc networks. IEEE J. Selected. Areas Commun. **26**(5), 748–760 (2008)
6. Cugola, G., Picco, G.P.: Reds: a reconfigurable dispatching system. In: Proceedings of the 6th International Workshop on Software Engineering and Middleware, pp. 9–16. ACM (2006)
7. Friedman, R., Kaplun Shulman, A.: A density-driven publish subscribe service for mobile ad-hoc networks. Ad Hoc Networks (2012)

8. Frömmgen, A., Heuschkel, J., Jahnke, P., Cuozzo, F., Schweizer, I., Eugster, P., Mühlhäuser, M., Buchmann, A.: Crowdsourcing measurements of mobile network performance and mobility during a large scale event. In: Karagiannis, T., et al. (eds.) PAM 2016. LNCS, vol. 9631, pp. 70–82. Springer, Heidelberg (2016). doi:10. 1007/978-3-319-30505-9_6

9. Frömmgen, A., Richerzhagen, B., Rückert, J., Hausheer, D., Steinmetz, R., Buchmann, A.: Towards the description and execution of transitions in networked systems. In: Latré, S., Charalambides, M., François, J., Schmitt, C., Stiller, B. (eds.) AIMS 2015. LNCS, vol. 9122, pp. 17–29. Springer, Heidelberg (2015)

10. Huguenin, K., Kermarrec, A., Kloudas, K., Taïani, F.: Content and geographical locality in user-generated content sharing systems. In: Proceedings of the NOSSDAV (2012)

11. Jaho, E., Stavrakakis, I.: Joint interest-and locality-aware content dissemination in social networks. In: Proceedings of the WONS (2009)

12. Karaliopoulos, M., Telelis, O., Koutsopoulos, I.: User recruitment for mobile crowdsensing over opportunistic networks. In: Proceedings of the INFOCOM, pp. 2254–2262. IEEE (2015)

13. Leclercq, M., Quéma, V., Stefani, J.B.: Dream: a component framework for the construction of resource-aware, reconfigurable moms. In: Proceedings of the 3rd Workshop on Adaptive and Reflective Middleware, pp. 250–255. ACM (2004)

14. Lee, K., Hong, S., Kim, S.J., Rhee, I., Chong, S.: Slaw: A new mobility model for human walks. In: Proceedings of the INFOCOM 2009, pp. 855–863. IEEE (2009)

15. Ma, H., Zhao, D., Yuan, P.: Opportunities in mobile crowd sensing. IEEE Commun. Mag. **52**(8), 29–35 (2014)

16. Martín-Campillo, A., Crowcroft, J., Yoneki, E., Martí, R.: Evaluating opportunistic networks in disaster scenarios. J. Netw. Comput. Appl. **36**(2), 870–880 (2013)

17. Meier, R., Cahill, V.: STEAM: Event-based middleware for wireless ad hoc network. In: Proceedings of the DEBS, pp. 639–644, Jul 2002

18. Olfati-Saber, R., Fax, A., Murray, R.M.: Consensus and cooperation in networked multi-agent systems. Proc. IEEE **95**(1), 215–233 (2007)

19. Paridel, K., Vanrompay, Y., Berbers, Y.: Fadip: lightweight publish/subscribe for mobile ad hoc networks. In: Meersman, R., Dillon, T., Herrero, P. (eds.) OTM 2010. LNCS, vol. 6427, pp. 798–810. Springer, Heidelberg (2010)

20. Pietzuch, P.R., Bacon, J.: Hermes: a distributed event-based middleware architecture. In: Proceedings of the DEBS (2002)

21. Pietzuch, P., Eyers, D., Kounev, S., Shand, B.: Towards a common API for Publish/Subscribe. In: Proceedings of the DEBS, pp. 152–157. ACM (2007)

22. Raychoudhury, V., Cao, J., Kumar, M., Zhang, D.: Middleware for pervasive computing: a survey. Pervasive Mobile Comput. **9**(2), 177–200 (2013)

23. Richerzhagen, B., Stingl, D., Hans, R., Gross, C., Steinmetz, R.: Bypassing the cloud: Peer-assisted event dissemination for augmented reality games. In: Proceedings of the P2P, pp. 1–10. IEEE (2014)

24. Richerzhagen, B., Stingl, D., Rückert, J., Steinmetz, R.: Simonstrator: Simulation and prototyping platform for distributed mobile applications. In: Proceedingd of the SIMUTOOLS. ICST (2015)

25. Richerzhagen, N., Stingl, D., Richerzhagen, B., Mauthe, A., Steinmetz, R.: Adaptive monitoring for mobile networks in challenging environments. In: Proceedings of the ICCCN, pp. 1–8. IEEE (2015)

26. Riley, G., Henderson, T.: The NS-3 network simulator. In: Wehrle, K., Güneş, M., Gross, J. (eds.) Modeling and Tools for Network Simulation. Springer, New York (2010)

27. Sivaharan, T., Blair, G.S., Coulson, G.: GREEN: a configurable and re-configurable publish-subscribe middleware for pervasive computing. In: Meersman, R., Tari, Z. (eds.) OTM 2005. LNCS, vol. 3760, pp. 732–749. Springer, Heidelberg (2005)
28. Sørensen, C.F., Wu, M., Sivaharan, T., Blair, G.S., Okanda, P., Friday, A., Duran-Limon, H.: A context-aware middleware for applications in mobile ad hoc environments. In: Proceedings of the MPAC, pp. 107–110. ACM (2004)
29. Stingl, D., Gross, C., Ruckert, J., et al.: PeerfactSim. KOM: a simulation framework for peer-to-peer systems. In: Proceedings of the HPCS. IEEE (2011)
30. Stingl, D., Richerzhagen, B., Zollner, F., Gross, C., Steinmetz, R.: Peerfactsim. kom: Take it back to the streets. In: Proceedings of the HPCS, pp. 80–86. IEEE (2013)
31. Vulimiri, A., Michel, O., Godfrey, P., Shenker, S.: More is less: reducing latency via redundancy. In: Proceedings of the HotNets (2012)
32. Yoo, S., Son, J., Kim, M.: A scalable pub/sub system for large mobile ad hoc networks. J. Syst. Softw. **82**, 1152–1162 (2009)

Cloud Flat Rates Enabled via Fair Multi-resource Consumption

Patrick Poullie$^{(\boxtimes)}$ and Burkhard Stiller

Communication Systems Group (CSG), Department of Informatics (IfI),
University of Zürich, Binzmühlestrasse 14, 8050 Zürich, Switzerland
{poullie,stiller}@ifi.uzh.ch

Abstract. Many companies rent Virtual Machines (VM) from cloud providers to meet their computational needs. While this option is also available to end-users, they do not always take advantage of this option. One reason may be that it is common to pay on a per-VM-basis, whereas the telecommunications sector has shown that customers prefer flat rates. A flat rate for cloud services needs to define utilization thresholds, to cap the usage of heavy customers and thereby limit their impact on the flat rate price and the cloud performance. Unfortunately, customers consume multiple heterogenous resources in clouds, *e.g.*, CPU, RAM, disk I/O and space, or network access. This makes the definition of a customer's fair "cloud share" and according utilization thresholds complex.

Backed by a questionnaire among more than 600 individuals, this paper designs the new Greediness Metric (GM) that formalizes an intuitive understanding of multi-resource fairness without access to consumers' utility functions. This GM enables the introduction of attractive cloud flat rates and fair sharing policies for private/commodity clouds and provides incentive to customers to wisely determine VM configurations.

1 Introduction

Cloud Computing (CC) is a computing paradigm enabled by the growing connectivity provided by modern communication systems combined with virtualization technology [8, 27]. CC allows server farms to provide their combined computing power on demand to customers, such as end-users and companies. To process a workload through CC a customer starts Virtual Machines (VM) in the cloud that process the workload. In particular, VMs are defined by Virtual Resources, *e.g.*, virtual CPU and virtual RAM [3, 8]. Resources in private/commodity clouds are often managed by quotas, *i.e.*, each user has a quota defining a maximum of VRs that his VMs may have in total.

As opposed to this, in commercial clouds, it is common practice that customers pay on a per-VM-basis [2]. However, the telecommunications sector has shown that customers often prefer flat rates [1, 21, 22], even if a volume-based tariff would reduce costs [18]. Contrary to a volume-based tariff, a flat rate induces a fixed cost cap. For private users this allows for care-free use and for commercial users an easy budgeting of costs. This suggests high demand for cloud flat

© IFIP International Federation for Information Processing 2016
R. Badonnel et al. (Eds.): AIMS 2016, LNCS 9701, pp. 30–44, 2016.
DOI: 10.1007/978-3-319-39814-3_3

rate schemes. With a cloud flat rate customers pay a monthly fee to get access to a cloud, where they can start VMs. Just as Internet flat rates come with a maximum bandwidth, cloud flat rate customers would get a certain quota to spawn VMs.

However, this mechanism is neither sufficient to cap costs that individual customers cause nor to ensure fairness between customers, because customers (i) often deploy different amounts of their quota and (ii) load VMs differently. In particular, (i) means that some customers may only operate a few VMs leaving most of their quota unused, while others fully utilize their quota. (ii) describes that even if customers create exactly the same number and types of VMs, the costs they cause varies depending on how they utilize their VMs. Because VMs on the same host compete for resources, a heavily loaded VM may impair the performance of other VMs on the same host. Therefore, in flat rate or private/commodity clouds, it is desirable to limit VMs of heavy customers in favor of VMs of more moderate customers, such that VMs of moderate customers are not impaired by VMs of heavy customers.

While technical means to enforce fairness in this way exist [3,10,12], cloud fairness is neither sufficiently enforced nor explored [7–9,15,28]. What makes the definition of cloud fairness problematic, is that multi-resource fairness has to be defined without access to utility functions. Here, *multi-resource* implies that *bundles*, which are allocated to the consumers, consist of heterogenous resources and the non-accessibility of utility functions implies that it is unknown how much consumers valuate different bundles (a consumer's *utility function* maps each bundle to a number quantifying the consumer's valuation for the bundle). Utility functions are unknown, because, depending on the workload a VM executes, dependencies between resources differ. Therefore, even for the owner of a VM, the VM's utility function is difficult to determine. Furthermore, no standardized format to describe utility functions exists. Lastly, even if cloud users could determine and express utility functions, they may not want to reveal it to the cloud operator, as it reveals private information about internal processes.

The problem of cloud fairness is often addressed by VM scheduling, *i.e.*, deciding which VM should be started next. This is insufficient to streamline resource utilization in clouds, because it makes static assumptions on utility functions necessary [4,7,9], while VM demands are dynamic. To reach a general applicability (including VM runtime), this paper defines the Greediness Metric (GM) in return to the research question how to quantify the commensurability of VMs' runtime resource utilization, *i.e.*, how fair VMs behave. Because fairness is an intuitive concept, *i.e.*, differs from person to person, the conformance of the GM with an intuitive understanding of fairness is verified by a questionnaire among more than 600 participants.

The remainder of this paper is structured as follows: Sect. 2 discusses related work leading to the research question stated in Sect. 2.1. Section 3 outlines the questionnaire, presents its results, and discusses key findings. Based on these outcomes, the new Greediness Metric (GM) is defined in Sect. 4. Section 5 draws conclusions and outlines future work.

2   Related Work and Problem

For a single resource, the size of bundles can be quantified, and thus, the value of bundles objectively compared. Therefore, fairness can be intuitively defined as Max-Min-Fairness [25] or Proportional Fairness [4] and quantified by metrics such as [14,19,30]. While such allocation problems were extensively studied in computer science [6,25], multi-resource allocation received much less attention.

In data centers, which comprise clusters, grids, and clouds, consumers share resources, such as CPU time, RAM, Disk I/O and space, and network access, wherefore it is necessary to define fairness, when every consumer receives a bundle of heterogenous resources. As noted in [7,9,15,17,23,28], multi-resource allocation in data centers is so far not fully investigated and often reduced to single-resource allocation problems at the cost of efficiency and fairness [9,20]. The assumption of more advanced approaches is that the resource utilization of jobs, which determine those entities consuming resources in clusters and grids, is static or at least follows static ratios [7,9]. This allows to introduce fairness by job scheduling, *i.e.*, which job should be started next. However, VMs, which are the entities consuming resources in clouds, change their resource utilization frequently and dynamically. This not only prohibits reducing cloud fairness to VM scheduling but also prohibits incorporating the concept of envy-freeness [9,11,28]. Envy-freeness, *i.e.*, no consumer prefers to swap his bundle with another, is essential for the definition of fairness in economics. However, this definition is not applicable, when consumer's utility functions are unknown or highly dynamic, as it is the case for clouds. Subsequently, approaches to multi-resource fairness in data centers (especially their cloud instances) are compared here, while ignoring numerous approaches focusing on a single resource.

Dominant Resource Fairness (DRF) is the most prominent approach to introduce multi-resource fairness in data centers [9]. DRF defines the value of a bundle as the biggest proportion relative to the total supply of any resource in it (cf. Sect. 3.2). Therefore, to define the value of a bundle only one resource is considered, which is also known as the L_∞ norm. A DRF fair allocation is the allocation that maximizes this value for every consumer. [11] points out that for many other functions (including all other $L_{i \in \mathbb{N}}$ norms) a unique allocation exists that can be found in polynomial time, but that the authors of DRF never argue

Table 1. Comparison of related approaches.

App.	Fairness	Area	Utility function
DRF	Max-min for L_∞ norm	Scheduling	Leontief
[4]	Proportional Fariness	Scheduling	Leontief
BBF	Equal share on a bottleneck	Scheduling	Perfectly complementary
[28]	Envy free and Pareto efficient	Micro resources	Cobb-Douglas
[17]	Priority based on metrics	Scheduling	Not needed
GM	Based on questionnaire	Runtime	Not needed

why their choice is superior. Leontief utility functions model that resources are required in static ratios, *i.e.*, increasing the amount a consumer receives of one resource does not increase his utility if his share of all other resources is not increased by the same factor. While all proofs for DRF's desirable properties are based on Leontief utility functions [9,23], the actual DRF scheduling policy, as proposed in [9], allows consumers to request different resource bundles. Therefore, in the scheduling process, consumers can have arbitrary utility functions, but DRF's properties are only proven for Leontief utility functions. [4] shows that proportional fairness is superior to DRF in terms of efficiency and comes with the same desirable characteristics under realistic assumptions.

Bottleneck-based fairness (BBF) was introduced in [7,8]. An allocation is bottleneck-based fair, if every consumer either is allocated all requested resources or at least the equal share on a congested/bottleneck resource and the other resource in proportion. [29] defines a multi-resource on-line scheduling policy that achieves BBF without knowing consumer's utility functions in advance.

[28] presents an allocation policy that achieves game-theoretic fairness, *i.e.*, sharing incentive, envy freeness, and pareto-efficiency, when allocating cache capacity and memory bandwidth. Different applications are profiled to convincingly argue that Cobb-douglas utility functions are well suited to model diminishing returns and substitution effects for these resources.

[17] considers the fair sharing of grids between customers and research groups. Contrary to all other approaches discussed in this section, [17] achieves fairness by a penalty/priority function, which is close to our approach. In particular, such function determines the priority of consumers when granting resource requests. Such approach is much more practically oriented, because no assumptions about utility functions need to be made.

Another research field on cloud resource allocation focuses on live-migration [16,26], *i.e.*, rescheduling VMs during runtime. While live-migration is applied during VM runtime it is, just as VM scheduling, orthogonal to this work here, because it does not change priorities of VMs.

Table 1 compares the approaches discussed in terms of the adopted fairness definition, the application area, and the assumed utility function. Most approaches are way too complex to be applied during VM runtime and none of these is based on an intuitive understanding of fairness. This motivates the general research undertaken and specifically this paper's problem statement.

2.1 Problem Statement

The characteristic of fair cloud resource allocations that is distinct for this context is that customers (between whom fairness is to be defined) utilize resources from different resource pools (hosts) by intermediaries (VMs). While fairness has to be achieved between customers, this has to be done by allocating resources to their VMs. Unfortunately resources can only be moved between VMs, which run on the same host. However, besides this structural dilemma, also a more general problem is faced: Defining and enforcing fairness of multi-resource allocations without knowing consumers' utility functions. In particular, because bundles consist of multiple heterogenous resources, bundles can contain resources in different amounts. This prohibits an objective comparison of bundles. For example, some customers may require more CPU for their workloads, while others require more RAM [20]. A third customer may deploy the cloud for backups and, therefore, mostly requires disk-space and bandwidth. Therefore, consumers can have different preferences over the same bundles.

Because utility functions of consumers in clouds are unknown, it is not possible to define fairness via utility functions here and, thus, fairness has to be defined via bundles that VMs serve themselves. In particular, hosts work as "self-serving stores" for VMs, which means that they provide all requested resources to VMs, if possible. Therefore, fairness in clouds has to be defined as constraining VMs of those customers whose VMs overcharge their self-serving stores, *i.e.*, are greedy. While also the concept of greediness has no formal definition, it can be better defined and quantified with the information that is available in clouds.

Therefore, the ***problem statement*** for this paper reads as follows: The greediness of VMs can be defined and quantified based on their multi-resource self-servings. An allocation is fair in such a case, when (i) the aggregates per customer of these quantifications are aligned and (ii) VMs of "greedy" customers are constrained in favor of VMs of "less greedy" customers.

3   Questionnaire

A questionnaire was developed to evaluate the intuitive understanding of fairness and greediness and to justify empirically the design of the new Greediness Metric (GM). The questionnaire can be found in the appendix of [24]. The questionnaire specified real-life resource allocation scenarios in terms of three questions Q1, Q2, and Q3 to not distract participants by technical terms and let them fully concentrate on the question of fairness. While these scenarios were specific, the questions were carefully designed to reach generic insights about intuitive understandings of fairness and greediness. To describe these questions subsequently, resources and consumers are denoted by r_i and c_j, respectively, where $i, j \in \mathbb{N}_{>0}$. Questionnaire participants had to chose between different options of allocations or define rankings of consumers. Additionally, participants were offered to explain their answers in text boxes. The questionnaire did not address any particular target group, to allow evaluating a popular and intuitive understanding of fairness that is not biased by technical notions established by experts. Out of 721 participants, who started the questionnaire, 604 completed it. Q2 addressed the question of how consumer requests should be taken into account, when allocating resources, but did not address the question of how fairness or greediness can be defined. Therefore, Q2 is not directly related to the design of the GM and only discussed in [24].

3.1   Choosing the Most Fair Allocation (Question 1)

DRF is the most prominent approach for fairness in data centers (cf. Sect. 2). Therefore, DRF's conformance with an intuitive understanding of fairness was

Table 2. The four Allocation Options A11, A12, A13, and A14.

	A11		A12		A13		A14	
Consumer	r_1	r_2	r_1	r_2	r_1	r_2	r_1	r_2
c_1	2	0	3	0	4	0	5	0
c_2	0	4	0	6	0	8	0	10
c_3	4	8	3	6	2	4	1	2

Table 3. The three Scenarios S31, S32, and S33.

	S31			S32			S33		
Consumer	r_1	r_2	r_3	r_1	r_2	r_3	r_1	r_2	r_3
c_1	4	3	3	4	2	4	4	1	4
c_2	2	1	5	1	4	3	1	4	3
c_3	4	2	1	1	6	2	1	6	2
Remainder	2	3	0	6	0	0	6	1	0

evaluated by Q1. In particular, DRF's centerpiece, which is using the L_∞ norm to measure the value of a bundle (*c.f.* Sects. 2 and 3.2), was evaluated. The scenario described covers two resources r_1 and r_2 of which six and twelve units where available, respectively. These resources have to be allocated to three consumers c_1, c_2, and c_3. c_1 only requires r_1, c_2 only r_2, and c_3 requires for each unit of r_1 two units of r_2. This results in seven possible allocations to allocate all resources and do not give consumers resources they have no use for. However, most of these allocations are intuitively unfair, *e.g.*, in two of these allocations at least one consumer receives no resources at all.

Because the scenario describes that resources are requested in static ratios, it is transferable to allocation problems in data centers, where these static ratios of resource requests, *i.e.*, Leontief utility functions, are the standard assumption [4, 7, 9]. Table 2 shows four of the seven allocations and their respective labels. These four allocations were presented to participants numerically and graphically and they had to choose *the* allocation that seemed most fair to them. As expected, A11 and A14 were only chosen by a minority of the 721 participants (0.4 % and 1.1 %, respectively) and most participants deterred between A12 and A13 (30.0 % and 68.5 %, respectively). The following arguments in support of A12 are summarized from textual comments received:

- c_1 and c_2 only compete with c_3 for resources, but not with one another. A fair allocation splits resources equally between those who contend for them.
- All receive an equal amount of what they want.
- This is the only allocation where nobody can complain that someone has more of the same resource.

For the following reasons A13 was supported:

- When prices are introduced based on available units, this option gives the same value to all consumers.
- c_1 and c_2 receive 2/3 of *one* resource and c_3 1/3 of *two* resources, which makes 2/3 for everybody. On a similar note, some participants rejected A12, because c_3 gets as much as c_1 and c_2 combined.
- Because c_1 and c_2 only want one resource, they should get more of it than c_3, as c_3 wants both resources.
- This option is the result of a simple auction or when all consumers get an equal share of both resources and then trade.

3.2   Estimating Greediness (Question 3)

Q3 was designed to collect information on how the greediness of consumers, who served themselves from a pool of common resources, is perceived. The transferability to clouds is evident, because in clouds VMs serve themselves from their host. Moreover, because in flat rate and commodity clouds no payment on a per VM basis occurs, such clouds are also a common resource shared among customers. In addition, insights were collected on how proportionality and value of resource bundles is perceived, when no information about consumers' utility functions is available. Thus, Q3 provides insights on how resources that different VMs on the same host utilize can be compared.

Q3 is based on three scenarios S31, S32, and S33, were three consumers c_1, c_2, and c_3 had served themselves from a pool of three common resources r_1, r_2, and r_3 (like VMs on the same host). To split these resources, each consumer had allocated himself a certain bundle as shown in Table 3. The three consumers had to be ranked according to how their greediness was perceived, all being based on the amounts the consumers had allocated themselves.

Metrics: Many participants tackled Q3 by proposing one of the four metrics discussed subsequently.

Price: The price metric is the simplest metric. The value of one unit of resource r_i is defined as $p/\overleftrightarrow{r_i}$, where p is a constant and $\overleftrightarrow{r_i}$ is the number of units available of r_i. The value of a bundle is the sum of values of its resources. For example, for $p = 1$ the value of c_2's bundle in S31 is $\frac{2}{12} + \frac{1}{9} + \frac{5}{9} = \frac{5}{6}$. This metric is equivalent to the sum-based-penalty function presented in [17].

P × S (Price×Scarcity): The P×S metric is a natural extension of the price metric. The value of one unit of resource r_i is defined as $a(r_i) \cdot p/\overleftrightarrow{r_i}^2$, where $a(r_i)$ is the amount that is allocated in total of r_i. The value of a bundle is defined as the sum of values of those resources contained. For example, for $p = 1$ the value of c_2's bundle in S31 is $\frac{2 \cdot 10}{12^2} + \frac{1 \cdot 6}{9^2} + \frac{5 \cdot 9}{9^2} = \frac{29}{54}$.

P∩S (Price∩Scarcity): The P∩S metric is another natural extension of the price metric and defines the value of a resource just as the price metric. However, the value of a bundle is defined only over resources that are depleted, *i.e.*, resources where $a(r_i) = \overleftrightarrow{r_i}$. For example, for $p = 1$ the value of c_2's bundle in S31 is $\lfloor\frac{10}{12}\rfloor \cdot \frac{2}{12} + \lfloor\frac{6}{9}\rfloor \cdot \frac{1}{9} + \lfloor\frac{9}{9}\rfloor \cdot \frac{5}{9} = \frac{5}{9}$.

DRF (Dominant Resource Fairness): The DRF metric defines the value of a bundle by the L_∞ norm, *i.e.*, by the biggest share of any resource relative to the overall amount of the resource. For example, the value of c_2's bundle in S31 is $\max\left(\frac{2}{12}, \frac{1}{9}, \frac{5}{9}\right) = \frac{5}{9}$. According to this DRF metric, the bundles of c_1 and c_2 in S33 are equally valuable. This tie is broken by the second biggest share in the bundles, wherefore c_1's bundle is more valuable.

Frequency Investigations: For some questionnaire rankings the free text indicated that the participant had assumed real life values of those resources and ranked the consumers accordingly. These rankings as well as incomplete rankings were removed, wherefore the presented results are based on 553 answers. Subsequently, consumer rankings are denoted by triplets. For example, the triplet (2,1,3) denotes the first consumer as moderate, the second consumer as most greedy, and the third consumer as least greedy.

Figure 1 illustrates for each scenario how many participants selected each ranking and highlights those rankings that correspond to all metrics discussed in Sect. 3.2. These numbers in Fig. 1 allow to compile Table 4 showing for each metric the respective ranking in the three scenarios and by how many participants this ranking was selected. Figure 1 and Table 4 show that the metrics discussed in Sect. 3.2 cover the majority of participants' rankings.

[24] analyses the combinations of rankings over the three scenarios, because these rankings given by most participants did not match the same metric over the three scenarios. This reveals that the most frequent combination was selected by 79 participants, conforming to the DRF metric. The second, third, and fourth most frequent combinations were selected by 55, 43, and 32 participants, conforming to the P×S, Price, and P∩S metric, respectively.

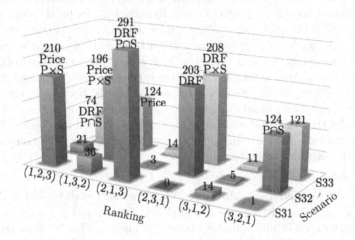

Fig. 1. Ranking frequencies (represented by triplets) in Q3 scenarios.

Table 4. Percentages of most frequent rankings in Q3.

Metric	S31	S32	S33
DRF	(2,1,3): 52.7 %	(2,3,1): 36.8 %	(2,3,1): 37.7 %
Price	(1,2,3): 38.0 %	(1,3,2): 35.5 %	(1,3,2): 22.5 %
P×S	(1,2,3): 38.0 %	(1,3,2): 35.5 %	(2,3,1): 37.7 %
P∩S	(2,1,3): 52.7 %	(3,2,1): 22.5 %	(1,2,3): 13.4 %

Table 5. A problematic DRF ranking.

	r_1	r_2	r_3	Price	P×S	P∩S	DRF
available	30	30	30				
c_1	18	0	0	1.80	1.68	0.00	0.60
c_2	0	14	17	3.10	3.04	1.40	0.56
c_3	10	16	12	3.80	3.69	1.60	0.53

3.3 Discussion

Only the first two arguments of the questionnaire's text replies in favor of A12 of the above presented Q1 are correct. The third argument is incorrect, because c_1 receives least of r_2 and c_2 least of r_1. Therefore, the arguments in favor of A13 are more versatile and sound than those in favor of A12. Because A12 and A13 were chosen by 30.0 % and 68.5 % of the participants, respectively, it is concluded that A13 determines the intuitively fair allocation.

In Q3, participants who ranked in conformance to the Price and P∩S metrics, stated that they had applied these metrics to arrive at the ranking. In contrast, participants who ranked conforming to the DRF and P×S metrics often argued not in conformance to the respective metric. In particular, for participants ranking in conformance to the DRF metric, only one participant argued in conformance to the DRF metric, while the majority argued that those consumers who exceed their equal share are greedy. Thus, in S31 c_2 is the greediest due to the disproportional consumption of r_3. Analog, in S32 and S33 c_3 is the greediest, because c_3 exceeds the equal share of r_2 by 50 % and c_1 is the second greedy, because c_1 exceeds the equal share of r_1 by 33 %. Participants who ranked conforming to the P×S metric mostly argued that the total amount of resources consumed is deceive (the tie of c_1 and c_3 in S33 according to this logic was broken by c_3's 50 % overconsumption of r_2). Further details can be found in [24].

Implications for Existing Metrics: While the metrics discussed in Sect. 3.2 cover the majority of participants rankings (cf. Table 4 and [24]), none of these metrics captures an intuitive understanding of fairness: The P∩S metric has a low conformance in S32 and S33 and for S33 results in the inverted ranking of S32. The latter implies that consumers can decrease their score by consuming more. This is not only counter-intuitive, but gives the undesirable incentive to consume more than needed. The Price metric has a low conformance in S33 and identifies c_1 as "greediest" in S31, although c_1 does not cause the bottleneck, but precisely sticks to his equal share (a behavior that is considered humble in S32 and S33). The sum- and the root-based-penalty functions, which [17] identifies as best metrics, result in the same rankings as the Price metric and, therefore, are also not satisfactory. Similar arguments hold for the P×S metric.

The DRF metric is satisfactory at a first glance: For all three scenarios of Q3 it results in the most frequent ranking and also in the most frequent combination of rankings (cf. Table 4 and [24]). However, only one participant argued according to DRF, while the majority argued that those who exceed their equal share are greedy. Therefore, the high conformance of DRF stems rather from the fact that every consumer exceeds the equal share on at most one resource (because DRF only considers these resources, this allows DRF to produce good results). Table 5 shows an allocation that proves that DRF's approach to ignore all but one resource can lead to undesirable results. For the depicted allocation, all other metrics discussed in Sect. 3.2 give the inverse ranking of DRF. Also, according to the arguments made by the participants, the DRF ranking is unfair: DRF classifies c_1 as the consumer with the most valuable bundle, although c_1 only receives the least loaded resource. c_3 cedes no resource at all and receives most of the only scarce resource, but DRF classifies c_3 as most humble. Also, Q1 of the questionnaire identified A13 as the intuitively fair allocation, while the DRF-fair allocation is A12. Because Leontief utility functions are assumed in Q1, $i.e.$, resources are required in static ratios, and DRF is defined based on this assumption, DRF should result in an intuitively fair allocation. Therefore, while DRF is often applied, when Leontief utility functions do not hold, Q1 shows that already for Leontief utility functions, DRF may result in allocations that are not intuitively fair. Moreover, consumers and resources can be added to this scenario, where consumer c_i requests only resource r_i (and as before one consumer requests all resources evenly). Thereby, the perceived unfairness of DRF can be increased arbitrarily, because the consumer requesting all resources receives as much as all other consumers combined.

Due to these shortcomings of all metrics presented so far, the new Greediness Metric (GM) was developed. This GM is aligned with arguments of this discussion and, thus, (i) classifies A13 in Q1 as the most fair allocation, (ii) results in the most frequent ranking for each of the three scenarios in Q3, (iii) gives the "correct" ranking for the allocation in Table 5, and (iv) captures an intuitive understanding of fairness, which allows defining attractive cloud flat rate models.

4   Greediness Metric

The Greediness Metric (GM) maps each resource bundle in an allocation to a rational number that can be associated to the *greediness* of the consumer, who served himself the bundle. In that sense this GM serves the same purpose as the other metrics presented in Sect. 3.2, which quantify the value of a bundle. As the most frequent textual comments of the questionnaire suggest, the GM sums up, what exceeds the equal share in each bundle. However, it also deducts what is not consumed of the equal share but handed over to other consumers instead.

Let $R = (r_1, r_2, \ldots, r_m)$ be a set of m resources, where resource $r_i \in R$ is available in the amount of $\overleftrightarrow{r_i}$. An *allocation* of R to n consumers $(c_1, c_2, \ldots, c_n)$ can be denoted by a matrix $A \in \mathbb{R}_{\geq 0}^{m \times n}$ with $\sum_{j=1}^{n} a_{ij} \leq \overleftrightarrow{r_i}$, for all $i \in \{1, 2, \ldots, m\}$, where c_j receives amount a_{ij} of r_i. The amount of r_i that c_j receives beyond his equal share is then $a_{ij} - \overleftrightarrow{r_i}/n$ (if the difference is negative, c_j does not utilize its entire equal share of the resource).

If $a_{ij} > \overleftrightarrow{r_i}/n$, consumers other than c_j have to cede some of their equal share of r_i in order to enable c_j's share of r_i. Therefore, the amount by which c_j exceeds his equal share is added to the greediness of c_j.

If $a_{ij} = \overleftrightarrow{r_i}/n$, c_j exactly receives his equal share, wherefore it does not change c_j's greediness. In particular, if $a_{ij} = \overleftrightarrow{r_i}/n$ for all $i \in \{1, 2, \ldots, m\}$, c_j's greediness is zero.

If $a_{ij} < \overleftrightarrow{r_i}/n$, c_j's cession of r_i is credited to c_j, i.e., subtracted from c_j's greediness, to the extent that other consumers profit from this cession, which is the case, when they utilize r_i beyond their equal share. This extension not only depends on how much of r_i is utilized beyond the equal share by other consumers, but also on how much of r_i is ceded by other consumers. Therefore, the *credit factor* for the cession of r_i is the ratio of what is ceded of r_i to what is consumed beyond the equal share of r_i. To capture this notion formally, the sum of what consumers receive beyond and cede of their equal share of r_i is defined by $\alpha(r_i)$ and $\beta(r_i)$, respectively. Therefore,

$$\alpha(r_i) := \sum_{j=1}^{n} \max\left(0, a_{ij} - \overleftrightarrow{r_i}/n\right) \quad \text{and} \quad \beta(r_i) := \sum_{j=1}^{n} \max\left(0, \overleftrightarrow{r_i}/n - a_{ij}\right).$$

Multiplying the amount that c_j cedes of r_i with $\alpha(r_i)/\beta(r_i)$ implements the considerations above. Therefore, the *greediness of c_j* is defined as

$$g(c_j) := \sum_{i=1}^{m} o(i,j) \cdot n/(m \cdot \overleftrightarrow{r_i}), \tag{1}$$

where $o(i,j)$ is the *offset* for c_j's consumption of r_i and defined as

$$o(i,j) := \begin{cases} a_{ij} - \overleftrightarrow{r_i}/n & \text{if } a_{ij} \geq \overleftrightarrow{r_i}/n, \\ \gamma \cdot \frac{\alpha(r_i)}{\beta(r_i)} \cdot \left(a_{ij} - \overleftrightarrow{r_i}/n\right) & \text{else.} \end{cases} \tag{2}$$

Note that, if $\beta(r_i) = 0$, no consumer cedes r_i and, therefore, the else-part of Eq. 2 is never reached (thus, no division by zero occurs). The factor $n/(m \cdot \overleftrightarrow{r_i})$ in Eq. 1 normalizes resource units. [24] discusses (i) the choice of this normalization factor in detail, (ii) detailed examples for the calculation of the GM, and (iii) how the GM is applicable to scenarios, where consumers have different endowments (instead of every consumer having an endowment of $\overleftrightarrow{r_i}/n$).

The parameter γ defines how strongly the ceding of resources is credited and, thereby, fine-tunes the greediness metric to best comply with the questionnaire results. Table 6 shows the results of the GM dependent on γ for the questionnaire's scenarios. As the table shows, already without the parameter γ (or, equivalently, $\gamma = 1$), the GM complies with results of Q1 and S31. However, for S32 and S33, the GM results in the ranking (3,2,1) (cf. Table 6), while the ranking most frequently selected by the participants is (2,3,1) (cf. Table 4). This mismatch for $\gamma = 1$ can be explained as follows: In S32 and S33, c_1 exceeds the equal share of r_3 by 33 % but also cedes 50 % of r_2 to c_3, while c_2 is "neutral". Thus, while c_2's greediness is zero independent of γ, c_1 has a negative greediness

Table 6. GM results for Q1 and Q3 of the questionnaire.

γ	Cons.	A12	A13	S31	S32 and S33
x	c_1	$0.25-0.5{\cdot}x$	$0.5-0.5{\cdot}x$	0	$0.\overline{1}-0.1\overline{6}{\cdot}x$
	c_2	$0.25-0.5{\cdot}x$	$0.5-0.5{\cdot}x$	$0.\overline{2}$	0
	c_3	0.5	0	$-0.\overline{2}{\cdot}x$	$0.1\overline{6}-0.\overline{1}{\cdot}x$
1	c_1	-0.25	0	0	$-0.0\overline{5}$
	c_2	-0.25	0	$0.\overline{2}$	0
	c_3	0.5	0	$-0.\overline{2}$	$0.0\overline{5}$
0.5	c_1	0	0.25	0	$0.02\overline{7}$
	c_2	0	0.25	$0.\overline{2}$	0
	c_3	0.5	0	$-0.\overline{1}$	$0.\overline{1}$

for $\gamma = 1$, *i.e.*, for $\gamma = 1$, the GM ranks c_2 greedier than c_1. However, most participants rated c_1 greedier than c_2, because c_1 over-consumes r_3 while c_2 never exceeds the equal share. Accordingly, $\gamma \in [0, 1]$ regulates how strongly the ceding of resources is credited (in addition to the dynamic regulation by $\frac{\alpha(r_i)}{\beta(r_i)}$), where, the smaller γ is chosen, the harder it gets to compensate for exceeding the equal share. [24] shows that for $\gamma \in \,]\frac{1}{4}, \frac{2}{3}[$ the GM perfectly complies with the questionnaire results and Table 6 lists that $\gamma = 0.5$ is an appropriate choice.

5   Conclusions and Future Work

Multi-resource fairness for clouds was so far not defined satisfactorily. Therefore, the Greediness Metric (GM) was defined and verified via a questionnaire among more than 600 participants. The GM defines an intuitive understanding of multi-resource fairness without access to utility functions. This questionnaire also revealed that DRF, which is the state-of-the-art in data center fairness, not always conforms with an intuitive understanding of fairness. Because the GM's definition is based on arguments of non-technical participants, it is intuitively comprehensible. This intuitive definition of cloud applicable fairness, allows for the design of attractive cloud flat rates. In particular, the telecommunications sector has shown that customers often prefer flat rates. Also private/commodity clouds are a perfect use case for the GM, as here no service level agreements guide the resource allocation making fairness an important allocation goal.

In addition to its intuitiveness, the GM is also well suited to be integrated into cloud sharing schemes, because the GM provides the right incentives to chose the configuration of a VM, such that it matches the VM's subsequent load: When a VM tries to exceed the resources it is configured with, it will receive them, if available. However, the customer's greediness increases with a potentially negative effect on other VMs of this customer. Because a customer's greediness only decreases, when resources that his VMs do not utilize are utilized by other VMs, it is not guaranteed that idle resources are credited to the consumer. Therefore, under- as well as over-provisioning VMs is costly. No metric known today (including those in Sect. 3.2) provides this incentive mechanism.

The GM is currently being evaluated within two different settings: the first setting allows for an evaluation of the GM under idealistic conditions to conclude on the effect of different design aspects, *e.g.*, the function to aggregate the VM greediness to customer greediness. The second setting defines a CloudSim [5] extension, which allows for evaluating the GM under realistic conditions in operation. In turn, the implementation to integrate the GM fairness mechanism into OpenStack [13] is ongoing.

References

1. Altmann, J., Rupp, B., Varaiya, P.: Effects of pricing on internet user behavior. Netnomics **3**(1), 67–84 (2001)
2. Amazon Web Services, Inc., Amazon EC2 Pricing (2016). https://aws.amazon.com/ec2/pricing/. Accessed 26 Jan 2016
3. Arcangeli, A., Eidus, I., Wright, C.: Increasing memory density by using KSM. In: 2009 Linux Symposium, vol. 1, pp. 19–28, Montreal, QC, Canada, July 2009
4. Bonald, T., Roberts, J.: Enhanced cluster computing performance through proportional fairness. Perform. Eval. **79**, 134–145 (2014)
5. Calheiros, R.N., Ranjan, R., Beloglazov, A., De Rose, C.A.F., Buyya, R.: CloudSim: a toolkit for modeling and simulation of cloud computing environments and evaluation of resource provisioning algorithms. Softw. Pract. Exper. **41**(1), 23–50 (2011)
6. Chandra, A., Adler, M., Goyal, P., Shenoy, P.: Surplus fair scheduling: a proportional-share CPU scheduling algorithm for symmetric multiprocessors. In: 4th Conference on Symposium on Operating System Design & Implementation, OSDI 2000, San Diego, CA, USA, p. 4, October 2000
7. Dolev, D., Feitelson, D.G., Halpern, J.Y., Kupferman, R., Linial, N.: No Justified complaints: on fair sharing of multiple resources. In: 3rd Innovations in Theoretical Computer Science Conference, ITCS 2012, Cambridge, MA, USA, pp. 68–75, January 2012
8. Etsion, Y., Ben-Nun, T., Feitelson, D.G.: A global scheduling framework for virtualization environments. In: 2009 IEEE International Symposium on Parallel Distributed Processing, IPDPS 2009, Rome, Italy, pp. 1–8, May 2009
9. Ghodsi, A., Zaharia, M., Hindman, B., Konwinski, A., Shenker, S., Stoica, I.: Dominant resource fairness: fair allocation of heterogeneous resources in data centers. Technical report UCB/EECS-2010-55, EECS Department, University of California, Berkeley, May 2010
10. Guo, F.: Understanding Memory Resource Management in VMware vSphere 5.0. In: Performance study, VMware, Palo Alto, CA, USA, (2011). http://www.vmware.com/files/pdf/mem_mgmt_perf_vsphere5.pdf
11. Gutman, A., Nisan, A.: Fair allocation without trade. In: 11th International Conference on Autonomous Agents and Multiagent Systems, AAMAS 2012, vol. 2, pp. 719–728, Valencia, Spain, June 2012
12. IBM: Best Practices for KVM. Technical report, Austin, TX, USA, November 2010. http://www.tdeig.ch/linux/pasche/12_BestPractices_IBM.pdf

13. Jackson, K.: OpenStack Cloud Computing Cookbook. Packt Publishing, Birmingham (2012)

14. Jain, R.K., Chiu, D.-M.W., Hawe, W.R.: A quantitative measure of fairness and discrimination for resource allocation in shared computer systems. Technical report TR-301, Digital Equipment Corp, Hudson, MA, USA, September 1984

15. Joe-Wong, C., Sen, S., Lan, T., Chiang, M.: Multi-resource allocation: fairness-efficiency tradeoffs in a unifying framework. In: 31st Annual IEEE International Conference on Computer Communications, INFOCOM 2012, pp. 1206–1214, Orlando, FL, USA, March 2012

16. Kapil, D., Pilli, E.S., Joshi, R.C.: Live virtual machine migration techniques: survey and research challenges. In: IEEE 3rd International Advance Computing Conference, IACC 2013, pp. 963–969, Ghaziabad, UP, India, February 2013

17. Klusáček, D., Rudová, H., Jaroš, M.: Multi resource fairness: problems and challenges. In: Desai, N., Cirne, W. (eds.) JSSPP 2013. LNCS, vol. 8429, pp. 81–95. Springer, Heidelberg (2014)

18. Lambrecht, A., Skiera, B.: Paying too much and being happy about it: existence, causes, and consequences of tariff-choice biases. J. Mark. Res. **43**(2), 212–223 (2006)

19. Lan, T., Kao, D., Chiang, M., Sabharwal, A.: An axiomatic theory of fairness in network resource allocation. In: 29th Annual IEEE International Conference on Computer Communications, INFOCOM 2010, San Diego, CA, USA, pp. 1–9, March 2010

20. Lee, G., Chun, B.-G., Katz, R.H.: Heterogeneity-aware resource allocation and scheduling in the cloud. In: 3rd USENIX Conference on Hot Topics in Cloud Computing, HotCloud 2011, Portland, OR, USA, p. 4, June 2011

21. Levinson, D., Odlyzko, A.: Too Expensive to meter: the influence of transaction costs in transportation and communication. Philos. Trans. R. Soc. Lond. A Math. Phys. Eng. Sci. **366**(1872), 2033–2046 (2008)

22. Odlyzko, A.: Internet pricing and the history of communications. Comput. Netw. **36**(5–6), 493–517 (2001)

23. Parkes, D.C., Procaccia, A.D., Shah, N.: Beyond dominant resource fairness: extensions, limitations, and indivisibilities. In: 13th ACM Conference on Electronic Commerce, EC 2012, Valencia, Spain, pp. 808–825, June 2012

24. Poullie, P., Stiller, B.: Cloud flat rates enabled via fair multi-resource consumption. Technical report IFI-2015.03, Universität Zürich, Zurich, Switzerland, October 2015. https://files.ifi.uzh.ch/CSG/staff/poullie/extern/publications/IFI-2015.03.pdf

25. Floyd, S. (ed.): Metrics for the evaluation of congestion control mechanisms. RFC 5166, IETF, Berkeley, CA, USA, March 2008

26. Strunk, A.: Costs of virtual machine live migration: a survey. In: 2012 IEEE 8th World Congress on Services, SERVICES 2012, Honolulu, HI, USA, pp. 323–329, June 2012

27. Wei, G., Vasilakos, A., Zheng, Y., Xiong, N.: A Game-theoretic method of fair resource allocation for cloud computing services. J. Supercomput. **54**(2), 252–269 (2010)

28. Zahedi, S.M., Lee, B.C.: REF: resource elasticity fairness with sharing incentives for multiprocessors. In: 19th International Conference on Architectural Support for Programming Languages and Operating Systems, ASPLOS 2014, Salt Lake City, UT, USA, pp. 145–160, March 2014

29. Zeldes, Y., Feitelson, D.G.: On-line fair allocations based on bottlenecks and global priorities. In: 4th ACM/SPEC International Conference on Performance Engineering, ICPE 2013, Prague, Czech Republic, pp. 229–240, April 2013
30. Zukerman, M., Tan, L., Wang, H., Ouveysi, I.: Efficiency-fairness tradeoff in telecommunications networks. IEEE Commun. Lett. 9(7), 643–645 (2005)

PhD Student Workshop — Management of Future Networks

Decentralized Solutions for Monitoring Large-Scale Software-Defined Networks

Gioacchino Tangari[(✉)], Marinos Charalambides, Daphné Tuncer, and George Pavlou

University College London, London, UK
gioacchino.tangari.14@ucl.ac.uk

Abstract. Software-Defined Networking (SDN) technologies offer the possibility to automatically and frequently reconfigure the network resources by enabling simple and flexible network programmability. One of the key challenges to address when developing a new SDN-based solution is the design of a monitoring framework that can provide frequent and consistent updates to heterogeneous management applications. To cope with the requirements of large-scale networks (i.e. large number of geographically dispersed devices), a distributed monitoring approach is required. This PhD aims at investigating decentralized solutions for resource monitoring in SDN. The research will focus on the design of monitoring entities for the collection and processing of information at different network locations and will investigate how these can efficiently share their knowledge in a distributed management environment.

1 Introduction

Effective resource monitoring is a fundamental requirement for the management of large-scale networks. Monitoring systems are designed to collect measurements from the network resources, process the acquired data and expose the resulting knowledge, in order to provide a reliable representation of the network state. Today, network monitoring mainly operates on long timescales producing periodic reports, which are mostly used for manual and infrequent network reconfigurations. However, with the advent of Software-Defined Networking (SDN) technologies, the monitoring requirements are changing since network operators will be able to reconfigure their resources at a faster pace to automatically react to emerging conditions.

By decoupling the control logic from the forwarding hardware, SDN enables easy and flexible network programmability. This key feature allows the implementation of complex high-level network policies [1–3] and the design of applications that reconfigure the network automatically and frequently [4–6]. These novel capabilities pose new monitoring requirements, which cannot be met by currently deployed approaches. As such, the overarching objective of this PhD is to design a monitoring framework that can provide frequent and consistent network state updates to complex and heterogeneous applications, thus enabling fast and effective reconfigurations.

© IFIP International Federation for Information Processing 2016
R. Badonnel et al. (Eds.): AIMS 2016, LNCS 9701, pp. 47–51, 2016.
DOI: 10.1007/978-3-319-39814-3_4

To address these requirements, the monitoring system has to be *scalable*, *flexible* toward heterogeneous applications and *adaptive* with respect to the network conditions. Our research starts from these considerations and focuses on a distributed monitoring system for large-scale software defined networks. The choice of a decentralized approach has its roots in recent research [7,8] which has demonstrated the weakness of centralized SDN proposals. First, using a central controller poses scalability limitations in terms of the number of switches and traffic flows. Second, as the network diameter grows, the associated latencies can become considerable, penalizing the responsiveness of the management operations. In contrast, decentralized solutions can cope with a large number of devices, distributed over wide geographic areas, and facilitate fast reconfigurations since monitoring information is acquired closer to the source.

2 Requirements and Research Challenges

This PhD aims to investigate decentralized solutions for resource monitoring in software-defined networks. The research will be based on the SDN framework proposed in [9] which introduces a clear separation between management and control functionality. A set of *managers*, distributed over the network, hosts various management applications that implement the necessary logic to decide on network (re)configurations, while corresponding *controllers* are in charge of enforcing those decisions. To communicate with the forwarding hardware, the controllers rely on OpenFlow [10], the *de facto* standard for the southbound communication in SDN. As described in [9], monitoring is part of the distributed management functionality with the objective to gather information from network devices and subsequently support applications for their decisions. Although of paramount importance, the authors did not elaborate on the technical challenges associated with collecting and disseminating information in a distributed environment. The objective of this PhD is to address this gap by investigating the challenges described below.

Design Considerations. Effective design of distributed monitoring functionality has to take into account a few key issues. The monitoring operations, if very intrusive, could adversely affect the network performance. At the same time, monitoring operations need to be frequent and fast to enable management applications to operate on short timescales. In addition, they should provide precise and high-granularity information to support accurate decisions. When the management system operates inside a large-scale SDN, the impact of these issues is amplified since the decisions might be taken far away from the locations where monitoring is performed. We identify below the two main features that need to be provided by monitoring entities.

1. **Programmability:** the frequency and the granularity level of the measurements have to be highly configurable based on the requirements of heterogeneous management applications.

2. **Adaptability:** the measurement rate should be frequently reconfigured, in such a way to follow the rate of change of the measured values. Adaptability, as argued in [11,12], enables a reduction of the monitoring overhead, while ensuring acceptable levels of accuracy.

We have identified the main operations composing the monitoring entity function in a distributed management framework. The first one is the analysis of the application requirements. By exposing a high-level API to the management applications, the monitoring entity receives a large variety of requirements. It interprets such requirements and translates them into sets of monitoring specifications, indicating the type of measurements to be performed and the targets of such measurements. Then, it efficiently schedules the individual monitoring operations, in such a way to limit the overhead and avoid the creation of bottlenecks [13]. For example, to gather statistics from an OpenFlow-enabled switch, the monitoring entity instructs the corresponding controller to query, through the OpenFlow interface, the target switches, or to configure them in order to push statistics upon flow expirations. Acquired statistics are finally processed and subsequently exposed to the management applications.

Distributing the Monitoring Function. In a distributed SDN environment, management applications operating at different locations may need statistics gathered from outside their local scope. In such a setting, the monitoring entities will need to share their local knowledge. Ensuring the right tradeoff in state distribution is an open issue, as argued in [8]. In our case, the distribution of the monitoring functionality poses a significant challenge: how can the monitoring entities frequently access reliable and detailed *knowledge* concerning remote resources at an acceptable *cost*? A solution where every local manager shares all the acquired statistics with every other manager is unlikely to scale due to the explosion of overhead and synchronization times. This would prevent decision-making entities to quickly react to emerging conditions and could therefore adversely affect the usage of resources. Part of our work will investigate the possible techniques to achieve the right balance between accuracy and overhead for a wide range of applications. Striking the right tradeoff in statistics aggregation, before the *knowledge* is exchanged, is a possible way to address the issue since this influences the overhead associated with state distribution. Another research challenge concerns the intelligent selection of managers between which knowledge should be shared according to the application requirements. Based on this, a suitable paradigm will be chosen for selective knowledge exchange.

3   Use Case: ISP-Managed Content Distribution

To experiment with the capabilities of the proposed approach, we will consider a distributed SDN network environment, where an ISP operates a content distribution service. In this scenario, a set of content items is cached within the ISP. The management system of the network periodically updates (*e.g.* in order

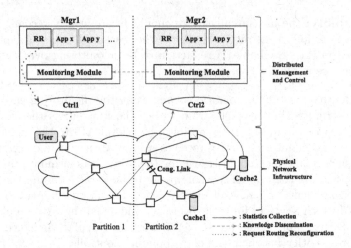

Fig. 1. Example representation of the use case.

of hours) the bandwidth allocation and the content placement, but also reconfigures in real-time the request routing (*i.e.* the routing of users' requests) by programming the underlying forwarding hardware.

Figure 1 depicts a simplified representation of this use case. Here, the network is divided in two partitions, each under the control of a local manager (*i.e.*, *Mgr1/2*). In addition, a controller is assigned to each partition (*i.e.*, *Ctrl1/2*) to interact with the network devices in the corresponding area.

Each manager implements an instance of a distributed Request Routing (RR) reconfiguration application which interacts with the monitoring modules to check the link utilization and the server load in the relevant partition. To collect network statistics, each monitoring module schedules periodic switch polls to acquire the values of the switch-port counters, together with periodic checks of the servers' CPUs and outbound traffic. The acquired data is then *processed* (filtered and aggregated) to form *knowledge* which is *disseminated* both locally (*i.e.* to the local applications) and to remote monitoring modules. We consider a simple example for this use case. Let us assume that, by default, all the requests received at a given *user* location are served by *Cache1* and that congestion occurs on a link located in partition 2. In this case the knowledge obtained by *Mgr2*, notifying the congestion, is exchanged with the monitoring module on *Mgr1*. This enables the *RR* application on *Mgr1* to modify the request-routing configurations by assigning part of the new requests to *Cache2*, thus reducing the utilization of the congested link. The performance of the reconfiguration performed by *Mgr1* depends on the timeliness, accuracy and level of granularity of the information shared between the two monitoring modules.

4   Summary and Future Work

We have presented the main research challenges associated with the design of a scalable monitoring framework that can provide heterogeneous management applications, distributed over a large-scale SDN, with reliable and accurate knowledge. In next steps of this research, we plan to demonstrate the capabilities of our approach by investigating (1) the type of information which can be extracted from the network infrastructure (not only the forwarding hardware), (2) how information can be efficiently exchanged, and (3) the possible implications in terms of delay and cost for the network. We will use the use-case described in the previous section as a baseline for the evaluation of the proposed approach in terms of generated overhead and synchronization time.

Acknowledgement. This research was funded by the UK EPSRC KCN project (EP/L026120/1) and by the Flamingo Network of Excellence project (318488) of the EU Seventh Framework Programme.

References

1. Kim, H., Feamster, N.: Improving network management with software defined networking. IEEE Commun. Mag. **51**(2), 114–119 (2013)
2. Yuan, Y., Alur, R., Loo, B.T.: NetEgg: Programming network policies by examples. In: Workshop on Hot Topics in Networks (Hotnets) (2014)
3. Shin, S., et al.: FRESCO: modular composable security services for software-defined networks. In: ISOC NDSS, February 2013
4. Al-Fares, M., Radhakrishnan, S., Raghavan, B., Huang, N., Vahdat, A.: Hedera: dynamic flowscheduling for data center networks. In: Proceedings of the NSDI 2010 (2010)
5. Heller, B., et al.: ElasticTree: saving energy in data center networks. In: Proceedings of the NSDI 2010 (2010)
6. Agarwal, S., Kodialam, M., Lakshman, T.: Traffic engineering in software defined networks. In: Proceedings of the INFOCOM 2013 (2013)
7. Tootoonchian, A., Ganjali, Y.: HyperFlow: A distributed control plane for OpenFlow. In: Proceedings of the 2010 Internet Network Management Conference on Research on Enterprise Networking (2010)
8. Levin, D., et al.: Logically centralized?: state distribution trade-offs in software definednetworks. In: HotSDN 2012 (2012)
9. Tuncer, D., Charalambides, M., Clayman, S., Pavlou, G.: Adaptive resource management and control in software defined networks. In: IEEE TNSM, March 2015
10. McKeown, N., et al.: OpenFlow: Enabling innovation in campus networks. In: ACM SIGCOMM Computer Communication (2008)
11. Chowdhury, S., Bari, M., Ahmed, R., Boutaba, R.: Payless: A low cost network monitoring framework for software defined networks. In: Proceedings of the NOMS (2014)
12. Moshref, M., Yu, M., Govindan, R., Vahdat, A.: Dream: dynamic resource allocation for software-defined measurement. In: SIGCOMM (2014)
13. Mogul, J.C., et al.: Devoflow: cost-effective flow management for high performance enterprise networks. In: Proceedings of the Hotnets 2010 (2010)

S3N - Smart Solution for Substation Networks, an Architecture for the Management of Communication Networks in Power Substations

Erwin Alexander Leal[(✉)] and Juan Felipe Botero

Electronic and Telecommunications Department,
Universidad de Antioquia, Medellin, Colombia
{erwin.leal, juanf.botero}@udea.edu.co

Abstract. Today, the communications network has become an essential element to the operation of any type of organization or infrastructure, such is the case of the electrical power substations. Such networks in particular, demand high levels of availability and reliability, as the substation is a key element in the chain of energy generation and distribution. However, although recent network modernization introduced new features that allow to optimize the operation of the substation, the variety of devices that integrate it (Intelligent Electronic Devices - IED: breakers, switches, Protection and Control, Merging Units - MU, Network Switches, IEEE 1588 Master Clock) and the huge set of application-level protocols (SMV - Sample Measure Value, GOOSE - Generic Object Oriented Substation Event, MMS - Manufacturing Message Specification, PTP - Precision Time Protocols, among others), increase the management complexity. In this context, the Applied Telecommunications Research Group (GITA), has decided to propose the development of S3N - Smart Solution for Substation Networks. S3N is defined as a network architecture that introduces the novel Software Defined Networks (SDN) and virtualization technologies, in order to simplify the management of communication networks in power substations.

Keywords: SDN · Network · Architecture · Substation · Power · Communication · IEC 61850 · Virtualization

1 Introduction

Smart Grid is a concept that aims to provide mechanisms for the generation and consumption of energy in a more efficient and intelligent manner. This concept proposes the appropriation of data networks advantages to the grid operation in the area of control, communications and monitoring [1]. To reach this purpose, the modernization of the infrastructure that supports the generation, transmission, distribution and consumption of power has caused the emergence, within the communication network, of a variety of IP compliant devices that are interconnected through a network based in Ethernet technology [2]. Currently, the automation process substation is oriented by the IEC 61850 standard [3], which covers almost all aspects of substation automation

© IFIP International Federation for Information Processing 2016
R. Badonnel et al. (Eds.): AIMS 2016, LNCS 9701, pp. 52–56, 2016.
DOI: 10.1007/978-3-319-39814-3_5

system (SAS), providing communication specifications for operations monitoring, control and protection real time. However, this process of modernization has caused that the communication network management, in power substations, has become complex due to the large number of elements that comprise it (Intelligent Electronic Devices - IED: such as Breakers, switches, Protection and Control; Merging Units - MU, Network Switches, IEEE 1588 Master Clock), where each device is responsible for executing functions, with different requirements of connectivity, delay, bandwidth provisioning, synchronization and security [4].

Nevertheless, in recent years, the field of data networks has been permeated by two major trends aiming to facilitate the administration of complex networks: SDN and virtualization technologies, which make the network management more flexible and enable the rapid development and deployment of network services. SDN allow to provide programmability to the network infrastructure, considerably facilitating their management, while virtualization technologies allow, through software, to create a virtual version of a technological resource as an operating system, a storage device, a hardware component or a network resource, where and when it is needed [5–7].

In this area, we propose an experimental architecture for communications networks in substations, based in SDN and virtualization technologies, which is functional, secure, scalable and easy to manage by the energy operator.

This paper is structured as follows: Sect. 2 presents the research problem and Sect. 3 describes the methodology approach. Foreseen impacts are presented in Sect. 4, and the expected contribution and the conclusion are presented in Sect. 5.

2   Research Problem

Although solutions reached through SDN and virtualization technologies are positively transforming the way large datacenters, corporate networks and campuses have begun to operate their networks; it is also seen how gradually these concepts can positively impact the performance and management of the increasing complexity of communications networks in electrical substations [8–10]. However, as proposed in [11], communication networks involved in the operation of electric grid, must meet requirements that are not the same as a corporate network. For example, a substation may contain hundreds of IEDs generating and consuming critical information in real time with different requirements of connectivity, delay, bandwidth provisioning, synchronization, and security, according to its purpose or scope; not to mention, IEDs require proper maintenance and configuration.

According to the above, it can be said that the efficient, reliable and safe operation of power substation data networks, which is a critical infrastructure whose operation can significantly impact a highly energy-dependent society, is limited by the constraints introduced by high number of devices on the network (the order of hundreds, only mentioning IEDs), complex network configuration (each IED can count with 4 network interfaces to guarantee redundancy and his configuration is manual), and traffic management complexity (GOOSE is a multicast protocol that does not tolerate delays greater than 3 ms).

In this context, considering that [8–10] have only presented provisional solutions to the problem exposed through testbeds where: (i) performance evaluation was always emulated [8–10], (ii) network traffic was emulated and only limited to GOOSE and SV messages [9, 10], (iii) SDN controllers based in Python were used in [8, 10] (Python is a interpreted language with low performance compared to other languages), and (iv) no research proposes a complete architecture for management of substation networks, or introduces technologies virtualization as a facilitator in this type of environment, they only present as the application of SDN concepts can improve performance of different tasks on this type of networks. We consider that it is necessary to implement a complete testbed to improve the mentioned limitations, where the experimentation on real network topologies, with traffic conditions matching the wide variety of environment specific protocols (GOOSE, SV, MMS, PTP, FTP, RTSP, etc.). Besides, the use of robust (production capable) SDN controllers is required. In addition, a special interest in identifying the advantages and disadvantages that SDN can bring to communications networks into Smart Grid is growing [11–15]. Therefore, we have decided to propose the development of: S3N - Smart Solution for Substation Networks. A proposal with the aim of defining an architecture for the management of communication networks in power substations, with a high degree of self-configuration, availability, scalability and security; which will use the concepts proposed by SDN and virtualization technologies, for its conception.

3   Research Objective and Methodology Approach

The objective of this research is to propose an architecture for the management of network communications in power substations using the concepts proposed by SDN and virtualization technologies. In this sense, we propose the development of a methodology composed by the following steps:

1. To establish what operation requirements are more restrictive for communications networks in power substations, operating under the IEC 61850 [3].
2. To review the operating characteristics offered by SDN and virtualization technologies in order to define attributes applicable to the field of communication networks in power substations, meeting the restrictions defined under the IEC 61850 standard [3]. The study, of open standards and state of art review of partial solutions in this field, is proposed.
3. To propose models describing the features of the physical/logical elements that integrate the architecture, as well as their schemes of interaction, for the corresponding description of the architecture. For the development of this stage, it is suggested to follow the recommendations specified in the ISO/IEC/IEEE 42010 standard, System and software engineering - Architecture description [16]. This standard provides a foundational ontology to describe system architectures or software architectures. The recommendations of this international standard present a common terminology and a conceptual base that facilitates the specification of requirements, as well as the definition, communication and review of architectures by using ADLs (Architecture description languages).

4. To validate the functionality of the proposed network architecture by implementing use cases in a real testbed. To verify that the architecture meets the operational requirements defined by the IEC 61850 standard, compliance testing will be executed according to the guidelines of IEC 61850-10: 2005 Communication networks and systems in substations - Part 10: conformance testing. Likewise, use cases will be implemented in the following categories: Disaster Recovery, QoS Management and Security.

4 Foreseen Impact

The first impact of the project will be the formulation of an architecture for the management of network communications in power substations by using the concepts around SDN and virtualization technologies. This will provide the opportunity to obtain a communication network with a high degree of self-configuration, availability, scalability and security, which could be replicated in other scenarios of the smart grid.

Another important impact, on the level of technological development and innovation, will be the design and implementation of a proof of concept for the management of communications network in power substations, based on SDN. The possibility of implementing this technology offers enormous potential for development and commercialization, since it contributes to reduced operating and capital costs associated with management in this specific field.

5 Conclusions

The concept of automated substation, which led to the transition from traditional wired connections to an Ethernet-based network with IP support devices, introduced new features in the network, but there are still challenges to be overcome before its proper implementation in current systems.

With the development of this project, we expect to answer research questions such as: (i) can the proposed architecture deliver solutions that improve the management of the communications network in substations, ensuring existing levels of reliability and availability?, (ii) is it possible, using virtualization technologies, to transfer functions that now reside on different hardware equipments (IED's - Intelligent Electronic Device) to a virtualized environment with the aim of optimizing the operation resources (physical space, maintenance, computing capacity)? (iii) can the experimental architecture proposed, contribute to the advancement of Smart Grid concept, in line with the standards and requirements set by the sector?

Acknowledgments. This research has partly been supported by the University of Antioquia, the CODI project 2014-856 and the Colciencias project COL15-2-09.

References

1. Farhangi, H.: The path of the smart grid. IEEE Power Energy Mag. **8**(1), 18–28 (2010)
2. Khan, R., Khan, J.: A comprehensive review of the application characteristics and traffic requirements of a smart grid communications network. Comput. Netw. **57**(3), 825–845 (2013)
3. IEC 61850-1 Ed.2: Communication networks and systems for power utility automation. International Electrotechnical Commission (2012)
4. Huang, Q.: Innovative Testing and Measurement Solutions for Smart Grid. Wiley, Singapore (2015)
5. Kreutz, D., Ramos, F.M.V., Esteves Verissimo, P., Esteve Rothenberg, C., Azodolmolky, S., Uhlig, S.: Software-defined networking: a comprehensive survey. Proc. IEEE **103**(1), 14–76 (2015)
6. Chowdhury, N.M.M.K., Boutaba, R.: Network virtualization: state of the art and research challenges. IEEE Commun. Mag. **47**(7), 20–26 (2009)
7. Mijumbi, R., Serrat, J, Gorricho, J., Bouten, N., De Turck, F., Boutaba, R.: Network function virtualization: state-of-the-art and research challenges. IEEE Commun. Surv. Tutorials **18**(1), 236–262 (2016)
8. Cahn, A., Hoyos, J., Hulse, M., Keller, E.: Software-defined energy communication networks: from substation automation to future smart grids. In: 2013 IEEE International Conference on Smart Grid Communications (SmartGridComm), pp. 558–563, October 2013
9. Molina, E., Jacob, E., Matias, J., Moreira, N., Astarloa, A.: Using software defined networking to manage and control IEC 61850-based systems. Comput. Electr. Eng. **43**, 142–154 (2015)
10. Lopes, Y., Castro, N., Malcher, C.: SMARTFlow: Uma Proposta para a Autoconfiguração de Redes de Subestação IEC 61850 Baseada em OpenFlow. In: WGRS 2014 - Anais do XIX Workshop de Gerência e Operação de Redes e Serviços (2014)
11. Bobba, R., Borries, D., Hilburn, R., Sanders, J., Hadley, M., Smith, R.: Software-defined networking addresses control system requirements. Government report. https://www.selinc.com/WorkArea/DownloadAsset.aspx?id=104399
12. Pfeiffenberger, T., Du, J.L.: Evaluation of software-defined networking for power systems. In: IEEE International Conference on Intelligent Energy and Power Systems (IEPS), pp. 181–185, June 2014
13. Dorsch, N., Kurtz, F., Georg, H., Hagerling, C., Wietfeld, C.: Software-defined networking for smart grid communications: applications, challenges and advantages. In: IEEE International Conference on Smart Grid Communications (SmartGridComm), pp. 422–427 (2014)
14. Dong, X., Lin, H., Tan, R., Iyer, R., Kalbarczyk, Z.: Software-defined networking for smart grid resilience: opportunities and challenges. In: Proceedings of the 1st ACM Workshop on Cyber-Physical System Security (CPSS 2015), pp. 61–68 (2015)
15. Kim, J., Filali, F., Ko, Y.-B.: Trends and potentials of the smart grid infrastructure: from ICT sub-system to SDN-enabled smart grid architecture. Appl. Sci. **5**(4), 706–727 (2015)
16. Systems and software engineering, Architecture description, ISO/IEC/IEEE 2010:2011(E)

Towards a QoS-Oriented Migration Management Approach for Virtualized Networks

Mahboobeh Zangiabady[✉] and Javier Rubio-Loyola

Centre for Research and Advanced Studies of the National Polythecnic Institute,
Carretera Victoria-Soto la Marina Kilómetro 5.5,
Ciudad Victoria, Mexico
{mzangiabady, jrubio}@tamps.cinvestav.mx

Abstract. Virtualization environments are dynamic and polymorphic, consequently they require complex management for both, physical and virtual elements. This research addresses the need for a management approach that can drive virtual network migration systematically to guarantee the required levels of Quality of Service (QoS) in virtual networks. This paper describes a framework that includes the processes needed to manage QoS in migration scenes. A selection of policies that will help in systematizing QoS-oriented virtual network migration are described as well. Test results are provided with the intention to emphasize the difficulty and need for formal research in this direction.

1 Introduction

Network virtualization continues attracting attention from academia and industry. This paradigm allows several Virtual Networks (VNs) deploy on top of the same physical infrastructure without interfering each other. VNs may come and go over time, they could change their Quality of Service (QoS) requirements and demands over time, and the underlying physical networks may experience their own dynamic changes. In the networking research area, the community has invested significant efforts developing VNs mapping approaches, exploiting majorly the use of metaheuristics to optimize metrics like VN acceptance ratio, embedding cost, and time to embed VNs onto physical infrastructures [1]. Moreover, although these solutions have been proved to be efficient to find trade-offs between physical resource usage and VN provisioning, the development of efficient VNs migration management approaches have received very little attention.

A selection of VN migration aspects have been addressed by three exceptional research works. The authors in reference [2] propose a VN mapping algorithm supporting path splitting and for such split paths a basic migration mechanism is proposed. The authors in reference [3] propose a selective VN migration scheme that prioritizes the hop count of virtual link to drive link migrations of the most critical VNs. More recently authors in reference [4] propose an embedding algorithm with a migration option in which physical link bandwidth (BW) utilization is driven to trigger virtual link migrations. Although these works have addressed VN migration issues, all of them

© IFIP International Federation for Information Processing 2016
R. Badonnel et al. (Eds.): AIMS 2016, LNCS 9701, pp. 57–61, 2016.
DOI: 10.1007/978-3-319-39814-3_6

leave aside node migration, as well as both, additive and non-additive QoS constraints of the VNs. It is taken for granted by the research community that VN providers (VNPs) must support virtual networks without having to operate under continuous human care, and VNs should be self-(re) configured taking into account the constraints of network elements, the dynamics in the network and the different levels of QoS of the deployed services. Our research work strives to contribute to the state of the art by defining a VN migration management approach intended to maintain QoS of virtual networks. More precisely, we intend to contribute with: (1) novel VN migration mechanisms that keep the required QoS levels of VNs; (2) VN migration strategies that consider the dynamics of the services deployed on VNs, the efficient use of network resources, and the potential costs involved in the migration process; (3) identifying the most appropriate VN migration strategies that converge to QoS delivery and efficient resources usage. This paper presents the initial steps in this direction. Namely, we present an initial migration framework, a selection of QoS-oriented policies and an overall procedure to systematize migration of virtual links.

2 Migration Framework

This section describes our ideas for a QoS-oriented migration framework. In order to maintain the required QoS in the VNs, migration management techniques should be implemented to decide which virtual elements (links, nodes) are subject of reconfiguration, and when to trigger such reconfigurations. The framework includes three components, namely monitoring, virtual network service management, and virtual network embedding management. Monitoring tasks provides information about usage and availability of physical resources (CPU, memory, bandwidth, etc.). QoS management in general requires static and online control over subscribed services [5]. In the context of our work, services are VNs that are first subscribed via VN requests, and they are mapped into the network via a VN embedding process to make them available to the SPs. VN service management includes VN-Subscription that handles the required topology, QoS requirements and the time to activate the VNs as they are requested. This information is used to draw estimates about additive and non-additive QoS constraints of the VNs to be considered in the mapping and also in the migration process. Virtual network embedding management includes two key elements of the framework, namely embedding and VN migration. Embedding deals with finding optimal mappings of VN requests onto the substrate network and it is addressed by means of metaheuristics. VN migration process (described later) is responsible to migrate virtual networks (nodes and links) between physical resources systematically. Both processes have impact on each other in terms of embedding cost, VN acceptance ratio, and revenue.

3 QoS-Oriented Migration Procedure

The foreseen technical approach for QoS-oriented VN migration management process consists of four stages described hereafter. First, resource bottlenecks in physical resources usage are identified through monitoring physical resources. Second, critical virtual links and/or virtual nodes with high potential to get migrated are identified based on the remaining time, arrival time and departure time of the VNs supported by the bottleneck resources. The third stage is a critical one, it is intended to define the physical resources that would support the virtual resources to-be-migrated. This process considers the additive (delay and hop count) and non-additive (CPU and BW) QoS parameters of the VNs supported by bottleneck resources. We define this process as the Virtual Link Migration Problem (VLMP), which consists of finding a physical path p from a given source, s to a given target t such that the path p meets three conditions: availability, feasibility and optimality. (1) Availability: the physical path p should have enough non-additive resources to support the virtual link to be migrated. Lower bound threshold values are defined to meet the CPU and BW constraints of the virtual link subject of reconfiguration. A basic pruning algorithm is used for this condition. (2) Feasibility: the path p should meet additive constraints. Upper bound threshold values are defined to meet the delay and hop count constraints of the virtual link to be migrated. A reverse-Dijkstra algorithm is used to evaluate this condition [6]. (3) Optimality: the path p is chosen based on options that are taken to meet the agreed QoS targets of virtual link to be migrated. The possible options are; minimize delay, minimize BW in use, minimize CPU in use, or a combination of them. A look ahead Dijkstra algorithm is used to evaluate this condition [6].

The three VLMP conditions described earlier are controlled by the threshold values for availability and feasibility conditions, and the optimality option in the third condition. These are critical aspects that drive the migration process. In this regard, we introduce the concept of migration policies as an important aspect to systematize QoS-oriented migration. We believe that the traffic characteristics and the QoS requirements of the VNs can be used to define, classify and prioritize appropriate VN migration processes. For this reason we propose policies that can be used to drive migration systematically, linking the three VLMP conditions with QoS-aware migration decisions. The objective of migration policies is to find paths with low delay (Policy 1), paths with high available BW (Policy 2), paths with high available CPU (Policy 3), paths with high available CPU and BW (Policy 4), paths with high available CPU and BW and low delay (Policy 5), and paths with high available CPU and BW, as well as low delay and hop counts (Policy 6). For example, the network administration would choose Policy 1 to migrate virtual links with low delay constraints, whereas Policy 6 should be used to find high available physical resources for virtual links with low delay and hop count requirements.

4   Partial Results

We have implemented the migration management process described in this paper in a discrete event simulator. This section describes the effect of QoS-oriented migration policies in the embedding process. Six metaheuristics for the embedding were implemented Genetic Algorithm (GA), Ant Colony (AC), Particle Swarm Optimization (PSO), Firefly Algorithm (FA) and Harmony Search (HS). The configuration parameters of our simulations are similar to the ones used in the literature for the same purposes [1]. We have defined three values of QoS parameters for the VN requests,

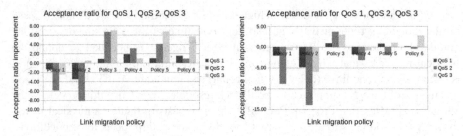

Fig. 1. Improvements (%) for HS (LEFT) and FA (RIGHT) embedding algorithms

modeled as follows: QoS (delay, hop-count, CPU, BW). The three QoS requirements used in our simulations are: QoS1 (20 ms, 3 hops, 60 %, 60 %), QoS2 (10 ms, 4 hops, 50 %, 50 %), and QoS3 (30 ms, 4 hops, 80 %, 80 %) respectively. For each QoS we executed one experiment. Each experiment consisted of 31 execution runs in order to get statistically valid results. Figure 1 shows the results of the HS metaheuristic (left), which outperformed the rest in acceptance ratio metric and the results of FA metaheuristic (right), which is the one with the worst performance out of the six metaheuristics implemented. Very little improvements are achieved for QoS1 in all policies; the highest improvement is 2 % with policy 4. QoS2 and QoS3 are majorly improved by policies 3, 5, and 6; the highest improvement is 6 % with policy 3. Migration policies 1 and 2 do not enhance the embedding in any case with our simulation settings. Through simulation, it is a fact that migration policy enforcement has an effect, which needs to be formally correlated with QoS requirement patterns, VN embedding algorithms and other aspects like topology features and dynamic changes in the physical network. These are important and relevant aspects that will drive our immediate research work.

5   Concluding Remarks and Future Work

We have presented our progress towards a QoS-oriented migration management approach for virtualized network environments. A preliminary framework has been proposed with the intention to identify the required processes needed to manage QoS in migration scenes. A novel contribution of this paper is a migration process driven by policies that systematize QoS-oriented migration. The migration policies are meant to give control capabilities to the network operator as they can be used to define, classify and prioritize appropriate VN migration processes depending on the traffic characteristics and QoS requirements of the VNs. Our preliminary results show that the migration policies have impact depending on the QoS of the VNs. However, more advanced analysis is needed to correlate effective migration policy enforcement with QoS patterns, physical and virtual topology patterns and dynamic changes in the physical network. This will allow the production of self-adapting mechanisms to find trade-offs between optimal resources usage and QoS delivery.

References

1. Chang, X.L., Mi, X.M., Muppala, J.K.: Performance evaluation of artificial intelligence algorithms for virtual network embedding. Eng. Appl. Artif. Intell. **26**, 2540–2550 (2013)
2. Yu, M., Yi, Y., Rexford, J., Chiang, M.: Rethinking virtual network embedding: substrate support for path splitting and migration. ACM SIGCOMM Comput. Commun. Rev. **38**, 17–29 (2008)
3. Zhu, Y., Ammar, M.: Algorithms for assigning substrate network resources to virtual network components. In: INFOCOM 2006, Barcelona, Spain (2006)
4. Hsu, W.-H., Shieh, Y.-P., Wang, C.-H., Yeh, S.-C.: Virtual network mapping through path splitting and migration. In: WAINA 2012, Proceedings of the 2012 26th International Conference on Advanced Information Networking and Applications Workshops, pp. 1095–1100 (2012)
5. Pavlou, G., Flegkas, P., Georgatsos, P., Asgari, A., Mykoniati, E.: Service-driven traffic engineering for intra-domain quality of service management. IEEE Netw. Mag. **17**, 29–33 (2003)
6. Korkmaz, T., Krunz, M: Multi-constrained optimal path selection. In: Proceedings of IEEE INFOCOM 2001, Twentieth Annual Joint Conference of the IEEE Computer and Communications Societies, vol. 2, p. 834 (2001)

Functional Decomposition in 5G Networks

Davit Harutyunyan[✉] and Roberto Riggio

CREATE-NET, via Alla Cascata 56/C, Trento, Italy
{dharutyunyan,rriggio}@create-net.org

Abstract. Mobile data traffic has been rapidly increasing over the last few years. To accommodate for such an ever–growing traffic demand, mobile network operators are required to perform costly network upgrades. Cell size reduction and network virtualization are known to be two of the most effective ways to increase capacity and lower the cost to deploy and operate future mobile networks. This PhD thesis will study the trade–offs associated with the different approaches to small cell virtualization in terms of the point at which base stations operations are decomposed into physical and virtual. Different functional splits will be compared using mathematical optimization tools (e.g., Integer Linear Programming) while novel heuristics will be devised in order to tackle problems of practical size. Finally, selected results will be empirically evaluated over the 5G-EmPOWER test-bed deployed at CREATE-NET premises.

Keywords: Mobile networks · Functional split · Component placement

1 Introduction

Recent advances in network virtualization enabled mobile network operators (MNOs) to move from the D–RAN (Distributed Radio Access Network) architecture, where base–band processing and radio elements are co–located, to the C–RAN (Cloud–RAN) architecture, where baseband units are decomposed from the radio elements and are consolidated in large data–centers. The vaunted benefits of C–RAN are enhanced radio resource utilization and coordination across multiple cells enabled by the centralization of the radio resource management tasks. The downside of such high level of centralization lies in the tight bandwidth and latency requirements imposed on the fronthaul, i.e. the link interconnecting RRHs (Remote Radio Heads) with the BBUs (Base–Band Units), which can *usually* be satisfied only using fiber links.

Nevertheless, although the link between RRHs and BBU Pool has been used as demarcation point in the C–RAN architecture, other functional splits can be in principle defined (see Fig. 1), each of them coming with different requirements. In general, the lower the functional split is executed within the RAN protocol stack, the higher is the centralization benefits, however the fronthaul requirements become also more stringent. For example C–RAN enables an MNOs to implement Coordinated Multi-Point (CoMP) transmission and reception, while

© IFIP International Federation for Information Processing 2016
R. Badonnel et al. (Eds.): AIMS 2016, LNCS 9701, pp. 62–67, 2016.
DOI: 10.1007/978-3-319-39814-3_7

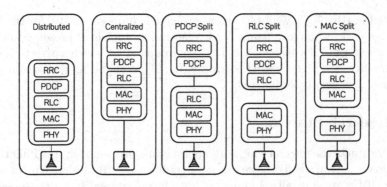

Fig. 1. Different functional splits for 5G small–cells [1].

a split above the Medium Access Control (MAC) layer cannot support CoMP only allowing higher–layers cooperation features (e.g., joint scheduling).

This PhD thesis will explore the trade–offs associated with the different functional splits, including, fronthaul requirements, centralization benefits, and deployment costs, with the ultimate goal of providing MNOs with a set guidelines to design cost–efficient mobile networks. In this paper we report on some preliminary results on the BBU placement problem over a reconfigurable wireless fronthaul while also presenting a roadmap for this PhD thesis.

2 Background

A detailed discussion on various functional splits can be found in [2–4]. The authors of [2] propose a novel RAN as a Service concept in which the level of centralization is flexible and can be adapted to the actual service demands. Several functional splits are introduced and the associated fronthaul requirements are provided in [3]. The authors of [4] survey several wired/wireless fronthauling technologies as well as the associated bandwidth and latency requirements for different functional splits.

Extensive work on C–RAN has been published in the recent years [5–8]. In [5] the authors propose the Colony–RAN architecture for cellular systems able to adjust the cell layout by dynamically changing the connections between BBUs and RRHs. An ILP problem is formalized in [7] for optimizing the assignment of cells to different BBU pools. The authors of [8] derive a mathematical model for optimizing C–RAN deployments combining fiber and microwave links.

The amount of literature on VNE (Virtual Network Embedding) is humbling, a comprehensive survey on this topic can be found in [9]. Likewise, also the amount of work on VNF (Virtual Network Function) placement is considerable [9–13]. In [14] SiMPLE is proposed to address the survivable VNE problem, exploiting a physical path diversity to provide survivability against single and multiple path failures. Similarly, the authors of [15] put forward a batch approach for survivable VNE. Joint node and link embedding algorithms are presented in [16,17]. A VNF placement problem is proposed in [10] for the radio access network, while a dynamic VNF placement problem is presented in [11]. The authors of [12] consider a hybrid environment in which part of the services are provided by dedicated hardware. In [13] an online VNF scheduling and placement problem is formulated.

3   Research Statement

Figure 2 depicts the reference network architecture envisioned in this PhD thesis. In the lower part of the figure we can see a traditional C–RAN deployment where all the BBUs are centralized and long fiber links are used in order to connect BBUs with RRHs (solid black lines). In the upper part of the figure instead, we can see the architecture envisioned in this work. In this case BBU Pools are co–located with macro cells and a reconfigurable wireless fronthaul is used to connect BBUs with RRHs (dashed black lines). A traditional backhaul is used in order to connect macro cells to the core network. This approach has the potential to reduce the length of the (expensive) fiber fronthaul links, thus improving operational and capital expenses, while still enabling advanced control and coordination mechanisms.

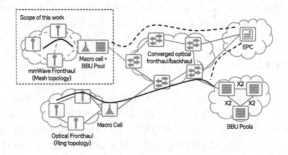

Fig. 2. The reference network architecture.

This architecture will be the starting point for this PhD thesis and will be extended in order to accommodate for different functional splits and for different fronhauling technologies. For each functional split we will formulate an optimization problem and we will study the associated trade–offs. The key performance indicators will include energy consumption as well as network performance (throughput, latency) and resiliency. Scalable heuristics will be developed in order to study networks of practical sizes. We will compare the performances of the ILP–based placement algorithm and of the heuristics using a custom discrete event simulator implemented in Matlab and based on the results we will implement a particular split in the 5G–EmPOWER testbed deployed at CREATE-NET premises[1]. Finally, we will address the economical implications

---

[1] http://empower.create-net.org/.

of the different splits with the overarching objective of providing MNOs a set of guidelines for designing and deploying future 5G networks.

4   Preliminary Result

As preliminary work we formalized and solved the BBU Placement problem over a reconfigurable wireless fronthaul. This approach is made possible by recent advances in microwave communications which allow for up to a few Gbps of bandwidth over short distances, (i.e., less than one Km). In the BBU placement problem the input consists of virtual network requests composed by a variable number of small cells and BBUs, whereas the substrate network provides the physical constraints in terms of bandwidth and computational capacity. In the evaluation we considered grid–shaped substrate networks and star–shaped virtual network requests. We formulate the BBU placement problem as an ILP problem and we propose a greedy heuristic. The ILP problem formulation, including the objective function and the associated constraints as well as the details of the greedy heuristic, have been omitted due to space limitations. Simulations are carried out in Matlab. In this study we assume that a fixed number of requests are embedded sequentially onto the substrate network. Figure 3 shows the percentage of accepted requests and the average embedding cost for different substrate networks. As expected the ILP–based placement algorithm is more efficient than the heuristic in mapping the incoming requests. Nevertheless the performance gap, in this particular case, is relatively small while, as expected, the time required to embed a single request using the greedy heuristic is roughly one order of magnitude smaller than the time required to perform the same embedding using the ILP–based algorithm.

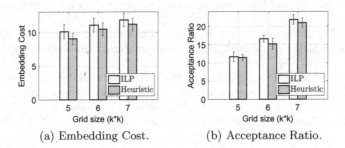

(a) Embedding Cost.   (b) Acceptance Ratio.

Fig. 3. ILP–based algorithm and heuristics performance for different networks.

5   Conclusion

In this paper we presented a roadmap for a comprehensive study on the trade–offs associated with different approaches to small cell virtualization in 5G mobile networks. The study will account for a broad range of key performance indicators ranging from energy consumption to deployment costs and will produce major results in terms of design guidelines and resource allocation algorithms for future mobile networks. Selected results will also be empirically evaluated over the 5G–EmPOWER testbed deployed at CREATE-NET premises.

References

1. Small cell virtualization functional splits and use cases. Small Cell Forum, Technical report, June 2015
2. Rost, P., Bernardos, C., Domenico, A., Girolamo, M., Lalam, M., Maeder, A., Sabella, D., et al.: Cloud technologies for flexible 5G radio access networks. IEEE Commun. Mag. **52**(5), 68–76 (2014)
3. Wubben, D., Rost, P., Bartelt, J.S., Lalam, M., Savin, V., Gorgoglione, M., Dekorsy, A., Fettweis, G.: Benefits and impact of cloud computing on 5G signal processing: flexible centralization through cloud-ran. IEEE Sig. Process. Mag. **31**(6), 35–44 (2014)
4. Maeder, A., Lalam, M., De Domenico, A., Pateromichelakis, E., Wubben, D., Bartelt, J., Fritzsche, R., Rost, P.: Towards a flexible functional split for cloud-ran networks. In: Proceedings of EuCNC, Bologna (2014)
5. Namba, S., Matsunaka, T., Warabino, T., Kaneko, S., Kishi, Y.: Colony-RAN architecture for future cellular network. In: Proceedings of IEEE FutureNetw, Berlin (2012)
6. Carapellese, N., Tornatore, M., Pattavina, A.: Placement of base-band units (BBUs) over fixed/mobile converged multi-stage WDM-PONs. In: Proceedings of IEEE ONDM, Brest (2013)
7. Holm, H., Checko, A., Al-obaidi, R., Christiansen, H.: Optimal assignment of cells in C-RAN deployments with multiple BBU pools. In: Proceedings of EuCNC, Paris (2015)
8. Al-obaidi, R., Checko, A., Holm, H., Christiansen, H.: Optimizing Cloud-RAN deployments in real-life scenarios using microwave radio. In: Proceedings of EuCNC, Paris (2015)
9. Fischer, A., Botero, J.F., Till Beck, M., De Meer, H., Hesselbach, X.: Virtual network embedding: a survey. IEEE Commun. Surv. Tutorials **15**(4), 1888–1906 (2013)
10. Riggio, R., Rasheed, T., Narayanan, R.: Virtual network functions orchestration in enterprise WLANs. In: Proceedings of IEEE ManFI, Ottawa (2015)
11. Clayman, S., Maini, E., Galis, A., Manzalini, A., Mazzocca, N.: The dynamic placement of virtual network functions. In: Proceedings of IEEE NOMS, Krakow (2014)
12. Moens, H., De Turck, F.: VNF-P: a model for efficient placement of virtualized network functions. In: Proceedings of IEEE CNSM, Rio de Janeiro (2014)
13. Mijumbi, R., Serrat, J., Gorricho, J.-L., Bouten, N., De Turck, F., Davy, S.: Design and evaluation of algorithms for mapping and scheduling of virtual network functions. In: Proceedings of IEEE NetSoft, London (2015)
14. Khan, M.M.A., Shahriar, N., Ahmed, R., Boutaba, R.: SiMPLE: survivability in multi-path link embedding. In: Proceedings of IEEE CNSM, Barcelona (2015)
15. Soualah, O., Fajjari, I., Aitsaadi, N., Mellouk, A.: A batch approach for a survivable virtual network embedding based on Monte-Carlo tree search. In: Proceedings of IEEE IM, Ottawa (2015)

16. Despotovic, Z., Hecker, A., Malik, A.N., Guerzoni, R., Vaishnavi, I., Trivisonno, R., Beker, S.A.: VNetMapper: a fast and scalable approach to virtual networks embedding. In: Proceedings of IEEE ICCCN, Shanghai (2014)
17. Guerzoni, R., Trivisonno, R., Vaishnavi, I., Despotovic, Z., Hecker, A., Beker, S., Soldani, D.: A novel approach to virtual networks embedding for SDN management and orchestration. In: Proceedings of IEEE NOMS, Krakow (2014)

Security Attacks and Defenses

An NFC Relay Attack with Off-the-shelf Hardware and Software

Thomas Bocek$^{(\boxtimes)}$, Christian Killer, Christos Tsiaras, and Burkhard Stiller

Communication Systems Group CSG, University of Zürich UZH,
Binzmühlestrasse 14, 8050 Zürich, Switzerland
{bocek,tsiaras,stiller}@ifi.uzh.ch, christian.killer@uzh.ch

Abstract. Passive Near Field Communication (NFC) devices, such as contactless smart cards, use NFC to communicate with other devices without any physical connection or an internal battery source, deriving power inductively via the radio field generated by the NFC reader device. Today, many Point-of-Sale (PoS) terminals, credit cards, and also mobile devices are NFC-capable and facilitate contactless payments. Although the communication range is typically limited to a few centimeters, NFC attacks exist that exploit such contactless communication channels.

This paper focuses on NFC relay attacks and shows that a practical relay attack on public transport PoS terminals, using off-the-shelf mobile devices and hardware, is feasible. Finally, countermeasures are discussed with the main finding that currently the best countermeasure against relay attacks is to physically shield an NFC device.

Keywords: NFC · Relay attacks · Countermeasures · Credit card

1 Introduction

Near Field Communication (NFC) technology is defined as a standardized wireless communication technology, which operates in the High Frequency (HF) band at 13,56 MHz. NFC devices do not necessarily need a battery in place to operate. Passive NFC devices, such as contactless smart cards, can operate deriving power inductively from the magnetic field generated by the NFC reader.

Europay, Mastercard, and Visa (EMV), is a protocol for smart card payments around the world [4]. The Point-of-Sales (PoS) exchanges EMV protocol messages with the chip on the smart card, while selected data is secured with a cryptographic Message Authentication Code (MAC) using symmetric encryption in the online mode, and asymmetric encryption in the offline mode (without access to a network). In the online mode, the key is known to the card issuer, so the identity of the card can be verified. Originally, EMV was designed to fight against the threat of magnetic stripe card fraud and the effort to establish a worldwide standard for chip-based payment-cards and PoS. While the deployment of EMV progressed, and the use of chip-based transactions increased, fraud incidents including magnetic stripe card fraud decreased. However, fraudulent

© IFIP International Federation for Information Processing 2016
R. Badonnel et al. (Eds.): AIMS 2016, LNCS 9701, pp. 71–83, 2016.
DOI: 10.1007/978-3-319-39814-3_8

card-not present transactions (especially card transactions over the Internet, phone, or fax) increased as well [24,26]. The widespread distribution of EMV-compliant payment-cards, immediately raised the question if security issues have to be further investigated. Prior research showed that the EMV protocol has major vulnerabilities that can be exploited [11,22,23]. Today, new PoS terminals, credit cards, and mobile devices are NFC-capable and designed according to the EMV contactless standard. Thus, many security sensitive applications, such as payment applications and electronic passports, already use contactless technologies [25].

One type of attack with NFC and Radio-frequency Identification (RFID) is the relay attack. This type of attacks in RFID communications is known for years, but still EMV-compliant PoS terminals are at least partially vulnerable. With relay attacks, the physical presence of the credit card near a PoS is not necessary anymore. This could disrupt security and privacy assumptions, mainly due to the fact that most of these contactless smart cards are based on the International Organisation for Standardization (ISO)/International Electronical Commission (IEC) 14443 standard and are intended to operate only over a distance of around 10 cm. With a relay attack, the distance assumption of 10 cm does not hold anymore. As an example, a credit card can be physically in the US, while in Germany, with relaying, this card can be used to pay for a public transport ticket using a contactless PoS terminal. Furthermore, in some countries, small amounts can be charged from the credit card via NFC without any user intervention or credential usage.

This paper shows the feasibility and proof-of-concept of relay attacks with off-the-shelf software and hardware by implementing a practical relay attack on EMV-compliant PoS machines for public transportation. It shows that its still feasible to exploit this known vulnerability. Furthermore, a discussion follows about countermeasures and its effectiveness.

The remainder of this paper is structured as follows. Related work is discussed in Sect. 2, followed by a generic NFC relay attack architecture in Sect. 3. While Sect. 4 presents technical details about the implementation of this work, Sect. 5 proposes possible countermeasures to prevent NFC relay attacks. Finally, Sect. 6 summarizes this paper and draws conclusions.

2   Related Work

Various EMV protocol attacks have been reported in the literature. After an overview over the EMV authentication methods, downgrading, yes-card, wedging, pre-replay, and relay attacks are presented in the following.

There are three different authentication methods for EMV cards, Static Data Authentication (SDA), Dynamic Data Authentication (DDA) and Combined Data Authentication (CDA) [3]. Weaknesses have been found for all these card authentication methods. Cards using SDA are vulnerable to the "yes-card" attack, where an attacker can copy the static data. Then, the attacker can use the copied card to conduct valid, statically signed transactions. As a result, DDA improved this by signing dynamic data with a card-unique asymmetric Rivest, Shamir and Adleman (RSA) key. CDA combines DDA, the signing of changing transaction data, with the use of an application cryptogram (AC) generated by the card.

All these authentication methods improve the security of contactless transactions. There are three main Cardholder Verification Methods (CVM) which are supported by EMV. There is an online and offline Personal Identification Number (PIN) verification, or the use of signatures (which is used for magnetic-stripe cards). Usually, for low amount transactions, no additional CVM is used. Prior research showed that the payment terminal itself can be forced to fall back to old Cardholder Verification methods (CVM), such as downgrading a full EMV credit card to perform an EMV magnetic-stripe transaction [26]. If such an attack is possible, all of the new authentication methods are rendered useless.

Another critical issue concerning EMV is the EMV PIN verification "wedge" vulnerability. This vulnerability allows an attacker to use stolen cards without knowing the correct PIN. To do so, the attacker uses a man-in-the-middle attack, where the stolen card will accept any PIN entered, for both offline and online transactions [23].

Prior research presented a proof-of-concept for the so-called Pre-Replay attack [11]. An attacker can use a tampered terminal to collect card details. Later on, the attacker can replay the data collected at a terminal of the same type that data were harvested on. The collected card details include the PIN and an Authorization Request Cryptogram (ARQC). These ARQCs are responses from the card, when presented with an Unpredictable Number (UN) by the PoS terminal. The flaw is that some PoS terminals generate predictable numbers instead of a random number. The protocol design flaw is that the terminal generates the number and the issuer relies on its random generation. Thus, for this attack to succeed, the attacker must compromise the terminal equipment and then harvest ARQCs, to be able to carry out indistinguishable transactions to the issuer.

Relay attacks on ISO/IEC 14443 Type A-based smartcards are introduced in [16,18]. The Radio Frequency (RF) communication was relayed up to a distance of 50 m. This work illustrates how the attacker can use commercially available tools. Moreover, it highlights the potential security implications for current contactless applications. Practical and generic relay attacks were implemented, only using two NFC-enabled mobile phones and software applications. It has been shown that many EMV-compliant systems still seem to be vulnerable [13,14]. Previous work has also shown that an extension of the classic relay attack is possible [20]. Such an extension could mean an increase of the distance between the reader device and the genuine card. The additional distance varies between 40 cm to 50 cm and the extra cost is less than 100 $. More precisely, a potential attacker could discreetly access a foreign card from about 50 cm far away. This is a fivefold increase in distance compared to the distance of a ISO 14443 contactless smart card transaction. Additionally, EMV transactions have a common structure. Thus, if a transaction is recorded and the static and redundant data, which is the same for every transaction, are omitted in the relayed communication, a relay attack transaction can be optimized.

Besides mobile payment, relay attacks in other scenarios, such as ticketing systems, have been successfully demonstrated as well as reported in [15].

This paper shows that while the relay attack vulnerability is well known and has been reported in many papers and articles before, its still exploitable as of today with off-the-shelf hard and software.

3   Background and Architecture

The relay attack presented in this paper applies to ISO/IEC 14443 smart cards of operation mode type A. These smart cards are passive and the inductively coupled RFID transponders have a transceiving range of up to 10 cm. The reading device is called Proximity Coupling Device (PCD) and the card is referred to as Proximity Integrated Circuit Card (PICC). In a typical usage scenario, the PICC interacts directly with a PCD.

For a relay attack, further devices are necessary. In addition, as shown in Fig. 1, two NFC devices (tablets) and at least one IEEE 802.11 wireless network (Wifi) are used. This enlarges the transceiving range up to the Wifi range to about 100 m. For larger ranges two Wifi devices connected to the Internet are required as shown in Fig. 2. In both cases, one NFC device is in a proxy mode that will relay the NFC traffic from the PCD (PoS) via Wifi and back, the other NFC devices is in relay mode that will relay the NFC traffic from Wifi to the PICC (credit card) and back. The Wifi network establishes a tunnel for the traffic between the two NFC devices in proxy mode respectively in relay mode. An attacker needs to place one NFC device on the contactless payment terminal, while placing the other NFC device close to the victim's NFC credit-card.

In consequence, the physical presence of the PICC is no longer required. This work here assumes that the delay occurring is below 1.5 s and, therefore, the attack is possible [11].

3.1   EMV Contactless Transaction

EMV Contactless [4] is the standard for contactless PICCs. The contact chips, for both contact and contactless PICCs, are usually based on the ISO/IEC 7816 standard and the "contactless integrated circuit" is designed according to ISO/IEC 14443.

Comparing ISO/IEC 7816 and ISO/IEC 14443 to the Open Systems Interconnection model (OSI model), in contact based systems, the ISO/IEC 7816-3 [8] standard specifies layer 1 (Physical), 2 (Data link), and 4 (Transport). In contactless systems, these three layers are specified in ISO/IEC 14443-2 [5], ISO/IEC 14443-3 [6], and ISO/IEC 14443-4 [7]. Even though the contact and contactless standards differ in various aspects (*e.g.* transport protocols, anti-collision, activation, bit transfer and power supply), the communication protocol as on OSI layer 7 (Application) is the same as specified in ISO/IEC 7816-4 [9] for contact

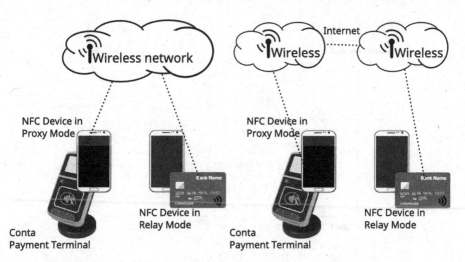

Fig. 1. Setup 1: simple relay attack setup

Fig. 2. Setup 2: internet relay attack setup

based systems. Further, the transaction protocol supports the use of so-called Application Protocol Data Units (APDU).

Before the APDU-based protocol can be started, PCD and PICC need to have the same configuration. First of all, the PCD polls for new PICCs by sending out a REQA. After that, PICCs that have not been activated yet, synchronously answer with their Answer-to-Request (ATQA). The PCD is now notified that a new PICC is available and, therefore, initiates the anti-collision procedure by starting a binary search tree algorithm and enumerating all PICCs based on their Unique Identifier (UID). If the anti-collision was successful, these PICCs send a Select Acknowledge (SAK), which indicates whether the card supports the standard data transmission of ISO/IEC 14443-4 or not. If supported, the PCD sends a request to answer the select (RATS) as a command and expects an answer to reset (ATS) as a response. The RATS contains parameters, such as the frame size the PCD can receive. In return, the ATS contains information about the chip's operating system. Now the PCD and PICC reached the same configuration. Hence, from there on the communication between PCD and PICC is always conducted in the form of APDU command-response pairs.

3.2 Visa Smart Debit/Credit (qVSDC) Protocol

Visa's payWave transactions are using the quick Visa Smart Debit/Credit (qVSDC) protocol as shown in Fig. 3, which is slightly more compressed than the MasterCard PayPass protocol. The main difference between the two protocols is that Visa transactions omit using the GENERATE AC command. The functionality is brought together in the GET PROCESSING OPTIONS (GPO) (message #5 in Fig. 3) request, because the card will respond to the GPO by calculating

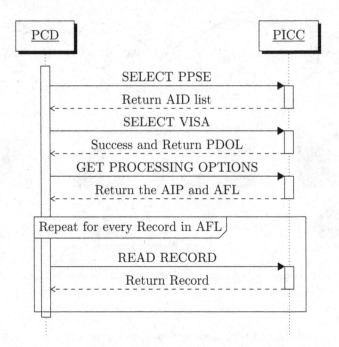

Fig. 3. EMV contactless transaction sequence diagram.

the Application Cryptogram (AC) and sign the data in the next response (message #6 in Fig. 3). The different steps in a Visa contactless transaction can be divided into 8 steps [13].

1st Message PCD → PICC: Command: SELECT PPSE
The PCD selects the Proximity Payment System Environment (PPSE).

2nd Message PICC → PCD: The PICC responds with the file control information template (FCI) which is list of the supported EMV applications, so-called Application Identifiers (AID) also combined with a priority indicator for every AID.

3rd Message PCD → PICC: Command: SELECT VISA
The PCD then selects the AID with the highest priority which it is supporting.

4th Message PICC → PCD: The PICC responds if the application was selected successfully. The response also contains the File Control Information (FCI) template with application details, such as the Processing Options Data Object List (PDOL) with all those fields (*e.g.* Amount, Terminal Country Code, Terminal verification Results, Transaction Date/Type and the Unpredictable Number) needed by the PCD for the next step.

5thMessage PCD → PICC: Command: `GET PROCESSING OPTIONS`
Following the application selection, the PCD requests processing options. In essence, the PCD responds with the PDOL related data encoded according to the PICC's previous PDOL received in the 4^{t}h message.

6thMessage PICC → PCD: The card responds with the Application Interchange Profile (AIP) and Application File Locator (AFL). The AFL is used by the terminal to read the data records from the PICC. These records contain a variety of information, such as the Primary Account Number (PAN), the expiry date, and more (except for the Card Verification Value (CCV)). The AFL also indicates, if any of the data will be provided for the Authentication Process. As a result, the card is in control, which files can be read.

7thMessage PCD → PICC: Command: `READ RECORD`
The PCD requests the records according to the AFL and the PICC follows these requests with the according responses. Which data is being read exactly depends on how the issuer configure the card.

8thMessage PICC → PCD: The PICC returns the records requested.

4 Implementation

For this work here, the NFCProxy [10] was selected to carry out the relay attack. The hardware requirements - as discussed above - are 2 NFC devices and one or more Wifi devices. Two commercially available off-the-shelf NFC-enabled mobile tablets were used. The NFCProxy requires a certain versions (9.1 and 10.1) of CyanogenMod [1]. The installation of those versions is mandatory, because the NFCProxy requires certain features for handling Host Card Emulation (HCE), which was removed in some Android versions. However, on never devices, these relay attacks work without installing a custom ROM [27]. To install Cyanogen-Mod on a mobile device, the device needs to be rooted and unlocked. Furthermore, these HCE extensions require the NXP PN544 NFC Controller, which is used on many commercially available devices. To carry out the relay attack, the setup as shown in Fig. 1 with a portable IEEE 802.11 b/g/n wireless router was used, which was powered on with a mobile power source.

4.1 Hardware/Software Specification

The following hardware and software was used to carry out the relay attack.

- 2 Tablets; brand/model: ASUS Nexus 7v1, CyanogenMod 10.1 operating system
- Wireless Router; brand/model: Alfa Network Hornet-UB, chip set: Atheros AR9331 SoC, 2.4 GHz, 802.11 b/g/n
- Credit-Card; brand: VISA, model: Visa Card Classic, payWave limit: 40 CHF
- NFCProxy [10], version 0.1.2.

4.2 Relay Attack Proof-of-Concept

The relay attack implementation was tested as described in [12] at two different public transport PoS terminals that were capable of handling contactless transactions. The attacker placed one Android device (proxy mode) on the PoS terminal and the other Android device (relay mode) next to an NFC credit card of the victim. Two relay attacks at two different terminals were video recorded and can be seen in a proof of concept (PoC) video as shown in Fig. 4. Note that for this attack purely the feasibility of the attack was targeted at, as the only purpose was to show and indicate vulnerabilities. At no times at all the public transportation authority was faced with fraud or any misuse of services obtained.

Fig. 4. Proof-of-concept [21]

4.3 Protocol Details

The Visa payWave logs that were recorded during the PoC implementation follow the protocol as described is Sect. 3. As a card authentication method, the offline CDA was used, following the Visa payWave Contactless EMV standards. In general, CDA verifies the card by generating an RSA signature on individual transaction data and additionally verifying using an AC generated by the card. For this reason, the message #5 as above also included an Unpredictable Number (UN). The card is expected to return a Signed Dynamic Application Data (SDAD) and an application cryptogram in message #6. SDAD is a dynamic signature generated by the card and validated by the reader during fast Dynamic Data Authentication (fDDA) processing. As the name implies, fDDA is faster than the standard DDA due to the fact that it utilizes a pre-defined list of data elements for authentication.

As indicated in Fig. 3, messages #7 and #8 are repeated for every record in the AFL. Therefore, the PCD starts to read data records (message #7) from the PICC. The first response (message #8) contains an Issuer Public Key Certificate (IPK), which is certified by a Certification Authority (CA). Further, the response contains more data, such as the Certification authority public key index (to identify the CA public key) and also an Issuer Public Key Exponent, which is used for verification of the SDAD and the IPK. In return, the PCD requests another data record with the message #7. In the second response of the card (message #8), the PAN, the expiration date, the issuer code, and the ICC Public Key Certificate is returned. If everything was accepted by the POS terminal, the transaction was successful.

Although, a successful relay attack was carried out on public transport PoS terminals, no fraudulent transactions were issued. At any point in time, equipment and credit cards were used belonging to a single person. All purchased tickets over the NFC relay were paid in full by the authors.

5   Countermeasures

To carry out this relay attack as presented above, an attacker does not have to decrypt any of the data, thus, there is no formal breaking of keying material or credentials involved. Hence, providing sufficient protection against such relay attacks is difficult, because the attack cannot be prevented by application-level cryptography [17]. Therefore, to supplement existing security mechanisms, additional countermeasures are required. These countermeasures have to focus according to today's knowledge on the essential and key aspects of the relay attack: (1) the added time delay and (2) any unnoticed access to the card [18].

Countermeasures can be classified into two key categories: either (1) the card is protected or (2) the system itself is [20]. The most simple, effective, and cost-efficient form to protect the card is to shield the chip (e.g., wrapping card in metal foil) and, thus, prevent almost certainly any unwanted remote activation. Additionally, the following selection of further possible countermeasure include (a) additional verifications, (b) time measurements, and (c) distance bounding.

5.1   Additional Verification

Relay attacks could be prevented by introducing secondary authentication procedures (e.g., password or biometrics). However, such additional verification countermeasures demand additional (typically unwanted - due to practicality reasons) user-interactions, which eliminates the convenience emerging from the use of the contactless smart cards. Another drawback that could arise is the resulting increase in transaction time, which might not be acceptable in every application anymore. Recent approaches in combining credit card and smartphone with NFC introducing an additional secure elemement could solve the problem e.g., by asking the user on the smartphone if a transaction should be carried out. Once a vendor is known with a previously approved transaction, further transcation with this vendor could be carried out again without any user interaction. Thus, making the relay attack much more difficult, without loosing the convenience and keeping the transaction times low.

5.2   Time Measurement

A valid and genuine contactless transaction has a certain time duration, depending on the specific PICC and PCD setup. Typically, relaying this communication results in a delayed transaction and, therefore, takes more time. Because these POS terminals would need to serve a variety [11] of contactless cards, setting a time limit could easily lead to valid transactions being rejected (false positive).

Theoretically, if an accurate response time is recorded for every PICC and PCD combination, it would be possible to implement a maximum time duration for a transaction as presented in this work [28]. The implementation of such a time measurement challenge-response protocol makes a relay attacks more difficult, but wold not be able to prevent them in full [26].

In contrary, prior research also concluded that the time variance observed on dynamic messages between various cards was even larger than the overhead by the relay [14]. Thus, simply using an overall time limit on static or dynamic data authentication (*e.g.,* using the GENERATE AC message response in MasterCard PayPass or the GET PROCESSING OPTIONS message response in Visas Pay-Wave) cannot be used as an efficient countermeasure against relay attacks due to different chips on cards, resulting in very different processing time.

The relay attacks in the PoC video [21] lasted between 671 ms and 2050 ms and those were accepted either way. Yet, the EMV Contactless standard allows for up to 500 ms of total time per transaction (*e.g.,* for Visa [2]). Prior research could also observe an equal behavior [14]. Transactions would be accepted even though the transaction took longer than 500 ms. Therefore, when performing a relay attack, the genuine card could be anywhere in the world and timing constraints are not sufficient on their own to provide a suitable protection against relay attacks.

5.3   Distance Bounding

Distance bounding protocols define countermeasure against relay attacks. In essence, a cryptographic distance bounding protocols enables the PCD to compute a maximum distance between the PCD and the PICC. Distance bounding protocols assume that the PICC and the PCD share a secret and measure thereafter the time it takes to exchange a number of bits. Combining the time measurement at the level of nano seconds and the knowledge of the speed of light, the distance can be estimated within an accuracy of a few meters. However, it would still be possible to perform a relay attack with specialized hardware that is able to relay communication close to the speed of light. However, such specialized hardware is very expensive today, resulting in a poor risk/reward ratio [14].

Distance bounding mechanisms have to be implemented into the physical communication layer, because all mechanisms above the physical layer, such as collision-avoidance, result in a fatal inaccuracy of the time measurement [19, 28]. This inaccuracy could be prevented using a dedicated and fast RF communication channel. Despite the aforementioned inaccuracy, distance bounding protocols are today and theoretically the best countermeasure against relay attacks.

A simplified distance bounding protocol has been proposed in [14]. The proposed PaySafe protocol is EMV-compliant and, therefore, uses existing fields within EMV (*e.g.,* Unpredictable Number and the ICC Dynamic Number). The main approach of PaySafe is to improve the protocol in such way, that time measurements can be used as an efficient countermeasure. For this reason, the protocol splits up the challenge and response command from the generation of the signed authentication and cryptogram. The PaySafe protocol also initiates the contactless transaction with the application selection. Now, before the PICC sends its PDOL (message #4 in Fig. 3) to the reader, the PICC generates a nonce it temporarily stores. Then the PCD sends a timed GET PROCESSING OPTIONS request to the PICC (message #5 in Fig. 3). The PICC immediately responses with the nonce generated in the previous step. This response does not need any computation and, therefore, the variance in the time it takes is very low. If the message was relayed, an additional overhead would be introduced and the PCD can easily detect such a deviation. The suggested upper bound for the respective time out is at 80 ms. Thus, the PaySafe protocol would stop relay attacks using mobile phones or off-the-shelf USB NFC readers.

6 Summary and Conclusions

This paper discussed security issues concerning the EMV protocol. Furthermore, the approach undertaken takes a deeper look at a practical path to relay attacks. As the approach was focused on public transportation PoS machines, it serves as an example only, which did not fraud any public or private body throughout the experiments. Thus, the PoC shows a successful relay attack over an IEEE 802.11 Wireless network, using two commercially available tablets, publicly available Software, and a Visa payWave credit-card.

Even though the EMV specification defines 500 ms as the maximum duration for a transaction, the transactions in those experiments have taken up to 2060 ms and were accepted! Similar behavior has been observed in prior research [14].

Possible countermeasures against relay attacks include additional verification mechanisms, which could prevent the attack by adding security, but giving away convenience emerging from the usage of contactless cards. Time measurement cannot be efficiently deployed due to the variance in dynamic messages and the possibility to cache static messages. Distance bounding requires stable performance and predictable time accuracy of those communication channels in use and in compliance with ISO/IEC 14443 systems. The PaySafe protocol is a simplified distance bounding protocol that is EMV-compliant.

Even though relay attacks have been a quite prominent research topic, the EMV-compliant payment systems in place today are still partially vulnerable. While effective countermeasures are theoretically available, they are not deployed everywhere yet. Since other cards use EMV as well, these cards are vulnerable too [14]. The ease to intercept and relay a full transaction shows that these systems need to be hardened against relay attacks, as currently the only effective defense strategy is to shield the chip as show in Fig. 5.

Fig. 5. NFC/RFID card protection

In general, there are further attack scenarios possible, *e.g.*, an attacker with his NFC device in relay mode, can stay at a PoS equipped with a contactless reader. A second attacker with his NFC device in proxy mode and an additional antenna can stay in a crowded place and try to activate foreign cards and relay the APDUs back and forth (cf. setup 2 in Fig. 2). However, such an attack does not scale well and the pay-off is not as high compared to the card-not-present fraudulent activities.

Explicit Note: This work performed did proof as its key and only objective the feasibility of this type of reply attack on public Point-of-Sales (PoS) terminals. Since this and only purpose was driven by research motivations on IT system security this work only shows, demonstrates as a proof-of-concept, and indicates technical vulnerabilities. At no times at all the publicly accessible PoS was faced or threatened with any fraud or any misuse of services obtained.

Acknowledgments. This work was partially supported by the FLAMINGO project funded under the EU FP7 Program (Contract No. FP7-2012-ICT-318488).

References

1. CyanogenMod. http://www.cyanogenmod.org. Accessed Jan 2016
2. EMV Contactless Specifications for Payment - Systems Book C-3 - Kernel 3 (Visa)
3. EMV Key Management - Explained. https://www.cryptomathic.com/hubfs/docs/cryptomathic_white_paper-emv_key_management.pdf. Accessed Jan 2016
4. EMVCo. http://www.emvco.com. Accessed Jan 2016
5. ISO, IEC 14443–2: 2010 - Identification cards - Contactless integrated circuit cards - Proximity cards, Part 2: Radio frequency power and signal interface (2010)
6. ISO, IEC 14443–3: 2011 - Identification cards - Contactless integrated circuit cards - Proximity cards, Part 3: Initialization and anticollision (2011)
7. ISO, IEC 14443–4: 2008 - Identification cards - Contactless integrated circuit cards - Proximity cards, Part 4: Transmission protocol (2008)
8. ISO, IEC 7816–3: 2006 - Identification cards - Integrated circuit cards, Part 3: Cards with contacts - Electrical interface and transmission protocols (2006)
9. ISO, IEC 7816–4: 2013 - Identification cards - Integrated circuit cards, Part 4: Organization, security and commands for interchange (2013)
10. NFCProxy. http://sourceforge.net/projects/nfcproxy/. Accessed Jan 2016
11. Bond, M., Choudary, O., Murdoch, S.J., Skorobogatov, S.P., Anderson, R.J.: Chip and skim: cloning EMV cards with the pre-play attack. In: IEEE Symposium on Security and Privacy (SP 2014), San Jose, CA, USA, May 2014

12. van den Breekel, J.: NFC Hacking: The Easy Way, DEF CON 2012, Las Vegas, Nevada, USA, July 2012
13. van den Breekel, J.: Relaying EMV Contactless Transactions using Off-The-Shelf Android Devices, BlackHat Asia, Singapore, March 2015
14. Chothia, T., Garcia, F.D., de Ruiter, J., van den Breekel, J., Thompson, M.: Relay cost bounding for contactless EMV payments. In: 19th International Conference on Financial Cryptography and Data Security, Puerto Rico, January 2015
15. Chu, X.: Relay attacks of NFC smart cards. Master Thesis, NTNU Trondheim, Norwegian University of Science and Technology, Department of Telematics, June 2014
16. Francis, L., Hancke, G., Mayes, K., Markantonakis, K.: Practical NFC peer-to-peer relay attack using mobile phones. In: Ors Yalcin, S.B. (ed.) RFIDSec 2010. LNCS, vol. 6370, pp. 35–49. Springer, Heidelberg (2010)
17. Hancke, G.P., Mayes, K.E., Markantonakis, K.: Confidence in smart token proximity: relay attacks revisited. Comput. Secur. **28**(7), 615–627 (2009)
18. Hancke, G.: A Practical Relay Attack on ISO 14443 Proximity Cards. Technical report, University of Cambridge Computer Laboratory, February 2005
19. Hancke, G., Kuhn, M.: An RFID distance bounding protocol. In: First International Conference on Security and Privacy for Emerging Areas in Communications Networks (SecureComm 2005), Athens, Greece, September 2005
20. Kfir, Z., Wool, A.: Picking virtual pockets using relay attacks on contactless smartcard. In: First International Conference on Security and Privacy for Emerging Areas in Communications Networks (SecureComm 2005), Athens, Greece, September 2005
21. Killer, C.: NFCProxy Relay Attack in the Wild. https://www.youtube.com/watch?v=fRtn4ZfkLkM. Accessed Jan 2016
22. Killer, C.: Security Challenges in Contactless Payments Solutions. Assignment Communication Systems Group, Department of Informatics, University of Zurich, June 2015
23. Murdoch, S., Drimer, S., Anderson, R., Bond, M.: Chip and PIN is broken. In: IEEE Symposium on Security and Privacy (SP 2010), Oakland, CA, USA, May 2010
24. Murdoch, S.J., Anderson, R.: Verified by visa and mastercard securecode: or, how not to design authentication. In: 14th International Conference on Financial Cryptography and Data Security (FC 2010), Tenerife, Spain, January 2010
25. Ngu, M., Scott, C.: How secure are contactless payment systems? In: RSA Conference, San Francisco, USA, April 2015
26. Roland, M., Langer, J.: Cloning credit cards: a combined pre-play and downgrade attack on EMV contactless. In: 7th USENIX Conference on Offensive Technologies (WOOT 2013), Washigton, D.C., USA, August 2013
27. Vila, J., Rodriguez, R.J.: Practical experiences on NFC relay attacks with android - virtual pickpocketing revisited. In: 11th Workshop on RFID Security (RFIDSEC 2015), New York City, USA, June 2015
28. Weiß, M.: Performing Relay Attacks on ISO 14443 Contactless Smart Cards using NFC Mobile Equipment. Master Thesis, Technische Universität München, May 2010

Analysis and Evaluation of OpenFlow Message Usage for Security Applications

Sebastian Seeber[1]([⊠]), Gabi Dreo Rodosek[1], Gaëtan Hurel[2],
and Rémi Badonnel[2]

[1] Department of Computer Science, Universität der Bundeswehr München,
85577 Neubiberg, Germany
{sebastian.seeber,gabi.dreo}@unibw.de
[2] Inria Nancy Grand-Est, Université de Lorraine,
Campus Scientifique, 54600 Villers-les-nancy, France
gaetan.hurel@inria.fr, remi.badonnel@loria.fr

Abstract. With the advances in cloud computing and virtualization technologies, Software-Defined Networking (SDN) has become a fertile ground for building network applications regarding management and security using the OpenFlow protocol giving access to the forwarding plane. This paper presents an analysis and evaluation of OpenFlow message usage for supporting network security applications. After describing the considered security attacks, we present mitigation and defence strategies that are currently used in SDN environments to tackle them. We then analyze the dependencies of these mechanisms to OpenFlow messages that support their instantiation. Finally, we conduct series of experiments on software and hardware OpenFlow switches in order to validate our analysis and quantify the limits of current security mechanisms with different OpenFlow implementations.

1 Introduction

Software-defined networking (SDN) has become a major paradigm for network programmability with the large-scale deployment of cloud infrastructures and the virtualization of network functions. It currently provides a convenient support to the design and implementation of different services, including security mitigation mechanisms, through the abstraction of higher-level functionality. In particular, it is often perceived or expected as a potential solution for enabling fast reconfiguration operations in order to address the growing complexity of networking environments. Indeed, decision making processes can be facilitated at the SDN controllers level, e.g. about forwarding paths, based on the logical global view of the network that is abstracted and given to applications. Moreover, the close relationship between network intelligence and the forwarding plane enables a faster reply and a more flexible way to react to security incidents, in comparison to other traditional solutions.

The abstraction induced by software-defined networking poses also important security issues with respect to the reliability and dependencies of solutions

© IFIP International Federation for Information Processing 2016
R. Badonnel et al. (Eds.): AIMS 2016, LNCS 9701, pp. 84–97, 2016.
DOI: 10.1007/978-3-319-39814-3_9

that are built on top of them. This statement is even more critical when these applications using network programmability facilities are intended to detect or prevent security attacks. Typically, these solutions are based on the OpenFlow standardized protocol, which is one of the most prominent software-defined solutions for supporting communications between network controllers and programmable switches. It therefore plays a central role in the effective reliability of applications. However, the various implementations of this protocol react in different ways. For instance, the timing and count of OpenFlow messages may differ for hardware and software implementations and among multiple vendors, which may have a direct impact on the overall performances of software-defined applications. In that context, a major challenge is to analyze the dependencies of security solutions to software-defined networking protocols, such as the exploitation of OpenFlow messages. It is also important to evaluate their performance impact on different hardware implementations to draw conclusions about the effectiveness of security approaches based on OpenFlow messages. Otherwise, vendors of OpenFlow-based security applications are bound to specific hardware and thus dashes the expectations of software-defined networking with respect to open vendor independent and standardized interfaces.

The rest of this paper is organized as follows: Sect. 2 gives an overview of security attacks that have been considered in this analysis and describes SDN-based security mitigation currently available to address them. In Sect. 3 we analyze the dependencies of these security solutions in terms of OpenFlow message usage through a dedicated mapping. We then evaluate in Sect. 4 the performance of different OpenFlow implementations and the induced impact on security applications. Section 5 details related work in the area of software-defined security. Section 6 concludes the paper and points out several research perspectives.

2 Network Attacks and SDN-Based Defences

Considering the traditional taxonomy of security attacks published in [12], our analysis has focused on SDN mitigation mechanisms for tackling two major categories of security attacks, namely overloading attacks and information gathering attacks. We remind in this section each of these categories and detail defence strategies designed in traditional and software-defined environments. These strategies will then serve as a basis for analyzing and quantifying the dependencies of security mechanisms to OpenFlow messages.

2.1 Mitigation of Overloading Attacks

These last years have seen an increase of overloading attacks, with in particular distributed denial-of-service (DDoS) [2] whose growth has been evaluated to 90 % in the last 12 months by a recent report from Akamai [1]. The main methods used in networking and software-defined networking are based on flooding techniques, where the attacker generates a very high amount of packets to overload the target environment. A typical example is given by smurf attacks which generate

ICMP echo/reply packets, where the source IP address is spoofed, with broadcast networks to multiply traffic. Following this approach, a couple of low-bandwidth sources can easily kill high-bandwidth connections. The overloading attacks may also rely on amplification techniques. In that case, the approach consists in turning a small amount of bandwidth coming from a few machines into huge attacks targeted on a specific device. For instance, in the case of NTP (Network Time Protocol) amplification attacks, this is made possible by the fact that no authentication is required in order to obtain a response. Therefore, the attacker is capable of forging their address so that the generated request looks like it originated from the intended victims machine. The attacker sends forged requests to a large distributed number of servers across the network. Since the response is up to 200 times bigger than the request, a large attack can be initiated by simply a single machine, once amplified through a number of distributed NTP servers. Such type of response is possible due to the `monlist` command, which is available in NTP servers. This command can return the addresses of up to the last 600 machines that the NTP server has interacted with. The amplification factor of domain name service (DNS) is much lower and ranges of around 40 to 100 depending on the effort that the attacker puts into the preparation of its attack. An overview of typical bandwidth amplification factors is presented in [3]. There exist many similar overloading attacks that are initiated via network, such as Teardrop, Bonk, Boink and Ping of Death. The impact is always to severely impair or disable an host or at least its IP stack, but through packet fragmentation techniques or vulnerability reassembling. However, these attacks require of course an host IP stack in order to receive packets from the attacker.

Mitigation strategies against overloading attacks within traditional networks are experiencing difficulties regarding their deployment, because most of them induce high network complexity and prohibitive operational cost [25]. In the meantime, SDN-based networks prove to be much more flexible due to their programmable nature. In an SDN-based network, the centralized view of the network state by the controller(s), as well as the capacity of the network to be dynamically reprogrammed, significantly ease the deployment of mitigation strategies, such as DDoS mitigation, initially designed for traditional networks. In particular, Moving Target Defense (MTD) is an intrusion prevention mechanism used to periodically change a deterministic attribute (typically the IP address) of a chosen host, in order to confuse attackers and thus protect the host. Usually, deploying MTD mechanisms within traditional networks is difficult and costly, because it involves the usage of dedicated hardware facilities for hosting the MTD intelligence [14]. In an SDN-based network, the MTD intelligence is hosted at the controller level, which is able of dynamically reconfiguring the network according to its dedicated algorithm [15]. Traffic analysis for intrusion and anomaly detection within a given network is another example of mitigation strategies simplified by the SDN paradigm [17]. In such a context, the controller can simply query the switches of the network in order to gather statistical information about the network traffic, and then detect potential intrusion or anomaly according to its detection algorithm(s). Once an attack has been detected, blocking the source of the attack or redirecting the associated malicious flows to security middleboxes - i.e. providing an intrusion response - can be done at the controller level by reprogramming the whole network [19]. Such reprogramming steps are important for implementing efficient intrusion tolerance mechanisms.

2.2   Mitigation of Information Gathering Attacks

Another important category of attacks corresponds to information gathering. The one refers to the process of determining the characteristics of one or more remote hosts (and/or networks). Information gathering can be used to construct a model of the target host, and to facilitate future penetration attempts. There exist several and complementary methods to perform a remote information gathering in the literature at various levels:

- **Host detection:** this method tries to identify if a host is available. In most of the cases this is done by a *ping* or *fping* which elicits e.g. an ICMP ECHO_REPLY from a victim.
- **Service detection:** service detection is typically performed based on port scanning. The objective is to detect the availability of UDP, RPC or TCP services, e.g. HTTP, DNS, through the execution of SYN or FIN scanning or slight variations like fragmentation scanning.
- **Network topology detection:** to get more information about a network, methods like TTL modulation, e.g. with *traceroute* or record route, e.g. *ping* -R can be performed. Another non-invasive method to learn more about a network is by network sniffing.
- **Operating system detection:** since the implementations of TCP/IP stacks of operating systems are different, the behavior of such an implementation can give information about the concrete operating system. This could be an interesting information to get access to the victim system, because the attacker can determine which vulnerabilities are present and exploitable. An additional name for this method is TCP/IP stack fingerprinting.

In the past, information gathering was performed with a one to one or one to many model; i.e. an attacker performs techniques linear against either one target host or a logical group of targets (e.g. a subnet). These methods were often optimized for speed and executed in parallel (e.g. nmap). Newer types of information gathering methods use distributed methods following the many to one or many to many model. Therefore, an attacker tries to use multiple hosts to execute some information gathering methods in random and non-linear ways. The aim of the distribution is to avoid detection either by human analysis or network intrusion detection systems.

Mitigation strategies for information gathering attacks within SDN-based networks prove to be quite similar to the ones mentioned for traditional networks. The main difference resides in the holistic view of the controller(s), which may ease both the statistic aggregation and the correlation steps, as well as blocking (after detection) by reprogramming the network. For instance, in the case of Moving Target Defence (MTD) solutions mentioned above, the mechanisms make the attacker task harder, since the information obtained from a scanning attack at a period p may not be correct anymore at the period $p+1$. Some other advanced MTD mechanisms have been designed in SDN-based networks to add network noise, such as dynamic fake servers and fake open ports [13], as well as to prevent OS fingerprinting and service version/banner grabbing. However, this last feature may induce overhead at the controller and/or the switch layer, since it requires to look and modify information in upper layers (e.g. httpd version in HTTP header), which might seem contrary to the SDN paradigm principles.

3   Analysis of OpenFlow Messages Used for Network Security Applications

Mitigation strategies take benefits from facilities offered by software-defined networking, even when they rely on similar models and methods well-known in traditional networks. These solutions often built on top of the software-defined layer introduce however dependencies of security mechanisms to these facilities, in particular to the OpenFlow protocol, that we analyze in the section. We typically consider three main deployment categories in software-defined infrastructures: reactive, proactive and hybrid deployments. In all of them, a flow-table lookup is performed when a network flow reaches a switch. Depending on the implementation, e.g. software vSwitch or hardware switch (ASIC (Application-Specific Integrated Circuit)) flow tables are accessed. In case no matching flow is found a request to the controller is sent for further instructions.

In a reactive approach, the controller acts upon these requests through the creation and installation of a rule in the switch's flow-table for the corresponding packet. In a proactive approach, the controller populates flow-table entries for all possible traffic matches possible for this switch in advance. This mode is comparable with typical traditional routing entries today, where all static entries are installed ahead in time. Following this proactive implementation, no request needs to be sent to the controller, since all incoming flows should find a matching entry. The major advantage of proactive deployments is due to the fact that all packets are forwarded in line rate (considering flow-table entries are stored in TCAM (Ternary Content-Addressable Memory)) and no delay is added. In addition, hybrid environments exist where the flexibility of a reactive environment for a set of traffic is used, while the low-latency forwarding (proactive) is used for the rest of the traffic.

Our analysis with respect to OpenFlow message usage for network security considers a reactive environment. Indeed, software-defined networking and in particular the OpenFlow protocol is typically leveraged for a dynamic reconfiguration and setup of the network. In addition, proactive deployments are quite inflexible. Therefore, proactive scenarios are often based on hybrid environments with a reactive part that is not necessarily activated. Our approach is applicable to all OpenFlow-enabled SDN environments that include a reactive part.

Table 1. Mapping of OpenFlow messages to security functionality addressing overloading attacks

OpenFlow message	Security functionality
PACKET_IN	Monitoring of e.g. number of new flows (detection)
OFPFlowMod	Traffic redirection and queuing (mitigation)
OFPMeterMod	Rate-limiting (detection)
OFP*StatsRequest	Detection based on statistics collection

This behavior allows us to gather and measure useful OpenFlow-related information, such as PACKET_IN messages, which are necessary for several types of security related applications. Based on this consideration, and within a security context, we specified for each attack category, a mapping of the OpenFlow message types that are used for serving security functionalities, such as detection, mitigation and reconfiguration purposes. These security mechanisms therefore rely on the reliability of these messages and the information they carry (e.g. counters). We considered the following OpenFlow message types in this security-oriented analysis and mapping:

- **PACKET_IN messages:** these are sent from the OpenFlow-enabled switch to the controller in case a new flow arrives at the switch and no matching flow-table entry is found. This behavior is useful for detection and mitigation approaches, like e.g. blacklisting or firewalling. In this case the number of new flows (e.g. IP addresses) can be counted (gathering stats on-the-fly) and if too many new IP addresses arrive, whether they are allowed or not this could be an indication for e.g. a DDoS attack or anomalous behavior in the monitored network. To gather these kinds of statistical data there, exist dedicated OpenFlow messages (e.g. MULTIPART_REQUEST). Compared to those messages, gathering PACKET_IN-based statistics is done on-the-fly for reactive environments inducing no additional OpenFlow communication between the controller and the switch(es). In proactive environments MULTIPART_REQUEST messages can assume this task.
- **OFPFlowMod,   OFPFlowStatsRequest/OFPFlowAggregateStats Request messages:** these are suitable for redirection and traffic mirroring. These messages can be useful to mirror traffic to different types of intrusion detection middleboxes or security appliances. In addition, there exist specific flags within these messages to reset packet and byte counters (OFPFF_RESET_COUNT) in the switch or modify the configuration of a switch in a sense that it sends a message once a flow rule has expired. As a last use-case these messages can be used to mitigate an attack by dropping malicious packets.
- **OFPMeterMod/OFPMeterStatsRequest messages:** these allow a rate-limiting configuration, which was originally designed for quality of service purposes. Nevertheless, this functionality can be used in the area of detection for sampling packets.

- **OFPQueueStatsRequest messages:** these can be used to gather statistics from existing queues. In the area of security applications an option is to set up two queues: one queue for legitimate traffic with high bandwidth and one queue for suspicious and malicious traffic with a limited throughput. The process of setting up such a queue states part of prevention or mitigating an attack. The statistics collection part is relevant for detection purposes. Using the set-queue attribute an application can set up a defined action (e.g. OUTPUT, DROP) for a specific queue.
- **Multipart messages:** these provide plenty of options useful for detection purposes. Using the OFP*Stats[Request—Reply] messages, statistics about flows and rules can be gathered from the switches. These methods are useful for applications to detect, e.g. possible anomalies in the traffic flows. In addition, considering pre-installed rule sets for security applications the statistics collection methods are necessary to derive possible security events. To reduce false-positives in such a detection approach correlation methods need to be developed.
- **PacketOut messages:** these enable forging packets and send them to security devices/middleboxes in order to reconfigure the network according to already detected incidents or to change configuration options to improve detection capabilities.
- **OFPFlowRemoved messages:** these are suitable for security diagnosis and testing purposes. With associated counters involved they could also be useful to improve detection capabilities.

Table 2. Mapping of OpenFlow messages to security functionality addressing information gathering attacks

OpenFlow message	Security functionality
PACKET_IN	Collection of new flows/packets (detection)
FlowMod	Traffic redirection and queuing (mitigation)
PacketOut	Confuse scanning by sending forged packets to the attacker

The different results of this security-oriented analysis of OpenFlow message usage are summarized in Table 1 corresponding to overloading mitigation strategies, and in Table 2 focusing on information gathering mitigation strategies. Keeping in mind these dependencies between security application goals (e.g. detection, mitigation, reconfiguration) and OpenFlow messages, there is a need to evaluate the implementation of OpenFlow messages in existing software-defined devices (software and hardware), in order to quantify the potential impact on these mitigation mechanisms.

4   Performance Evaluation

Based on this analysis, we have performed a series of experiments in order to evaluate the accuracy and reliability of OpenFlow messages. The objective of this quantification is then to infer the potential impact of this performances on security applications developed on software-defined networking infrastructures. In that context, we have built dedicated testbeds based on hardware and software SDN solutions and have focused on two different types of messages, namely PACKET_IN and OFPQueueStatsRequest messages. However, this approach is generic and can be easily applied to the other messages identified in the previous section. The main reason of this focus was to gather statistics comparable to NetFlow/sFlow data from an OpenFlow-enabled switch.

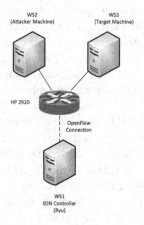
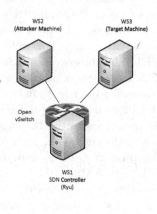

(a) Experimental Setup with an HP 2920 switch

(b) Experimental Setup with an Open vSwitch [4] on WS1

Fig. 1. Experimentation with SDN-enabled software and hardware switches

We have considered the following experimental setup for performing our evaluation, with two different testbeds. Our first testbed consists of three workstations (4xCore i3 2.93 GHz and 4 GB RAM) with the Debian 7 (kernel 3.2.0) operating system. All workstations have a gigabit network card installed that is connected directly to an HP2920-24G OpenFlow-enabled switch running the WB.15.16.005 firmware and OpenFlow version 1.3 enabled. On the switch, two workstations (W2 and W3) are connected within the same VLAN which is managed via the OpenFlow protocol. The other workstation (W1) directly connected to a switch port which is dedicated for OpenFlow controller messages (OpenFlow Management VLAN). For this purpose, the machine W1 is running an SDN controller. The Ryu framework in version 3.18 [5] is chosen, because it supports OpenFlow version 1.3 and is well maintained. The motivation of having two workstations (W2 and W3) connected to each other is to replay pcap files containing attacks on one machine (W2) and receive attacks from the pcap on the other machine (W3). Thus, the machine W2 can be seen as an attacker and the machine W3 as the target. Figure 1a corresponds to the first testbed. A modification of the experimental setup was done to verify the behavior of a software switch. For this second testbed, we installed Open vSwitch [4] on the machine W1 where the SDN controller with the Ryu framework is located and is connected to the Open vSwitch [4] locally. Moreover, we installed an additional 2 port gigabit network card and bridged the ports via the Open vSwitch [4] to connect the attacker (represented by the machine W2) and the target machine W3 (see Fig. 1b corresponding to the second testbed). During our experiments, we replayed network traces derived from the DEFCON 22 hacking conference [7]. We used *tcpprep* in order to change IP addresses and simulate the traffic flow from the attacker workstation (W2) to the target workstation (W3). Furthermore, we deduced the statistics from the traces to assess the results with respect to OFPQueueStatsRequest messages. We modified the existing Ryu [5] controller code so that no new flow rule is pushed to the switch and make sure that all PACKET_IN messages are counted in time when they arrive at the controller. In addition, a flow-mod message is introduced during the initialization phase of the controller in order to insert a flow-rule that matches any packet (relevant for the OFPQueueStatsRequest messages evaluation).

In order to quantify the capacity of sending PACKET_IN messages from the switch to the controller, we replayed traces at different speeds from the attacker workstation W2. We considered respectively the following bandwidth speeds: 0.1 Mbps, 0.25 Mbps, 0.5 Mbps, 1.0 Mbps, 2.0 Mbps, 5.0 Mbps, and 10.0 Mbps. In order to verify the speed and number of packets on the attacker and target workstations, we used common Linux tools, namely *ip -s link*, *iftop* or *nload*. In parallel, we counted on our modified Ryu [5] controller the number of Open-Flow PACKET_IN messages. In order to test our modified Ryu [5] controller script, we also counted the number of packets via the interface statistics on the workstation W1 on which the SDN controller is running. Based on these experiments, we evaluated the difference between the replayed packets and the effective received PACKET_IN messages. We then calculated the percentage of received PACKET_IN messages with respect to the replayed packets. This value permits to quantify how much traffic in respect of bandwidth we can utilize from the switch without losing PACKET_IN messages, and therefore distorsing statistic values collected from the SDN switch, this distorsion having a direct impact on the security application performance.

The results are given in Fig. 2a and b where we plotted the ratio of lost PACKET_IN messages while varying the bandwidth used when replaying traces for respectively the HP 2920 hardware SDN switch and the Open vSwitch software SDN switch. The results clearly show that the distorsion can be quite important in both cases, even with the bandwidth dedicated to the generated traffic is low. When we compare the two figures, it appears that the phenomenon is even more important with the first testbed, corresponding to the hardware SDN switch in our case. In a second serie of experiments, we quantified the

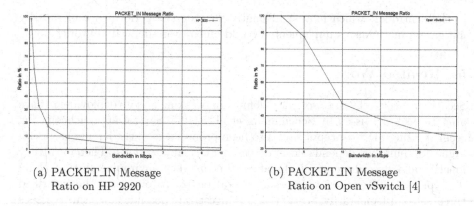

(a) PACKET_IN Message
Ratio on HP 2920

(b) PACKET_IN Message
Ratio on Open vSwitch [4]

Fig. 2. PACKET_IN message ratio on SDN-enabled switches

performance with respect to the OFPQueueStatsRequest messages. We assessed the counters for the installed flow rules. Figure 3a and b illustrate the relationship between the bandwidth and the ratio of correct packet counters for the earlier mentioned HP switch and the Open vSwitch. We can observe on the figures a similar trend as the one obtained with the experiments with the PACKET_IN messages. These results are particularly interesting, when we know that counters from matching flow-rules are preferably used to implement detection solutions, such as Defense4All [8], a module for the commonly used SDN Controller Open-Daylight [18].

These results raise important concerns about the implementation of Open-Flow in hardware as well as software solutions, and the implication that may directly have these differences in the context of security applications. It highlights severe differences in sending OpenFlow messages from the SDN switch

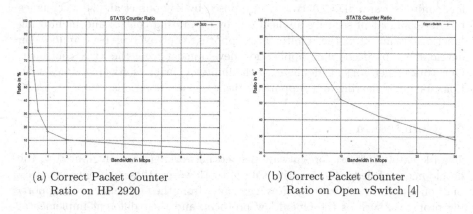

(a) Correct Packet Counter
Ratio on HP 2920

(b) Correct Packet Counter
Ratio on Open vSwitch [4]

Fig. 3. Correct packet counter ratio on SDN-enabled switches

to the controller, which may significantly degrade the performance of security mitigation mechanisms implemented based on software-defined networks.

5   Related Work

Security aspects related to software-defined networking and its deployments have already been discussed by Schehlmann et al. in [20]. Several approaches facing security using SDN concepts have also been proposed recently. Kreutz et al. [16] argue for building dependable and secure SDN applications. Therefore, they identify and describe current threat vectors in SDN environments that could be exploited. They then propose a general design to overcome the identified threats. Complementarily, Scott et al. [21] investigate possible new security issues introduced through SDN and identify the affected layers. Focusing on network security approaches using SDN capabilities, François et al. [10] reviews recent research efforts and provides a qualitative comparison, complementary to our analytical and empirical evaluation.

Furthermore, existing work has been focusing on more specific attacks and their mitigation. Shishira et al. summarizes several types of distributed denial-of-service (DDoS) attacks and recently developed mitigation approaches in [22]. Vizváry et al. have analyzed the detection and mitigation of DDoS attacks using an OpenFlow enabled SDN environment in [23]. Using self-organizing maps, the authors of [6] propose a method to detect DDoS attacks based on flow analysis. Feamster et al. [9] investigated possibilities to detect botnet traffic by using distributed monitoring approaches. Jafarian et al. presented an approach to hide the real IP addresses by introducing a virtual IP address to hide real hosts from unauthorized scanners. A similar approach was introduced by Kampanakis et al. [15] to obfuscate the attack surface. Combining traditional network features (sFlow) and OpenFlow, Giotis et al. [11] proposed a mechanism to detect anomalies and mitigate attacks by modifying flow tables. A different architecture for monitoring and SDN control was proposed by Zaalouk et al. [24] to enhance the development of security applications by separating control and monitoring functions. In addition, the architecture supports a controller-agnostic application development by decoupling application development from the SDN controller. Our work rather aims at highlighting the limits of current software-defined solutions for implementing and supporting these security solutions.

6   Conclusion

The increasing interest for software-defined networking has contributed to the development of dedicated security solutions. However, these solutions typically built on top of these infrastructures may suffer from the performance of supporting protocols, such as the OpenFlow protocol, and their different implementations. In that context, we have proposed in the paper an analysis and evaluation of OpenFlow message usage by network security applications, in order to quantify these dependencies and their impact.

We have first describe two categories of security attacks, namely overloading attacks and information gathering attacks, that are quite common in these environments, and have detailed regular and SDN-based mitigation mechanisms that have been designed for tackling them. We have then analyzed for each category the dependencies of these mechanisms to the OpenFlow protocol commonly supporting the communications between SDN controllers and switches. These dependencies have been identified through the mapping of OpenFlow messages to security functionalities in that context. Based on this analyzis, we performed series of experiments for comparing and evaluating the accuracy and reliability that can be expected with respect to these messages based on two different testbeds. We first considered OpenFlow PACKET_IN messages that are typically generated when a new flow arrives to an SDN switch and no matching rule is found in the existing rule-set. We observed that the number of PACKET_IN messages sent to the controller strongly depends on the line speed of flows sent to the switch. For a higher line speed, the switch was not able to send PACKET_IN messages at the same speed when new packets arrived. This is particularly impacting, because this directly influences the statistics gathered from the switch, which are used by security solutions as a starting point for several detection approaches. We then performed experiments with respect to OFPQueueStatsRequest messages that are used to provide statistics on existing queues, and observed a similar degradation of performance. When the line speed is high, the precision of counters per flow-rule can significantly decrease.

As future work, we are interested in performing complementary experiments, in order to extend our methodology to additional OpenFlow message types. This analysis will permit to further investigate the dependencies of security applications and their limits regarding SDN implementations. This could directly influence the design of these security mechanisms, and allow us to infer and specify guidelines and patterns with that respect, in order to maximize security performance.

Acknowledgment. The authors wish to thank the member of the Chair for Communication Systems and Internet Services at the Universität der Bundeswehr München, headed by Prof. Dr. Gabi Dreo Rodosek, for helpful discussions and valuable comments for this paper. This work was partly funded by FLAMINGO, a Network of Excellence project (ICT-318488) supported by the European Commission under its Seventh Framework Programme.

References

1. Akamai - Q4 2014 State of the Internet - Security Report. http://www.stateoftheinternet.com/resources-web-security-2014-q4-internet-security-report.html. Accessed on 04 Feb 2016
2. Arbor Networks - Worldwide Infrastructure Security Report 2014. http://pages.arbornetworks.com/rs/arbor/images/WISR2014.pdf
3. US-CERT Alert (TA14-017A) UDP-Based Amplification Attacks. https://www.us-cert.gov/ncas/alerts/TA14-017A. Accessed on 04 Feb 2016

4. Open vSwitch Community: Open vswitch. http://openvswitch.org/. Accessed on 04 Feb 2016
5. Ryu SDN Framework Community: Ryu sdn controller. http://osrg.github.io/ryu/. Accessed on 04 Feb 2016
6. Braga, R., Mota, E., Passito, A.: Lightweight ddos flooding attack detection using nox/openflow. In: 2010 IEEE 35th Conference on Local Computer Networks (LCN), pp. 408–415. IEEE (2010)
7. DEF CON Communications, Inc.: Defcon pcap traces. https://www.defcon.org/html/links/dc-torrent.html. Accessed on 04 Feb 2016
8. Defense4All: Defense4all module. https://wiki.opendaylight.org/view/Project_Proposals:Defense4All. Accessed on 04 Feb 2016
9. Feamster, N.: Outsourcing home network security. In: Proceedings of the 2010 ACM SIGCOMM Workshop on Home Networks, pp. 37–42. ACM (2010)
10. François, J., Dolberg, L., Festor, O., Engel, T.: Network security through software defined networking: a survey. In: IIT Real-Time Communications (RTC) Conference-Principles, Systems and Applications of IP Telecommunications (IPT-Comm). ACM (2014)
11. Giotis, K., Argyropoulos, C., Androulidakis, G., Kalogeras, D., Maglaris, V.: Combining openflow and sflow for an effective and scalable anomaly detection and mitigation mechanism on sdn environments. Comput. Netw. **62**, 122–136 (2014)
12. Hansman, S., Hunt, R.: A taxonomy of network and computer attacks. Comput. Secur. **24**(1), 31–43 (2005)
13. Jafarian, J.H., Al-Shaer, E., Duan, Q.: Openflow random host mutation: transparent moving target defense using software defined networking. In: Proceedings of the First Workshop on Hot Topics in Software Defined Networks, pp. 127–132. ACM (2012)
14. Jajodia, S., Ghosh, A.K., Swarup, V., Wang, C., Wang, X.S.: Moving Target Defense: Creating Asymmetric Uncertainty for Cyber Threats, vol. 54. Springer Science & Business Media, New York (2011)
15. Kampanakis, P., Perros, H., Beyene, T.: Sdn-based solutions for moving target defense network protection. In: 2014 IEEE 15th International Symposium on A World of Wireless, Mobile and Multimedia Networks (WoWMoM), pp. 1–6, June 2014
16. Kreutz, D., Ramos, F., Verissimo, P.: Towards secure and dependable software-defined networks. In: Proceedings of the Second ACM SIGCOMM Workshop on Hot Topics in Software Defined Networking, pp. 55–60. ACM (2013)
17. Lara, A., Kolasani, A., Ramamurthy, B.: Network innovation using openflow: A survey. IEEE Commun. Surv. Tutorials **16**(1), 493–512 (2014)
18. OpenDaylight: Sdn controller opendaylight. https://www.opendaylight.org/. Accessed on 04 Feb 2016
19. Sahay, R., Blanc, G., Zhang, Z., Debar, H.: Towards autonomic ddos mitigationusing software-defined networking. In: 2015 Network and Distributed SystemSecurity Symposium (NDSS 2015), pp. 1–6, February 2015
20. Schehlmann, L., Abt, S., Baier, H.: Blessing or curse? revisiting security aspects of software-defined networking. In: 2014 10th International Conference on Network and Service Management (CNSM), pp. 382–387. IEEE (2014)
21. Scott-Hayward, S., O'Callaghan, G., Sezer, S.: Sdn security: A survey. In: 2013 IEEE SDN for Future Networks and Services (SDN4FNS), pp. 1–7. IEEE (2013)
22. Shishira, S., Pai, V., Manamohan, K.: Current trends in detection and mitigation of denial of service attacks-a survey. Int. J. Comput. Appl. (2014)

23. Vizváry, M., Vykopal, J.: Future of DDoS attacks mitigation in software defined networks. In: Sperotto, A., Doyen, G., Latré, S., Charalambides, M., Stiller, B. (eds.) AIMS 2014. LNCS, vol. 8508, pp. 123–127. Springer, Heidelberg (2014)
24. Zaalouk, A., Khondoker, R., Marx, R., Bayarou, K.: Orchsec: An orchestrator-based architecture for enhancing network-security using network monitoring and sdn control functions. In: 2014 IEEE Network Operations and Management Symposium (NOMS), pp. 1–9. IEEE (2014)
25. Zargar, S., Joshi, J., Tipper, D.: A survey of defense mechanisms against distributed denial of service (ddos) flooding attacks. IEEE Commun. Surv. Tutorials 15(4), 2046–2069 (2013)

On the Readiness of NDN for a Secure Deployment: The Case of Pending Interest Table

Hoang Long Mai[1]([✉]), Ngoc Tan Nguyen[1], Guillaume Doyen[1], Alain Ploix[1], and Remi Cogranne[2]

[1] HETIC/ERA, Institut Charles Delaunay – UMR CNRS 6281,
Troyes University of Technology, 10004 Troyes Cedex, France
hoanglong00792@gmail.com
[2] ROSAS/LM2S, Institut Charles Delaunay – UMR CNRS 6281,
Troyes University of Technology, 10004 Troyes Cedex, France

Abstract. Named Data Networking (NDN) is one the proposals for the Future Internet design relying on the Information Centric Networking paradigm and probably the most promising. To enable a large-scale deployment by Internet Service Providers, however, a well-established security is fundamental. While numerous prior works study the security of NDN, a large amount of those works have been conducted using simulation frameworks which prevent the consideration of potential threats and flaws in a real deployment context. Toward this effort, this paper studies the practical vulnerabilities exposed by NDN Forwarding Daemon (NFD), the current implementation of NDN, and especially its Pending Interest Table. An attack scenario, based on the Interest Flooding Attack, is implemented on NFD routers deployed in a Network Function Virtualization environment. We show that the current implementation, though designed to be flexible, has some flaws that can ease the mounting of attacks in a real NDN network. We have found that there is no mechanism to protect NFD router when Pending Interest Table (PIT) is overloaded and identified the set of parameters which can increase the attack success. Several recommendations are proposed for the security of future implementations.

1 Introduction

The foundations of current Internet architecture have not been deeply changed since the first proposal back in the 70s. In contrast, the use of the Internet has dramatically changed over the last decades with, to cite a few aspects, a tremendous growth of traffic, connected devices and needs for mobility and security. Such a profound change in the usage of the Internet challenges the current IP network. Therefore, there are currently many efforts to design the Future Internet and the Information Centric Networking (ICN) paradigm is a clean-slate approach that essentially proposes to move from the current host-based IP network to a content-based network.

To date, Named Data Networking (NDN) [1] is one of the most accomplished and studied ICN proposals and, hence one of the first candidates for a deployment in an operated context by Internet Service Providers (ISP). This evolution

© IFIP International Federation for Information Processing 2016
R. Badonnel et al. (Eds.): AIMS 2016, LNCS 9701, pp. 98–110, 2016.
DOI: 10.1007/978-3-319-39814-3_10

of the paradigm can be assessed by different recent efforts which all focus on providing solutions for a reliable deployment. Among the academic contributions, the NDN Testbed [1] and the CONET solution [2] deployed over the OFELIA testbed provide tools and an experimental feedback on early deployments, Ren et al. [3] address the hosting features which could facilitate ICN deployments by, for instance, leveraging Network Function Virtualization (NFV), which is a concept that leverages virtualization technologies to emulate network elements, while A. Afanasyev [4] proposes NDNS, a resolution framework which solves operational issues such as key registrations and retrievals. Jointly, from the standardization perspective, some Internet-Drafts are under publication by the Internet Engineering Task Force (IETF) such as [5,6] to respectively identify ICN management considerations or propose NDN Message Format.

Moving from a lab restricted solution to a fully deployable solution, the NDN security must also be assessed and bound with operational constraints. If a first step of early security flaws identification, detection and mitigation has already been achieved in prior works (e.g. denial of service [7], cache pollution [8] and poisoning [9], . . .), their assessments only rely on simulated environments which provide a partial NDN behavior. As such, they are insufficient to address all threats which can occur in real implementations and a real context.

Taking part in this effort, this paper proposes to deploy a real NDN testbed based on the last version of the NDN Forwarding Daemon (NFD) in a NFV context. We implement an Interest Flooding Attack (IFA) in order to observe the behavior of the NFD process and especially the Pending Interest table (PIT). The main goals of such experiments are (1) to exhibit unexpected behaviors when the network is stressed by the IFA, (2) to compare the empirical limits of the current implementation with the theoretical and simulated ones, and (3) to eventually provide a set of recommendations regarding the NFD security.

The paper is organized as follows. Section 2 presents in more details the related works focusing on NDN security issues and especially on the IFA. Then, Sect. 3 details the experimental setup that is implemented in the current study. Section 4 presents the numerical results and shows how an IFA can actually be implemented with success thanks to vulnerabilities of NFD. Finally, Sect. 5 concludes the paper and proposes some recommendations for the future development of NFD.

2 Related Work

In this section we briefly introduce the NDN data-plane architecture and router components. Then, we review the set of literature which focuses on potential attacks related to the router overloading and especially the Pending Interest Table. Finally, we introduce the set of design and architectural solutions which have been proposed previously to protect NDN from these attacks.

2.1   Named Data Networking

Among all the proposals which aim at bringing a novel Internet protocol design, NDN [1] is considered as one of the most promising Future Internet solution. As part of the ICN paradigm, which relies on the key concept of naming content objects instead of naming hosts with IP addresses, NDN uses a hierarchical naming scheme for content objects, like a Uniform Resource Identifier (URI). Communication in NDN is achieved by two types of packets: (1) *Interest* and (2) *Data*. A user issues his/her demand for some content by sending an *Interest* packet. In return, a *Data* packet containing the requested content is sent back to the user. In NDN, a router exhibits many faces which stand for a generalization of interfaces in IP networks and it owns three main components which are combined to build the forwarding process. Firstly, the *Content Store* (CS) is a local cache that improves content delivery by storing recently requested content. Secondly, the *Forwarding Information Base* (FIB) contains routing information for *Interest* packets. Finally, the *Pending Interest Table* (PIT) contains routing information for *Data* packets. More precisely, for each forwarded *Interest*, its incoming faces are saved in a PIT entry, so that the corresponding *Data* can be sent back to the user. For each received *Data*, the corresponding PIT entry is then removed. Consequently, NDN defines a full-state data-plane which, although enabling an efficient routing of *Interest* and *Data* packets, also brings novel threats related to the state maintenance in each routers. Especially, the PIT overload phenomenon, which can occur due to a malicious traffic activity or a legitimate network overload, has been extensively studied, such as in [10] which, with the help of a custom simulator, provides guidelines for the design and implementation of this component.

2.2   Detection and Mitigation of PIT Overload Attacks

A large set of studies has proposed various solutions against the IFA [7], a variation of the Denial of Service (DoS) attack in NDN, which consists in overloading the PIT by sending a large amount of malicious *Interest* packets for non-existent content. Such *Interests* cannot be resolved by any *Data* packet. As such, the corresponding PIT entry cannot be removed by a *Data* packet, but only by the entry lifetime expiration. When the PIT is overloaded, new *Interest* packets cannot be handled and, thus, are dropped. This attack induces serious consequences on network for two reasons. Firstly, it can cause large scale damage by targeting the network infrastructure. Secondly, *Interests* for non-existing content can be easily generated by any user.

In [11], Dai et al. present their *Interest* trace back mitigation strategy. Whenever the PIT's size exceeds a threshold, a spoofed *Data* packet is created by the router to resolve a long-unsatisfied *Interest*. These *Data* are eventually forwarded back to the source of attack by tracing PIT entries. At the same time, routers also limit the incoming packet rate of faces to which they send fake *Data*. Profiting from statistics to identify harmful faces, the Poseidon approach, proposed by Compagno et al. in [12], maintains two measures: (1) the satisfaction ratio and (2) the PIT space used by *Interests* from the affected face. Once an alarm occurs, a router issues an alert message to its neighbor on the malicious face. When the latter receives an alert, it also triggers the same counter-measure, but with a lower threshold, in order to better identify the compromised face. In [13], Afanasyev et al. proposed the satisfaction-based push-back counter-measure. The idea of this proposal is similar to the Poseidon proposal: routers exchange announcements with neighbors and adjust their reactions based on these messages. Although this solution monitors the satisfaction ratio, it does not have a separate detection phase. The ratio is actually used to periodically calculate the *Interest* limit exchanged in announcements between routers. Leveraging the statistical hypothesis testing theory, in our previous work [14,15], we have also proposed a low-computation-cost detector against IFA which enables the theoretical performance assessment of the detector: assessment of the confidence given in results, setup of the detection threshold at the design stage and independence from the attack behavior.

Although all these solutions provide different strategies for the detection and mitigation of IFA, they are all based on a theoretical behavior of routers and an evaluation performed in a simulation environment (e.g. ndnSim). As such, they only consider a restricted behavior of NDN components (e.g. memory management) and attack patterns while omitting practical solutions that could mitigate this attack as well as the set of related threats which occur in case of a real deployment and lead to a different behavior of a NDN topology.

2.3 Design and Implementation Considerations

In an effort to mitigate IFAs, the authors of [16] introduce the *Interest NACK* packet to extend the forwarding mechanism of NDN. When a NDN router can neither satisfy nor forward an *Interest*, an *Interest NACK* is generated and sent to the downstream router. In other words, an *Interest NACK* is a packet which carries an error code to notify and prevent the downstream router from sending further *Interests* with the same content name. More precisely, there are currently three types of error codes for *Interest NACK* defined as follows:

- *Duplicate NACK*: the router is still waiting for *Data* for an identical *Interest* packet;
- *Congestion NACK*: the *Interest* packet cannot be forwarded due to a congestion occurring on the outgoing link;
- *No data NACK*: the router cannot receive any *Data* to satisfy the *Interest* packet for some reason (e.g. no path available in FIB or PIT entry times out).

As such, *Interest NACK* has two benefits on a NDN topology: (1) the routers release the PIT entries much faster than waiting for the lifetime expiration, thus bringing a natural mitigation of the IFA and (2) it also helps the downstream routers to determine the cause of *NACK* in order to decide the further forwarding strategies.

To conclude this literature review, we state that in order to make NDN a secure and efficient data-plane solution deployable by ISP, the efforts must now target the implementation of components which reveal novel weaknesses that could not be handled at the design stage nor through simulation environments. In this effort we propose in this paper to feature the PIT overload phenomenon from a practical perspective to assess its feasibility, understand its consequences on operated routers, identify potentially unrevealed aspects of the phenomenon and eventually provide a set of guidelines for the implementation roadmap.

3   Experimental Framework

In order to evaluate the readiness of NDN for a realistic deployment use-case, we leveraged system and networking virtualization, thus fitting with a NFV [17] scenario. Such a deployment hypothesis is currently considered as an opportunity to accelerate and facilitate the deployment of novel networking functions, or even full data-planes, while preserving legacy ones without increasing Capital Expenditure (CAPEX) and it is the most credible hypothesis for a NDN deployment [3]. In this context, we present in this section different scenarios we have considered to implement the IFA on a real NDN infrastructure, the subsequent test architecture we have deployed and the set of tools we have implemented.

3.1   Scenarios

We consider a set of attack scenarios which goes beyond the basic generation of a large amount of *Interest* packets in a short time to overload the PIT as described in current literature. By contrast, this set considers realistic flaws in NDN and brings IFA from a pure simulated attack to reality.

Scenario 1: Congestion on the Link Between Provider and Router. This first scenario deals with the straightest way to implement an IFA. For the attacker, it consists in sending a large amount of *Interests* in a short time to, rather than try to fill the PIT of upstream routers, make the link between routers and a provider congested. When the link between the provider and the last upstream router is congested, the provider cannot send *NACK* packets to notify the router anymore. Therefore, at the time of congestion, the router is under attack without the presence of *NACK*. One drawback of this scenario resides in the congestion point which can happen on any link separating the attacker from the provider (e.g. on any intermediate router), thus making it strongly dependent from the capacity of each link in the end-to-end path. Even more, if the *Congestion NACK* mechanism has still not been implemented to date, its acknowledgment by the NDN community for an integration in future implementations make this scenario almost obsolete and as such, we do not consider it in the following of our study.

Scenario 2: Exploit the *No Data NACK* to Accumulate PIT Entries. This scenario exploits the vulnerability design of the *No Data NACK*, which allows the PIT to keep an *Interest* until its lifetime expires even if it received an *Interest NACK* [16]. This scenario is simple to deploy. For example, we consider an intermediate router *R*1 owning an entry in FIB to forward all *Interests* of a given prefix to a router *R*2. But in turn, this router does not own a route in FIB to forward the *Interest*. It will thus generate a *No Data NACK* packet to and send it to the downstream router *R*1. However, when *R*1 receives the *No Data NACK* packet, it will not remove the PIT entry of the affected *Interest* because its face bound to *R*2 is still available. The PIT entry will be removed only when the router has no available face in FIB to send the *Interest*. This design leads to a potential vulnerability in the accumulation of PIT entries which can be exploited to perform an IFA.

Scenario 3: Stretch the Data Providing Delay by a Malicious Provider. As mentioned above, the *NACK* mechanism makes the forwarding decisions on downstream routers totally dependent from the upstream router. Therefore, when a top upstream node (e.g. a data provider) does not send the *NACK* downstream, the whole topology cannot detect the attack. To illustrate this case, we propose in this third IFA scenario to create a malicious data provider exhibiting an abnormal long response delay to *Interests* which however is lower than the lifetime of *Interests*. As a consequence, the downstream router will not receive any *NACK* packet while its PIT will accumulate entries. This scenario, while requiring the cooperation of both the consumer and provider sides, remains easy to implement especially given the opportunity of the current Internet to let end-users operate their own virtualized content servers.

3.2   Testbed Architecture

Figure 1 illustrates the overall architecture of the experimental framework we have deployed for our study. In order to emulate the presence of several physical servers hosting NDN network functions, we have deployed it in OpenStack[1]. The latter provides an Infrastructure as a Service (IaaS) enabling the testbed[2] scalability for future larger experiments. Each virtual machine, emulating an ISP server, follows the *large* template configuration of OpenStack and hosts Linux Ubuntu as an operating system.

On that basis we have setup and implemented a set of tools which enables the deployment of NDN in an NFV context. As such, each emulated server hosts Docker[3] as a container-based virtualization framework of network functions and OpenVSwitch[4] as the infrastructure-layer networking component. In order to enable the communication between containers in a realistic NFV use-case, we have leveraged VXLan as a transport framework for all data from one container

---

[1] https://www.openstack.org/.
[2] One can note that OpenStack is used as a sole background experimental means which does not take part of the subsequent architecture.
[3] https://www.docker.com/.
[4] http://openvswitch.org/.

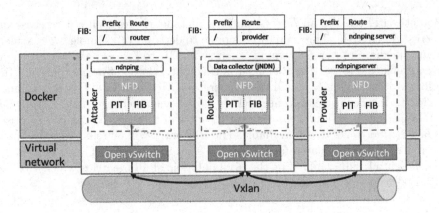

Fig. 1. Architecture of our experimental framework

to another. The network function we consider here is NFD (NDN Forwarding Daemon), configured as an overlay which encapsulates all *Interest* and *Data* packets in IP/UDP channels. In order to collect all data related to our experiments, we have developed a dedicated module based on the jNDN[5] client which collects every second all status information (e.g. number entries in the PIT, total number of In and Out packets) as well as all face statistics (e.g. number of In *Interest* packets, number of Out *Data* packets) of the instrumented router through the NFD Management Protocol[6]. All this information is registered in a JSON format for further processing. Finally, as a traffic producer and consumer, we use *ndnping*, a tool originally designed to test the connection between two NDN routers. We have modified its source code to generate dedicated packets as an attacker with a similar intention could easily do. Especially, we generate *Interest*s with the following prefix: */test/ping/123456789*, where *test* is a static prefix configured to identify an experiment, *ping* identifies the packets belonging to *ndnping* and finally *123456789* is a unique identification number of *Interest*, randomly generated at start of the tool and then increased by one for each packet generation. This value is also used in the *Nonce* field of NDN packets to ensure that there are no duplicate *Interests*.

The set of tools we have considered is summarized in Table 1. One can note that we used the latest NFD version. The latter allows NFD to support the *Interest NACK* packet and creates dedicated incoming and outgoing *NACK* pipelines. More specifically, the *Duplicate NACK* is implemented in a *Interest* loop pipeline while the *No Data NACK* is implemented in the forwarding strategy of NFD. However at the date of the experiments, the *Congestion NACK* was still not supported.

---

[5] https://github.com/named-data/jndn.
[6] http://redmine.named-data.net/projects/nfd/wiki/Management/.

Table 1. Experimental tools implemented for our study

Component	Software	Version
Forwarding engine	NFD	0.4.0
Content provider and attacker	ndnping	N.A.
Measurement client	jNDN	0.9
Virtualization layer	Docker	1.9.1
Network virtualization	Open vSwitch	2.0.2
Operating systems	Ubuntu	14.04 LTS

4 Results

We have implemented the second scenario presented above to reproduce the IFA because it stands for the straightest case for an attacker while actually exploiting vulnerabilities in the current NDN design and its NFD implementation. In order to capture its operating mode, we have first identified the set of factors which impact the attack success. In a second time, we have quantified them with several iterations, all varying the factor values. In order to get reliable results, for each value of a factor, the experiments were performed five times and the following results provide the average of each measured factor bounded with a 95 % confidence interval. The set of factors we consider in our experiments are:

- The memory size allocated to the NFD process;
- The attack rate given by the number of *Interests* per second generated by the attacker;
- The lifetime of *Interests*;
- The prefix size given by its number of characters;
- The number of levels which compose the prefix.

4.1 The PIT Overload Phenomenon

The first result we observed as an immediate consequence of a PIT overload is the system crash of the NFD process. This result is unexpected since all previous works, based on simulations, feature the PIT overload process by a packet drop which does not impact the forwarding process proper execution. To illustrate this phenomenon, we provide in Fig. 2 an extract of the NFD log related to a PIT entry insertion. The log clearly shows that, when overloaded, the NFD process simply stops without an error message. We conclude that currently, no protection scheme prevents NFD from a memory overload, whose consequences are highly damageable in case of a real deployment by an ISP. Consequently, in all subsequent experiments, we consider the router crash, denoted as the collapse point, as the main output of our experiments and we address the different factors which lead to such a phenomenon.

```
1454422643.526260 TRACE: [LinkService] [id=264,local=tcp4://173.16.1.33:6363,remote=tcp4
://173.16.1.11:40521] receiveInterest
1454422643.551709 DEBUG: [Forwarder] onIncomingInterest face=264 interest=/ping
/1971374167
1454422643.581967 TRACE: [NameTree] lookup /ping/1971374167
1454422643.602334 TRACE: [NameTree] insert /
1454422643.623407 TRACE: [NameTree] Name / hash value = 0 location = 0
1454422643.647951 TRACE: [NameTree] insert /ping
1454422643.676848 TRACE: [NameTree] Name /ping hash value = 465469377468200915 location =
30675
1454422643.699100 TRACE: [NameTree] insert /ping/1971374167
1454422643.726028 TRACE: [NameTree] Name /ping/1971374167 hash value =
1245908298819173469l location = 56227
1454422643.746207 TRACE: [NameTree] Did not find /ping/1971374167, need to insert it to
the table
```

Fig. 2. Log trace of NFD for a PIT entry insertion when the router crashes

4.2   Factors Impacting the PIT Overload

Memory Allocation. As mentioned in [10], the memory capacity allocated to the NFD process has an important impact on the PIT capacity. A router with a larger memory has undoubtedly a larger capacity of PIT entries. As such, in order to clearly evaluate the impact of the allocated memory on the collapse point, we have configured Docker with different amounts of memory for the NFD container. In order to exacerbate the overload phenomenon, we have considered extra-long prefixes containing 256 levels and 522 characters in total. Regarding the attack pattern, in this experiment, 5 *Interest* packets per second have been sent, each set with a 1000ms lifetime. The result, depicted in Fig. 3a, although predictable, indicates that the PIT collapse point is proportional to the amount of allocated memory. However, the internal structure of the PIT, called the *nameTree*, is actually implemented in a structure shared with other NFD components relying on both a tree and a hashtable for fast-lookup[7]. This data structure leads to the average use of 0,27 entries per MByte of allocated memory to the NFD process, which also indicates that extra-long prefixes are very costly to store. While such result is highly surprising, its deep understanding is left for future work.

Attack Pattern. Secondly, we have studied the impact of lifetime and frequency of *Interest* packets on the PIT collapse point which together form an attack pattern. The lifetime of *Interests* is an important aspect, because the longer *Interests* stay in the PIT, the faster the PIT collapse point is reached. Furthermore, the default lifetime of *Interest* in NDN is 4 s, but content consumers can arbitrarily fix the lifetime of their *Interests*. As a consequence, a malicious user can intentionally flood NFD with large *Interest* lifetime values in order to multiply the impact of the IFA and currently there is no protection in NFD which could prevent this phenomenon. In order to understand the relation

---

[7] See section 3.6 of the NFD developer guide, available at http://named-data.net/
wp-content/uploads/2014/07/NFD-developer-guide.pdf.

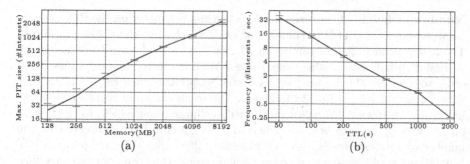

Fig. 3. Collapse point of the forwarding daemon according to **(a)** the NFD container memory (log-log scale) and **(b)** *Interest* frequency and lifetime (log-log scale)

which binds the lifetime with the packet frequency to reach the PIT collapse point, we have modified the source code of *ndnping* to generate *Interests* with a prefix containing 32 levels and 72 characters and allocated 128 MB of memory to the Docker container hosting NFD. The results of these experiments are depicted in Fig. 3b. The smallest lifetime we have measured to successfully overload the PIT is 50 s. However, our scenario only considers a basic implementation of IFA with a single attacker. We can imagine that in the reality of such an attack, a system of botnets would generate a larger frequency of *Interests* without any congestion issue. Therefore, the 50-s value is not the definitive smallest lifetime to perform an IFA and an attacker can perform the attack with a smaller *Interest* lifetime by leveraging more attack sources. Furthermore, these results also assess the potential vulnerability of NDN to the accumulation of PIT entries in case of *No Data NACK*. It especially shows that an attacker can perform flooding attacks with a small packet frequency by simply extending the *Interest* lifetime. A mechanism dedicated to the PIT cleaning before the *Interest* lifetime expires or a limit on the *Interest* lifetime is required to prevent this phenomenon.

Length of *Interests*. We have then studied the impact of the size of *Interests* on the PIT collapse point since the implementation of the PIT in NFD is designed as a data-structure hosted directly in the NFD process memory. Hence, the more complex the *Interests*, the more space in memory is needed to host them. As a first feature of *Interests*, we have considered the length of *Interests*, which is indicated in [10] as an important factor. To that aim, we have generated in this case different prefixes with a fixed number of two levels but with a variable length given by the number of characters which form the prefix. In a similar way with previous experiments, we have considered a container with 128MB to host NFD. The results, presented in Figure 4a show that the length of *Interest* has an impact on the number of entries required to reach the PIT collapse point, but this impact is reasonable. Indeed, one can note that a growth of the *Interests* length of the interest by a factor of 8 –in term of number of characters– only decreases the PIT collapse point by 28 %.

Number of levels of *Interests*. As a last impact factor on the PIT collapse point, we have considered the number of levels which form a prefix in an *Interest*. The naming convention of content in NDN follows a hierarchical scheme, which is similar to URI and at this time, there is no limit to the number of levels. In order to measure this impact, we have created prefixes with various levels, but with a constant length of 522 characters. The result shown in Fig. 4b reveals the important impact of this factor on the PIT collapse point which, to the best of our knowledge, has not been identified to date. Specifically, we observe that the number of *Interests* levels, growing from 2 to 256, drastically reduces the PIT collapse point of almost three orders of magnitude, thus providing an easy flaw to exploit for any attacker to successfully perform an IFA with small means.

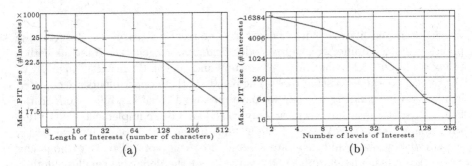

Fig. 4. Collapse point of the forwarding daemon according to **(a)** the packet size of *Interests* (semi-log scale) and **(b)** the number of *Interests* levels (log-log scale)

5   Conclusion and Future Work

In this paper, we have studied the *Interest* Flooding Attack from a practical perspective, by implementing it on the last version of the NDN Forwarding Daemon deployed in a NFV context. The goal of this study relies in the security assessment of NDN since it is now considered as a promising solution for a real deployment by ISP. We have especially implemented a scenario which, despite the integration of *Interests NACK* in the NDN protocol specification demonstrates the feasibility of this attack. From this scenario, we have first shown that the practical consequence of a PIT overload is the crash of the forwarding daemon which is highly damageable in an operated context. Then, we have identified the set of factors which impact the attack success. These are: the *Interest* packet frequency, the lifetime of *Interest*, the size of prefixes in *Interests* and especially the number of levels it counts.

From this results, we conclude that basic security enforcement mechanisms are missing and have to be integrated in NFD to enable this implementation to be actually deployed in any production environment. Especially, as recommendations, we state that some basic upper limits must be implemented in NFD on especially (1) the lifetime of *Interest* which is currently freely fixed by the user, (2) the number of levels in the prefix of *Interests* which leads to an exponential memory exhaustion and (3) the amount of memory allocated to the sole PIT data structure in order to prevent the daemon crash but rather drop exceeding *Interests*.

As a future work, we plan to extend this study to other NDN protocol fields to evaluate their potential vulnerabilities. We also plan to extend our testbed to implement more advanced attack scenarios such as distributed ones. Finally, from a long term perspective, we plan to couple our testbed with an existing content delivery service to estimate to what extend existing services carried by a NDN protocol stack could suffer from this kind of attack.

Acknowledgments. This work is partially co-funded by (1) the French National Research Agency (ANR), DOCTOR project, <ANR-14- CE28-0001>, started in 01/12/2014 and supported by the French Systematic cluster and (2) the CRCA and FEDER CyberSec Platform, <D201304601>.

References

1. Zhang, L., et al.: Named data networking. ACM SIGCOMM Comput. Commun. Rev. **44**(3), 66–73 (2014)
2. Salsano, S., et al.: Information centric networking over SDN and OpenFlow: architectural aspects and experiments on the OFELIA testbed. Comput. Netw. **57**(16), 3207–3221 (2013)
3. Ren, J., et al.: On the deployment of information-centric network: programmability and virtualization. In: 2015 International Conference on Computing, Networking and Communications (ICNC), pp. 690–694. IEEE (2015)
4. Afanasyev, A.: Addressing operational challenges in named data networking through NDNS distributed database. Ph.D. thesis, UCLA (2013)
5. Vidal, I., et al.: ICN management considerations. Technical report Version 6th, IETF, Internet-draft (2014)
6. Stapp, M.: NDN message format proposal. Technical report Version 1st, IETF, Internet-draft (2015)
7. Gasti, P., et al.: DoS and DDoS in named data networking. In: International Conference on Computer Communications and Networks (ICCCN), pp. 1–7. IEEE (2013)
8. Xie, M., Widjaja, I., Wang, H.: Enhancing cache robustness for content-centric networking. In: 2012 Proceedings of IEEE INFOCOM, pp. 2426–2434. IEEE (2012)
9. Ghali, C., Tsudik, G., Uzun, E.: Needle in a haystack: mitigating content poisoning in named-data networking. In: Proceedings of NDSS Workshop on Security of Emerging Networking Technologies (SENT) (2014)
10. Virgilio, M., Marchetto, G., Sisto, R.: PIT overload analysis in content centric networks. In: Proceedings of 3rd ACM SIGCOMM Workshop on Information-Centric Networking, pp. 67–72. ACM (2013)
11. Dai, H., et al.: Mitigate DDoD attacks in NDN by Interest traceback. In: Proceedings of IEEE INFOCOM NOMEN Workshop (2013)

12. Compagno, A., et al.: Poseidon: mitigating interest flooding DDoS attacks in named data networking. In: International Conference on Local Computer Networks (LCN), pp. 630–638. IEEE (2013)
13. Afanasyev, A., et al.: Interest flooding attack and countermeasures in named data networking. In: IFIP Networking Conference, pp. 1–9. IEEE (2013)
14. Nguyen, T., Cogranne, R., Doyen, G.: An optimal statistical test for robust detection against Interest flooding attacks in CCN. In: IFIP/IEEE International Symposium on Integrated Network Management (IM), pp. 252–260 (2015)
15. Nguyen, T.N., et al.: Detection of Interest flooding attacks in named data networking using hypothesis testing. In: IEEE International Workshop on Information Forensics and Security (WIFS), pp. 1–6 (2015)
16. Yi, C., et al.: A case for stateful forwarding plane. Comput. Commun. 36(7), 779–791 (2013)
17. Jain, R., Paul, S.: Network virtualization and software defined networking for cloud computing: a survey. Commun. Mag. 51(11), 24–31 (2013)

In Whom Do We Trust - Sharing Security Events

Jessica Steinberger[1,2]([✉]), Benjamin Kuhnert[1], Anna Sperotto[2],
Harald Baier[1], and Aiko Pras[2]

[1] da/sec - Biometrics and Internet Security Research Group,
Hochschule Darmstadt, Darmstadt, Germany
{Jessica.Steinberger,Benjamin.Kuhnert,Harald.Baier}@h-da.de
[2] Design and Analysis of Communication Systems (DACS),
University of Twente, Enschede, The Netherlands
{J.Steinberger,A.Sperotto,A.Pras}@utwente.nl

Abstract. Security event sharing is deemed of critical importance to
counteract large-scale attacks at Internet service provider (ISP) networks
as these attacks have become larger, more sophisticated and frequent.
On the one hand, security event sharing is regarded to speed up organization's mitigation and response capabilities. On the other hand, it is
currently done on an ad-hoc basis via email, member calls or in personal
meetings only under the premise that participating partners are personally known to each other. As a consequence, mitigation and response
actions are delayed and thus security events are not processed in time.
One approach to reduce this delay and the time for manual processing is to disseminate security events among trusted partners. However,
exchanging security events and semi-automatically deploying mitigation
is currently not well established as a result of two shortcomings. First,
the personal knowledge of each sharing partner to develop trust does not
scale very well. Second, current exchange formats and protocols often
are not able to use security mechanisms (e.g., encryption and signature)
to ensure both confidentiality and integrity of the security event information and its remediation. The goal of this paper is to present a trust
model that determines a trust and a knowledge level of a security event in
order to deploy semi-automated remediations and facilitate the dissemination of security event information using the exchange format FLEX in
the context of ISPs. We show that this trust model is scalable and helps
to build a trust community in order to share information about threats
and its remediation suggestions.

Keywords: Sharing security events · Attack mitigation · Internet
service provider · Network security

1 Introduction

Nowadays, large-scale cyber attacks (e.g., Distributed Denial of Service (DDoS)
attacks) have become larger, more sophisticated (e.g., multi-vector attacks) and

© IFIP International Federation for Information Processing 2016
R. Badonnel et al. (Eds.): AIMS 2016, LNCS 9701, pp. 111–124, 2016.
DOI: 10.1007/978-3-319-39814-3_11

frequent [1]. These large-scale cyber attacks are responsible for network and service outages and thus are causing brand damage and financial loss. To counteract these attacks, one approach that gained increasing attention in recent years is to semi-automatically disseminate cyber threat information among trusted partners [2,3] to facilitate collaboration. However, current collaborative cyber defense is founded on an ad-hoc basis via email, member calls or in personal meetings and thus a manual process [4,5]. This slows mitigation and response times and impedes mitigation and reaction efficacy [6]. Besides the fact that collaboration and information sharing often only takes place in case participating partners are personally known to each other, some legally binding orders (e.g., Executive Order 1363 [7,8]) have been published recently that force owners and operators of critical infrastructures to establish procedures to increase the volume, timeliness and quality of cyber threat information sharing.

To improve the timeliness of cyber defense, support collaboration among trusted partners and facilitate the dissemination of security events, a common data representation and security mechanisms to establish trust are required. Even though several exchange formats (e.g., Incident Object Description Exchange Format (IODEF) [9], Intrusion Detection Message Exchange Format (IDMEF) [10], Abuse Reporting Format (ARF) [11], Extended Abuse Reporting Format (x-arf v0.1 and v0.2) [12] and Flow-based Event eXchange Format (FLEX) [13]) have been published [14] to exchange security events or incidents, the majority of the exchange formats and protocols do not provide any security mechanisms to sign or encrypt a security event [14].

Besides the lack of a standardized exchange format and protocol, the development of trust is deemed of critical importance to share security events. Despite well-known and established trust models are used in other application contexts, the personal knowledge of each sharing partner to develop trust in order to share security events does not scale very well.

To overcome the constraint of personal knowledge of each sharing partner to develop trust in context of mitigation and response to large-scale cyber attacks and to establish an effective collaboration among trusted partners, this paper presents a trust model, called MiRTrust. MiRTrust determines a trust and a knowledge level of a security event in order to deploy semi-automated remediations and facilitate the dissemination of security events using FLEX in the context of ISPs. MiRTrust is based on the well known PGP trust model [15,16] and used to establish different levels of trust, determine the prioritization of the shared security event, sanitize the occurrence of security events and contributes to build a trust community in order to share information about cyber threats and its remediation suggestions.

The paper is organized as follows. In Sect. 2, we describe the scenario in which the trust model is going to be used. Next, we present the requirements that are derived from the presented scenario. Section 3 presents the foundation and related work. Our trust model MIRTrust is presented in Sect. 4. In Sect. 5, we evaluate our trust model MiRTrust. Finally, the paper is concluded in Sect. 6.

2   Scenario and Requirements

In this Section, we describe the main focus of this work. First, we define the networks in which we are going to place our trust model to facilitate the semi-automated assessment and deployment of remediation suggestions. Second, we define the requirements that a trust model should fulfill, as they emerged by the scenario described in Sect. 2.1. In the following, we will use these requirements to evaluate the trust model. Attacks targeting the trust model are out of scope of this work.

2.1   Scenario

The primary focus of this work are multiple high-speed networks using a link speed of 10 Gbps and higher [17]. In addition, we focus on network operators that cooperate among trusted partners to minimize or prevent damages caused by network-based attacks and use an automated threat information exchange. The collaboration is established using an infrastructure based overlay network [18] to prevent a full mesh within the network and to ensure scalability. Each participating partner receives security events from different origins as shown in Fig. 1. Security events originating from a detection engine within the own network infrastructure is defined as an internal security event and shown in Fig. 1a. Further, each participating ISP possesses a list of directly connected collaborating partners. In case of ISP a a directly connected collaborating partner is ISP c as shown in Fig. 1b. The networks of ISP b, ISP d and ISP e are not directly connected to ISP a and thus are regarded as external non collaborating partners as shown in Fig. 1c.

2.2   Requirements

In this section, we introduce five requirements that a trust model should fulfill in order to establish collaboration among trusted partners. These requirements are derived from European Network and Information Security Agency's (ENISA) position paper no. 2 [19] and the work of [20].

Ease of Deployment: The trust model and its underlaying implementation should support platform independency to ensures that they easily integrates with the existing infrastructure.

Access Control: The trust model should support the use of the Traffic Light Protocol (TLP) [21]. The reason is that the TLP provides a scheme for sharing different detail of information tailored for its intended receivers. The reason is that the amount of provided threat information depends on the trust and sharing relationship between collaborating ISPs.

Subjectivity: The trust model should provide the possibility that network operators are able to form their own trust options. These trust options represent the degree of belief about the behavior of collaborating partners.

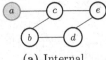 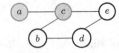 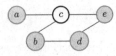

(a) Internal   (b) External collabo-   (c) External non col-
                          rating   laborating

Fig. 1. Origin of security events

Asymmetry: The trust model should support asymmetric levels of trust for both collaborating partners as they do not need to have similar trust in each other.

Decentralized: Each trust model within the mitigation and response (MiR) system should act as a self-contained unit and thus calculates its trust decisions locally. The MiR system should exchange these decisions in form of recommendations with its directly connected collaborating partners.

3   Related Work

In this section, we introduce the terminology by defining trust, review reputation-based trust models and analyze existing collaboration communities used to mitigate and response to large-scale attacks.

3.1   Terminology

Currently, there is no consensus in the definition of trust available. The authors of [22] reported that there are various definitions of trust based on the use-case context. In this paper, we adhere to the following definition of trust: "Trust is the quantified belief by a trustor with respect to the competence, honesty, security and dependability of a trustee with a specific context [22]." Besides trust, we also adhere to the following definition of distrust: "Distrust is the quantified belief by a trustor that a trustee is incompetent, dishonest, not secure or not dependable within a specific context [22]."

3.2   Collaboration Communities

The majority of the collaboration communities are private communities that require a membership application and are charging an annual fee. Recent well-known collaboration communities that require a membership application and are charging an annual fee are the Anti-Phishing Working Group (APWG), the Messaging, Malware and Mobile Anti-Abuse Working Group (M³AAWG), the Research and Education Networking (REN) Information Sharing and Analysis Center (REN-ISAC) and the Forum of Incident Response and Security Teams (FIRST). In contrast to the fee-based collaboration communities are non-fee-based collaborations. The Advanced Cyber Defence Centre (ACDC), the Gigabit

European Academic Network (GÉANT) Task Force on Computer Security Incident Response Teams[1] (TF-CSIRT) and the Gigabit European Academic Network (GÉANT) Special Interest Group on Network Operations Centres[2] (SIG-NOC) and the DDoS Open Threat Signaling[3] (DOTS) working group within the IETF are well-known collaboration communities in context of security event sharing.

The collaboration of APWG focuses on eliminating the identity theft and fraud that result from the growing problem of phishing and email spoofing [23]. M³AAWG is working against bots, malware, spam, viruses, DoS attacks and other online exploitation [24]. REN-ISAC is sharing sensitive information regarding cyber security threat, incidents, response, and protection located in United States, Canada and New Zealand [2], and FIRST cooperatively handles computer security incidents and promote incident prevention programs from around the world. ACDC focus on detection, mitigation and response of botnets. Further, ACDC also supports the mutal data sharing between partners (e.g., ISPs, government agencies, law enforcement, research groups, industry partners). TF-CSIRT and SIG-NOC facilitates knowledge exchange and collaboration in a trusted environment in order to improve cooperation and coordination. DOTS is developing a standards based approach related to DDoS detection, classification, traceback and mitigation in context of a larger collaborative system at service provider level.

All of the aforementioned collaboration communities require and provide different level of memberships, whereas the fees vary from $250 to $25 000. In addition, each application initiates a review process which is performed by the community and decides about acceptance to join. Some communities perform collaboration following the following the Chatham House Rules[4] (e.g., M³AAWG). The number of community members within a fee-based community vary from $200 to $1 800 and FIRST is mentioned to be the oldest and biggest international collaboration community for CERTs [25].

3.3   Reputation-Based Trust Models

e-Commerce: The trust model of e-Commerce is often a centralized reputation-based system that rely on feedback of the involved parties. This feedback system is used in eBay, AirBnB, Booking and Amazon and is a primary resource for potential buyers to determine the trustworthiness of the seller. A feedback consists of comments and five different ranking levels to evaluate several aspects (e.g., price, condition, timeliness). Further, the overall feedback score consists of a positive, neutral or negative rating. A positive feedback adds +1, a negative feedback adds −1 and a neutral feedback 0 to the overall feedback score. To calculate the overall feedback percentage, the ratio of feedback scores is computed.

---

[1] http://www.geant.org/Innovation/SIG_TF/Pages/TF-CSIRT.aspx.

[2] http://www.geant.org/Innovation/SIG_TF/Pages/SIG-NOC.aspx.

[3] https://datatracker.ietf.org/wg/dots/charter/.

[4] https://www.chathamhouse.org/about/chatham-house-rule.

Web of Trust: The trust model *web of trust* (WOT) describes a decentralized public-key infrastructure (PKI) relying on trust decisions of individual participants [16]. It is used in PGP, GnuPG and OpenPGP. The basic WOT uses three levels of trust: complete, marginal and no trust. In addition, PGP, GnuPG and OpenPGP distinguish unknown trust from no trust and thus differentiate between 5 trust levels [15,16]. Each participating partner owns a personal collection of certificates called the key ring and is allowed to sign a key for any other participant. [16] reported that the trust model accepts a given public key in the key ring as completely valid, if either (i) the public key belongs to the owner of the key ring, (ii) the key ring contains at least C certificates from completely trusted certificate issuer with valid public keys and (iii) the key ring contains at least M certificates from marginally trusted certificate issuer with valid public keys. The default values in PGP are $C = 1$ and $M = 2$, whereas GnuPG uses $C = 1$ and $M = 3$. The calculation of the trust level is described by [16] as follows: The key legitimacy $L = \frac{c}{C} + \frac{m}{M}$, where c and m represents the number of certificates from completely/marginally trusted certificate issuers with valid keys. A key is completely valid for $L \geq 1$, marginally valid for $0 < L < 1$, and invalid for $L = 0$.

4   Trust Model

Our mitigation and response trust model (MiRTrust) is based on hTrust [26], a trust management model to facilitate the construction of trust-aware mobile systems and applications and on the PGP trust model [15,16]. In contrast to hTrust, MiRTrust uses the four GnuPG [27] trust levels: *unknown, none, marginal* and *full* and additionally the trust level *distrust*. Moreover, MiRTrust takes into account the EU Trusted Lists [28] and the Alexa top 10 million websites list in order to extract the use of certification authorities using a 3 months average ranking. Unlike hTrust, MiRTrust does not consider contexts as the security events are identified in the context of ISPs and result from a large-scale attack.

MiRTrust consists of several input parameters (yellow colored) and three components: trust formation (blue colored), trust dissemination (brown colored) and trust evaluation (green colored) as shown in Fig. 2. The component trust formation is responsible to determine the trustworthiness of a security event before a semi-automated mitigation and response action is taken. In case a security event from a new collaborating partner or an unknown source was received, the trust dissemination guarantees a minimum set of information upon the predication of trust can be calculated. The last component, trust evaluation, is responsible to continuously self-adapt the trust information kept in the ISP's local trust list.

A trusted-based collaboration relies on two participating partners exchanging security events, where as trust has the following three characteristics: (i) Trust is not symmetric. If ISP a trusts ISP b, it does not follow ISP b trusts ISP a. (ii) Trust is not inherently transitive. If ISP a trusts ISP b and ISP b trusts ISP c, it does not automatically follow that ISP a trusts ISP c. (iii) Trust of own detection engines varies in a range from marginal trust to full trust, as false

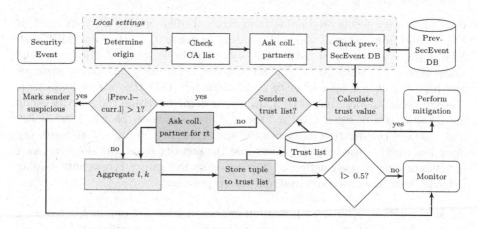

Fig. 2. Trust level calculation of MiRTrust (Color figure online)

positives are possible. A security event is described as the quadruple (a, b, s, t). The quadruple can be described as follows: ISP a informs ISP b about a security event of type s occurring at time t. The sender of a security event is referred to as trustee, whereas the receiver of a security event is called trustor. ISP b is a trustor that forms a trust opinion about the trustee ISP a based on b's previous trust experiences with a. The process to form a trust opinion about a trustee is shown in Fig. 2. The trust experiences are stored locally at each MiR system and are described by a 6-tuple: (a, b, s, l, k, t). The tuple can be described as follows: ISP b trusts ISP a at level l about the security event type s in context of large-scale attacks. The trust level l is denoted as $l \in [-2, 2]$, whereas -2 represents distrust, -1 represents unknown trust, 0 represents no trust, 1 represents marginal trust and 2 represents full trust. In accordance to [26], MiRTrust also considers only partial knowledge about the trustworthiness of collaborating partner. The reason is that only directly interconnected networks are collaborating and thus their trust opinions contain a level of uncertainty. This uncertainty is expressed as knowledge k and varies from a trust based decision *do not trust* to a lack of evidence based decision *do not know*. The knowledge k is denoted as $k \in [0, 1]$, whereas 0 represents unknown and 1 perfect knowledge. Both, the trust level l and the knowledge k is retrieved from local settings and past experiences. The better the experience in the past, the higher the trust level l and the knowledge k. To relate trust and knowledge to time, MiRTrust uses the variable t to refer at which time t the trust t and knowledge k was calculated.

Local Settings: In a first step, MiRTrust computes a trust range $\Upsilon[lb, ub]$ and an initial knowledge value based on the origin of the security event. In case of an internal security event $\Upsilon[lb, ub]$ is set to $\Upsilon[1, 2]$ and the knowledge value is set to $k = 1$. The trust range of security events originating from external collaborating partners is set to $\Upsilon[0, 1]$, where as the trust range of security events originating from external non collaborating partners is set to $\Upsilon[-2, 0]$. The knowledge value of security events originating from external collaborating partners is set to $k = 0.5$ and from external non collaborating partners to $k = 0$. Next, MiRTrust takes into account several local settings ls. The basic setup of MiRTrust considers three local settings: $ls_1 = $ *check CA list*, $ls_2 = $ *ask collaborating partners* and $ls_3 = $ *check previous security event database* (DB) that all evaluate to a boolean value. ls_1 describes if IP addresses or domains within the security event are listed on the merged CA list. This CA list combines the EU Trusted list and the used certification authorities of the Alexa top 10 million websites. ls_2 describes whether the behavior that cause the security event has also been seen in collaborating partner networks [29]. ls_3 refers to security events with similar behavior that have been received and stored previously.

Trust Formation: The trust formation enables a trustor to predict a trustee's trustworthiness before mitigation and response actions are initiated. Therefore, the function p is used to calculate a trust value as shown in Eq. (1). p uses a weight w to emphasize the importance of a local setting ls. The importance of these values are defined by each participating ISP. The function $c(ls_i)$ is used to decide which value of the trust range $\Upsilon_{[lb,ub]}$ is multiplied with weight w.

$$p(w_1, \ldots, w_n, ls_1, \ldots, ls_n, \Upsilon_{[lb,ub]}) = \sum_{i=1}^{n} w_i \cdot c(ls_i), c(ls_i) = \begin{cases} \Upsilon_{lb} & \text{if} \quad ls_i = 0 \\ \Upsilon_{ub} & \text{if} \quad ls_i = 1 \end{cases} \tag{1}$$

Next, MiRTrust looks up the sender of the security event in the local trust list. In case, the sender is listed within the trust list, the previous level of trust within the trust list and the current level of trust of the function p are compared. If $|$ prev. l $-$ curr. l $| > 1$, the sender is marked as suspicious. Otherwise, the past trust experiences v and the current trust value p are aggregated using the weighted average, as the trust experiences evolve over time. The trust level l is set to $l = \frac{v+p}{2}$. In case, the sender is not listed within the trust list and thus no aggregated trust experience tuple is available, collaborating partners are asked for recommendations r. As a recommendation is transferred over the network, it uses encryption to ensure confidentiality and a signature to prove the recommendation's authenticity. Thus, the current trust value p and the trust value of the recommendation r are aggregated depending on the quality q of the recommendation and determined as shown in Eq. (2). Only those recommendations are considered that provide a quality q greater than a minimum level of trust. In addition, only recommendations with a time stamp $t(p) > t(r)$ are used. The trust value rl takes into account the inherent knowledge uncertainty k of the given recommendation. T represents the time interval in which security events are observed and the total number of security events.

$$q_i = max\left(l_{min}, l_i \cdot k_i \cdot max\left(0, \frac{T - (t_n - t)}{T}\right)\right) \tag{2}$$

Due to the collaboration, multiple recommendations r_n are received. Therefore, a unique recommendation trust value rl is computed using a weighted average of the individual trust range of the recommendations with a quality greater than the minimum level of trust as shown in Formula (3) [15].

$$rl(r_1, \ldots, r_n) = \frac{1}{n} \sum_{i=1}^{n} l_i \cdot q_i | q_i > l_{min} \tag{3}$$

rl and the current trust value p are aggregated using the weighted average. The trust level l is set to $l = \frac{p+rl}{2}$.

Trust Dissemination: The trust formation is used to predict the trustworthiness of an ISP. In case no aggregated tuples are available, an ISP exchanges recommendations r with its collaborating partners to guarantee a minimum set of information to decide about the trustworthiness. As a consequence, recommendations contain sensitive data that require the use of security mechanisms (e.g., encryption & signature). Therefore, the exchange format FLEX is used to disseminate the recommendations.

Trust Evaluation: MiRTrust continuously updates its local settings during the occurrence of a security event and based on the received recommendations. These updates are included with equal weight to ensure that a trust opinion can not change rapidly (e.g., caused by false good recommendation). In case a recommendation r is received that conflicts with the own calculated trustworthiness, the level of trust of ISP x is not aggregated into previous trust opinions and ISP x is marked as suspicious. In case, several security events of ISP x occur with conflicting trustworthiness, the level of trust of ISP x tends to drop to -2, that represents distrust and thus identifies x as an ISP with a suspect behavior. As a consequence, recommendations of x will be disregarded.

5   Evaluation

In this Section, we describe the qualitative and quantitative evaluation of our trust model MiRTrust. First, we describe the characteristics of the evaluation criteria. Second, we introduce five evaluation criteria for our trust model. Further, we evaluate MiRTrust using multi-method-modeling, describe the setup of the testbed and present the test scenario of the trust model. Finally, we present and summarize the results of the evaluation.

5.1   Qualitative Evaluation Methodology

The trust model MiRTrust is evaluated based on the following five criteria: Ease of deployment, authorization, subjectivity, asymmetry and decentralization. These criteria were derived from the requirements described in Sect. 2.2.

The criterion 'Ease of Deployment' describes the ability to use the trust model and its underlying implementation on different operating systems, infrastructure devices, exchange formats and protocols. The criterion 'authorization' refers to the ability to support the TLP protocol. The 'subjectivity' describes the possibility that network operators are able to form their own trust opinions. The criterion 'asymmetry' describes the possibility that two collaborating partners do not need to have the similar trust in each other. The criterion 'decentralization' refers to the ability that each participating ISP acts as a self-contained unit, calculates and stores its trust decisions locally.

5.2 Quantitative Evaluation Methodology

MiRTrust is evaluated using a multi-method-modeling approach consisting of an agent-based and a discrete event model using AnyLogic[5]. The model of MiRTrust is based on a scale-free network of ISPs that share security event information and perform mitigation actions based on the trust and knowledge level of each security event. The ISPs are modeled as agents. Each ISP has an individual behavior and attitude towards the trustworthiness of a sender of a security event. The process of mitigation is modeled in a discrete event way at each single ISP.

Initially, MiRTrust models a weekly contact rate to describe the assumption that 1 % of potential ISPs will want to join the MiRTrust community. Besides this contact rate, non-community members are able to join the community by using a sponsoring join process. Each community member possesses a list of directly connected collaborating partners and assigns an initial trust value range of $[0, 1]$ and a knowledge value of 0.5. Based on the findings in [30], each ISP receives 5 security events per month. The sender of the security event is set using a triangular distribution. This triangular distribution is used to create security events sent from an internal detection engine of an ISP, an external collaborating ISP and an unknown ISP. Based on the sender of the security event, an ISP starts its trust formulation calculation and looks up its past trust experiences w_1 with the sender of the security event. In case no trust experiences are available and thus no previous security events have been exchanged between the sender and receiver of the security event, the receiving ISP asks its collaborating partners to send recommendation tuples about the trustworthiness of the sender. Therefore, ISPs interact and share their trust experiences. Further, MiRTrust takes into account a local created trusted CA list w_2 and if this security event has also been seen by collaborating partners w_3. These local settings are weighted based on the formula (1) as follows: $w_1 = 0.5, w_2 = 0.15$ and $w_3 = 0.45$ with $w_1 + w_2 + w_3 = 1, 0 \leq w_i \leq 1$. Next, the trust level and the knowledge values are calculated. Finally, mitigation and response actions are deployed, if the trust level pass a threshold of 0. The duration of the mitigation process is set using a triangular distribution with lower limit $a = 20$ and upper limit $b = 1440$ min. These mitigation values are derived from [30]. Finally, the ISPs are waiting for the next occurring security event that restarts the trust formation process.

---

[5] The model can be downloaded on https://bitbucket.org/dasec/mirtrust.

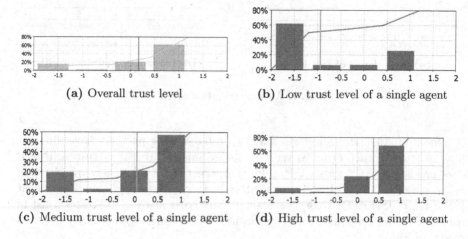

(a) Overall trust level   (b) Low trust level of a single agent

(c) Medium trust level of a single agent   (d) High trust level of a single agent

Fig. 3. Distribution of trust levels

5.3 Evaluation Results

In this paragraph, we present and discuss the results of the qualitative and quantitative evaluation of MiRTrust.

Ease of Deployment: The heterogeneity of network devices and used operating systems requires a platform independent trust model that easily integrates within the existing infrastructure. Therefore, the implementation of MiRTrust is based on Java and thus can easily be deployed on different operating systems. Further, MiRTrust encodes its recommendation tuples in FLEX. The dissemination of those tuples among trusted partners is using STOMP and thus ensures platform independency.

Access Control: MiRTrust supports the semi-automated dissemination of security threat information based on the different level of trust. Therefore, MiRTrust differentiates between the following five different trust levels: distrust, unknown, none, marginal and full trust. The use of different trust levels allows to encode security event information using the TLP protocol and thus provide different detail of information within a security event tailored for its intended receivers. The trust level distrust, unknown and none trust are mapped to the color red of the TPL protocol. The color amber is used to encode the trust level margial trust and the color green is used to represent full trust.

Subjectivity: Through the different level of trust and sharing relationship between collaborating ISPs, MiRTrust supports that each collaborating partner is able to form its own trust opinion. The quantitative evaluation of MiRTrust shows the distribution of different level of trust in Fig. 3.

From	To	l	k	s		t
iSPs[359]	iSPs[11]	0.98	0.6	DDoS		2016-02-08 18:27:27.103+01
iSPs[289]	iSPs[11]	−1.5	0.1	DDoS		2016-02-08 18:27:29.571+01
iSPs[168]	iSPs[11]	0.83	0.6	DDoS		2016-02-08 18:27:30.253+01

(a) Trust levels of ISP 11

From	To	l	k	s	t
iSPs[11]	iSPs[359]	0.5	0.5	I	2016-02-08 18:27:27.457+01
iSPs[11]	iSPs[289]	0.5	0.5	I	2016-02-08 18:27:29.429+01
iSPs[11]	iSPs[168]	0.5	0.5	I	2016-02-08 18:27:32.089+01

(b) Trust of other ISPs in ISP 11

Fig. 4. Asymmetric trust level

Asymmetry: MiRTrust supports that two collaborating partners have different level of trust in each other as trust is not symmetric. If ISP a trusts ISP b, it does not follow ISP b trusts ISP a. Further, trust is not inherently transitive. If ISP a trusts ISP b and ISP b trusts ISP c, it does not automatically follow that ISP a trusts ISP c. Therefore, each single MiRTrust instance possesses a list of calculated trust level and knowledge values of each exchanged security event as shown in Fig. 4.

Decentralization: MiRTrust is deployed at each collaborating partner and thus acts as a self-contained unit that calculates and stores trust opinions locally. Further, the recommendation tuples are transfered to collaborating partners using FLEX and thus are signed. Each ISP is able to form its own trust opinion about collaborating partners similar to the principle of web of trust.

6 Conclusion

Nowadays, large-scale cyber attacks have become larger, more sophisticated and frequent. One approach to mitigate and respond to large-scale network-based attacks focuses on collaboration. In this paper, we introduced the trust model MiRTrust that facilitates the semi-automated assessment and deployment of remediation suggestions within a security event. MiRTrust is used to determine different levels of trust, set the prioritization of the shared security event, sanitize the occurrence of security events and contributes to built a trust community in order to share information about cyber threats and its remediation suggestions. We have shown that MiRTrust is able to support the formation of a subjective and asymmetric trust level and can be used to encode cyber threat information using TLP for dissemination.

Based on our qualitative and quantitative evaluation, MiRTrust constitutes a viable and collaborative approach to assess the trust level of collaborating ISPs and thus deploy semi-automated remediations of a security events.

Acknowledgment. The work has been funded by CASED and by EU FP7 Flamingo (ICT-318488).

References

1. Anstee, D., Bussiere, D., Sockrider, G., Morales, C.: Worldwide Infrastructure Security Report. Technical Report IX, Arbor Networks Inc., January 2014. http://www.arbornetworks.com/resources/annual-security-report

2. Research and Education Networking Information Sharing and Analysis Center: REN-ISAC Research and Education Networking Information Sharing and Analysis Center (2015). http://www.ren-isac.net/

3. Advanced Cyber Defence Centre: ACDC Deliverables (2015). http://acdc-project.eu/acdc-deliverables/

4. Reitinger, P.: Enabling Distributed Security in Cyberspace. U.S. Department of Homeland Security (2011). https://www.dhs.gov/xlibrary/assets/nppd-cyber-ecosystem-white-paper-03-23-2011.pdf

5. Internet Architecture Board, the Internet Society: CARIS Workshop Template Submissions. Internet Architecture Board and the Internet Society, June 2015. https://internetsociety2.wufoo.com/reports/caris-workshop-template-submissions/

6. Morrow, C., Dobbins, R.: DDoS Open Threat Signaling (DOTS) Working Group Operational Requirements. IETF 93, July 2015. https://www.ietf.org/proceedings/93/slides/slides-93-dots-3.pdf

7. The White House: Executive Order - Improving Critical Infrastructure Cybersecurity (2013). https://www.whitehouse.gov/the-press-office/2013/02/12/executive-order-improving-critical-infrastructure-cybersecurity

8. National Parliament of the Federal Republic of Germany: Gesetz zur Erhung der Sicherheit informationstechnischer Systeme (IT-Sicherheitsgesetz) (2015). http://dipbt.bundestag.de/extrakt/ba/WP18/643/64396.html

9. Danyliw, R., Meijer, J., Demchenko, Y.: The Incident Object Description Exchange Format RFC 5070 (Proposed Standard), December 2007

10. Debar, H., Curry, D., Feinstein, B.: The Intrusion Detection Message Exchange Format (IDMEF) RFC 4765 (Experimental), March 2007

11. Shafranovich, Y., Levine, J., Kucherawy, M.: An Extensible Format for Email Feedback Reports RFC 5965 (Proposed Standard), August 2010

12. abusix GmbH: x-arf Network Abuse Reporting 2.0. http://www.x-arf.org/

13. Steinberger, J., Sperotto, A., Baier, H., Pras, A.: Exchanging security events of flow-based intrusion detection systems at internet scale. Internet Architecture Board and the Internet Society, June 2015. https://www.iab.org/wp-content/IAB-uploads/2015/04/CARIS_2015_submission_3.pdf

14. Steinberger, J., Sperotto, A., Golling, M., Baier, H.: How to exchange security events? overview and evaluation of formats and protocols. In: 2015 IFIP/IEEE International Symposium on Integrated Network Management (IM 2015), May 2015

15. Abdul-Rahman, A., Hailes, S.: A distributed trust model. In: Proceedings of the 1997 Workshop on New Security Paradigms, NSPW 1997, pp. 48–60. ACM, New York (1997)

16. Jonczy, J., Wüthrich, M., Haenni, R.: A probabilistic trust model for GnuPG. In: 23C3, 23rd Chaos Communication Congress, Berlin, Germany, pp. 61–66 (2006)

17. Golling, M., Hofstede, R., Koch, R.: Towards multi-layered intrusion detection in high-speed networks. In: 2014 6th International Conference On Cyber Conflict, June 2014

18. Esposito, C., Ciampi, M.: On security in publish/subscribe services: a survey. IEEE Commun. Surv. Tutorials **17**(2), 966–997 (2015)

19. European Union Agency for Network, Information Security: Reputation-based Systems: a security analysis (2007). https://www.enisa.europa.eu/publications/archive/reputation-based-systems-a-security-analysis

20. Fullam, K.K., Klos, T.B., Muller, G., Sabater, J., Schlosser, A., Topol, Z., Barber, K.S., Rosenschein, J.S., Vercouter, L., Voss, M.: A specification of the agent reputation and trust (art) testbed: experimentation and competition for trust in agent societies. In: Proceedings of the Fourth International Joint Conference on Autonomous Agents and Multiagent Systems, AAMAS 2005, pp. 512–518. ACM (2005)

21. The Department of Homeland Security's United States Computer Emergency Readiness Team: Traffic Light Protocol (TLP) Matrix and Frequently Asked Questions (2015). https://www.us-cert.gov/tlp

22. Grandison, T.: Trust management for internet applications. Ph.D. thesis, Imperial College of Science, Technology and Medicine University of London (2003). http://www.doc.ic.ac.uk/~tgrand/PhD_Thesis.pdf

23. Anti-Phishing Working Group: Charter and Saga - Unifying the global response to cybercrime though data exchange, research and public awareness (2015). http://apwg.org/

24. Messaging, Malware, Mobile Anti-Abuse Working Group: Member application (2015). https://www.m3aawg.org/

25. European Union Agency for Network, Information Security: CERT cooperation and its further facilitation by relevant stakeholders (2006). https://www.enisa.europa.eu/activities/cert/background/coop/files/cert-cooperation-and-its-further-facilitation-by-relevant-stakeholders

26. Capra, L.: Engineering human trust in mobile system collaborations. In: Proceedings of the 12th ACM SIGSOFT Twelfth International Symposium on Foundations of Software Engineering, SIGSOFT 2004/FSE-12, pp. 107–116. ACM, New York (2004)

27. The Free Software Foundation: Trust in a key's owner (1999). https://www.gnupg.org/gph/en/manual.html

28. General, European Commission's Directorate for Communications Networks, Content & Technology: EU Trusted Lists of Certification Service Providers (2014). https://ec.europa.eu/digital-agenda/en/eu-trusted-lists-certification-service-providers

29. Steinberger, J., Kuhnert, B., Sperotto, A., Baier, H., Pras, A.: Collaborative DDoS defense using flow-based security event information. In: 2016 IEEE/IFIP Network Operations and Management Symposium (NOMS 2016), April 2016

30. Steinberger, J., Sperotto, A., Baier, H., Pras, A.: Collaborative attack mitigation and response: a survey. In: 2015 IFIP/IEEE International Symposium on Integrated Network Management (IM 2015), May 2015

PhD Student Workshop — Security Management

Network Defence Using Attacker-Defender Interaction Modelling

Jana Medková[✉] and Pavel Čeleda

Institute of Computer Science, Masaryk University, Brno, Czech Republic
jana.medkova@mail.muni.cz, celeda@ics.muni.cz

Abstract. Network security is still lacking an efficient system which selects a response action based on observed security events and which is capable of running autonomously. The main reason for this is the lack of an effective defence strategy. In this Ph.D., we endeavour to create such a defence strategy. We propose to model the interaction between an attacker and a defender to comprehend how the attacker's goals affect his actions and use the model as a basis for a more refined network defence strategy. We formulate the research questions that need to be answered and we discuss, how the answers to these questions relate to the proposed solution. This research is at the initial phase and will contribute to a Ph.D. thesis in four years.

Keywords: Network defence · Defence strategy · Attacker-defender interaction modelling

1 Introduction

In network security, we can consider the reaction to an attack to follow a recurring cycle of detecting and understanding security events, making decisions and taking response actions [6]. However, if the defence is carried out by a human and the attack is automated, the response action might occur too late. In order to react quickly to an attack, the network defence has to be able to operate autonomously. In order to create an autonomous defence system, each part of the cycle has to be fully automated.

This has already been partly accomplished: the gathering of information from various sources is automated by Intrusion Detection Systems (IDS), which generate security alerts when malicious or suspicious activity is observed [2,11]. The received information is automatically processed to form situation awareness by Security Information and Event Management systems (SIEM), which provide a real-time analysis of security alerts [10]. The selected response actions can be carried out automatically using Software Defined Networking (SDN) [5,8].

However, the selection of response actions is still performed by a security expert or unsophisticated decision algorithms, which take actions only where certain thresholds are exceeded. These thresholds are usually very high to avoid

© IFIP International Federation for Information Processing 2016
R. Badonnel et al. (Eds.): AIMS 2016, LNCS 9701, pp. 127–131, 2016.
DOI: 10.1007/978-3-319-39814-3_12

blocking legitimate users. Such systems are not capable of handling more complicated situations. If we want to be able to create a system capable of selecting response actions autonomously or work as a decision support for a security expert, we need a more efficient, refined defence strategy. In the proposed Ph.D. thesis, we would like to address this issue.

We propose to create a mathematical model of the interaction between an attacker and a defender and use it as a basis for a network defence strategy. Through modelling, we gain insight. Through insight, we gain understanding. Through understanding, we can form a strategy. However, to form a strategy based on the model several challenges have to be overcome.

1. The interaction between an attacker and a defender on the network is very complex. The network can be large, change over time and the number of attack vectors is ever growing. Moreover, each action has to be considered not individually but in the context of its future implications.
2. We are always uncertain about the state of the network, the attacker's objectives and previous actions (and whether he is an attacker at all). The best we can do is to operate on our beliefs – a probability distribution over the possible states updated whenever we receive new information.

Attempts have been made towards an autonomous network defence strategy. The Response and Recovery Engine [13] selects a response action using game theory. The system showed promising results in simulated scenarios, however, it has limited usability since it assumes that an agent system is installed on each host. In [1] the authors propose a network defence system using reinforcement learning and dynamic risk assessment. However they admit that the overall performance was not optimal and further improvement is needed. A general overview of the model's requirements applicable for modelling the interaction between an attacker and a defender was given in [9].

2   Research Questions

The main goal of the proposed research is **to model the interaction between an attacker and a defender and use the model as a basis for a network defence strategy**. We have defined following research questions, which need to be answered to achieve this goal:

1. **How can we model the interaction between an attacker and a defender?** The model of the interaction between an attacker and a defender provides a formal description of the workings of the interaction. It is necessary that the description is accurate, so that it captures the underlying principles of the interaction. At the same time, the model has to simplify the situation since we want to use the model to optimise the defender's actions. Balancing the accuracy and simplicity is crucial. We have to define the model that can be solved with reasonable computational complexity even for large networks and still be capable of capturing the essence of the interaction.

2. **How can we use the model to form a network defence strategy?** The model of the interaction between an attacker and a defender only describes the interaction in a simplified manner. However, it enables us to better comprehend the dynamics of the interaction between an attacker and a defender, which in turn enables us to find the best response actions for the defender. We will use these actions to form a defence strategy.

3. **Can human instinct and experience be included in the defence strategy?** While the model can capture principles applicable in real life, it has its limitations. It is not unusual that the security expert observed similar attacks in the past or has better intuition. It would be therefore very desirable to use this information to improve the decision based on the model. Such a concept exists in economics, namely the Black-Litterman model [3].

3   Proposed Approach

Our approach to creating a defence strategy consists of modelling the interaction between an attacker and a defender. We consider the interaction only on the defended network. Without the loss of accuracy, we also assume that the attacker's malicious intent is targeted on the network and he tries to maximise his utility by employing a series of attacks. On the other hand, the defender makes his best effort to defend the network based on his observations and available response actions. We assume both the observation and the response actions are made at the network level since it allows us to cover all connected hosts. Moreover, in reality, the defender usually does not have administration rights on the hosts in the network. In a fully autonomous defence, the role of the defender is taken on by a system capable of network monitoring and reconfiguration.

In this Section, we outline the steps that need to be taken in order to answer the research questions. We describe each step and a proposed approach.

Modelling the interaction between an attacker and a defender – We believe that game theory is a suitable mathematical tool for modelling the interaction between an attacker and a defender since it can model situations in which multiple parties with conflicting interests compete with each other [4]. We can use a game-theory toolset to compute the optimal strategies (in a game-theoretic meaning) for the defender and base the defence strategy (in a network defence meaning) on them. When defining the model, we have to keep in mind, that at some point in future we will need to compute the optimal actions of the defender and the attacker. Therefore, the model should be designed so that this task is computationally feasible.

Translating network information into model parameters – We have to estimate the input parameters of the model from information about the network in an automated fashion. The information should be passed in the form of a formal network description: the topology of the network, the hosts and services present in the network, the required levels of confidentiality, availability and integrity of these services and their interdependence. Based on this information, we can compare how desirable different outcomes are for the defender.

Network defence strategy – When formulating the strategy, we have to take into account uncertainty about the state of the network and the attacker's previous actions and goals. A possible approach would be to use the alerts generated by an intrusion detection system to maintain beliefs about the current state of the network, the attacker's past actions and his goals. Based on these beliefs we can use the model and select the best response action in a given situation. Since the computational complexity of optimising the response action is most likely going to be very high, we do not suppose that this selection would be computed at runtime, more likely it would be computed for the network in advance and only the precomputed results will be used.

Strategy verification – The efficiency of the decision algorithm has to be verified. First, we plan to test the proposed strategy in a simulated environment using a cloud-based testbed for simulating cyber attacks [7]. Then, we plan to compare the strategy with decisions made by teams in the Computer Security Incident Response Team (CSIRT) training exercise [12]. In this exercise, teams of CSIRT employees defend their network and are scored based on the success of the attacks. The strategy would represent the fifth team and its score will be compared to the "real" teams score.

Adding human intuition to decision output – The strategy will base the defence on beliefs about the state of the network, the attacker's past and future actions and his goals. Any refinement of these beliefs will lead to better results. Humans have expertise and intuition which cannot be emulated by any model, no matter how sophisticated. They could have seen similar situations before, guess what will the attacker do next or have additional information which is not included in the strategy. We can include human opinion on the situation into the decision by updating the current beliefs.

4   Conclusion

The role of a defender in network security is difficult. If the defender cannot protect his network, he fails. If he impairs a legitimate user by his actions, he fails. Moreover, the defender is never certain about the state of the defended network since the observations of the network might be incorrect. Currently, automated network defence systems select response actions based only on the observed security events. They react only in unambiguous situations and the rest of the events must be investigated by security experts. We want to refine the decision making process by including also the motivation of the attacker. By comprehending how his goals affect his actions, we gain more information and we can select the response action more accurately.

Acknowledgement. This research was supported by the Security Research Programme of the Czech Republic 2015–2020 (BV III / 1 VS) granted by the Ministry of the Interior of the Czech Republic under No. VI20162019014 Simulation, detection, and mitigation of cyber threats endangering critical infrastructure.

References

1. Beaudoin, L., Japkowicz, N., Matwin, S.: Autonomic computer network defence using risk state and reinforcement learning. Cryptol. Inf. Secur. Ser. **3**, 238–248 (2009)
2. Bhuyan, M.H., Bhattacharyya, D.K., Kalita, J.K.: Network anomaly detection: methods, systems and tools. IEEE Commun. Surv. Tutor. **16**(1), 303–336 (2014)
3. Black, F., Litterman, R.: Global portfolio optimization. Finan. Anal. J. **48**(5), 28–43 (1992)
4. Hamilton, S.N., Miller, W.L., Ott, A., Saydjari, O.S.: The role of game theory in information warfare. In: 4th Information Survivability Workshop (ISW-2001/2002), Vancouver, Canada, March 2002
5. Hu, F., Hao, Q., Bao, K.: A survey on software-defined network and openflow: from concept to implementation. IEEE Commun. Surv. Tutor. **16**(4), 2181–2206 (2014)
6. Kott, A., Wang, C., Erbacher, R.F.: Cyber Defense and Situational Awareness. Springer, New York (2014)
7. Kouřil, D., Rebok, T., Jirsík, T., Čegan, J., Drašar, M., Vizváry, M., Vykopal, J.: Cloud-based testbed for simulation of cyber attacks. In: 2014 IEEE Network Operations and Management Symposium (NOMS), pp. 1–6, May 2014
8. Kreutz, D., Ramos, F., Esteves Verissimo, P., Esteve Rothenberg, C., Azodolmolky, S., Uhlig, S.: Software-defined networking: a comprehensive survey. Proc. IEEE **103**(1), 14–76 (2015)
9. Liu, P., Zang, W., Yu, M.: Incentive-based modeling and inference of attacker intent, objectives, and strategies. ACM Trans. Inf. Syst. Secur. **8**(1), 78–118 (2005)
10. Miller, D., Harris, S., Harper, A., VanDyke, S., Blask, C.: Security Information and Event Management (SIEM) Implementation. McGraw Hill Professional, New York (2010)
11. Shameli-Sendi, A., Ezzati-Jivan, N., Jabbarifar, M., Dagenais, M.: Intrusion response systems: survey and taxonomy. Int. J. Comput. Sci. Netw. Secur. **12**(1), 1–14 (2012)
12. Čeleda, P., Čegan, J., Vykopal, J., Tovarňák, D.: KYPO - a platform for cyber defence exercises. In: STO-MP-MSG-133: M&S Support to Operational Tasks Including War Gaming, Logistics, Cyber Defence. NATO Science and Technology Organization (2015)
13. Zonouz, S.A., Khurana, H., Sanders, W.H., Yardley, T.M.: RRE: a game-theoretic intrusion response and recovery engine. IEEE Trans. Parallel Distrib. Syst. **25**(2), 395–406 (2014)

Evaluating Reputation of Internet Entities

Václav Bartoš[1,2(✉)] and Jan Kořenek[1]

[1] Faculty of Information Technology, Brno University of Technology,
Brno, Czech Republic
korenek@fit.vutbr.cz
[2] CESNET a.l.e., Prague, Czech Republic
bartos@cesnet.cz

Abstract. Security monitoring tools, such as honeypots, IDS, behavioral analysis or anomaly detection systems, generate large amounts of security events or alerts. These alerts are often shared within some communities using various alert sharing systems. Our research is focused on analysis of the huge amount of data present in these systems. In this work we focus on summarizing all alerts and other information known about a network entity into a measure called *reputation score* expressing the level of threat the entity poses. Computation of the reputation score is based on estimating probability of future attacks caused by the entity.

1 Introduction

Network operators today often recognize the need to monitor their networks. This includes security monitoring, *i. e.* deployment of various detectors of malicious or unwanted traffic, such as honeypots, IDS, behavioral analysis or anomaly detection. These systems can generate large amounts of *security events* or *alerts*. In large networks with many such detectors, or when alerts are exchanged among several organizations via some alert sharing system (such as Warden, AbuseHelper, n6, *etc.* [6]), the number of such alerts may be very large (millions per day [1]). We believe that analysis of such amount of data can reveal interesting characteristics of sources of malicious traffic. In particular, we want to label them by estimated measure of threat they pose, which we call *reputation score*.

It is known that network attacks are generated mostly by hosts infected with malware allowing attackers to control them remotely. Once a host is compromised, it often stays compromised for some time and therefore many security events can be caused by this single host. This fact is often used for spam mitigation, where lists of known malicious IP addresses (blacklists) are used to block known sources of spam. The same principle can be used to deal with other kinds of malicious traffic as well. For many attack[1] types, it is common to see the same IP address reported as malicious repeatedly for a long time [1,2,9].

However, while blacklists are easy to use, the information they provide is very limited. It is a binary information only – an address is either listed or not, surely bad or surely good, nothing in between. Moreover, there is no information about

---

[1] For simplicity, all kinds of malicious or unwanted traffic, including spam or port scanning, are called *attacks* in this paper.

© IFIP International Federation for Information Processing 2016
R. Badonnel et al. (Eds.): AIMS 2016, LNCS 9701, pp. 132–136, 2016.
DOI: 10.1007/978-3-319-39814-3_13

why it was listed or when. Also, it has been shown that malicious IP addresses are distributed non-uniformly both geographically and in IP space [1,3,10]. Some networks, autonomous systems or countries (called *bad neighborhoods* in [10]) host significantly more malicious hosts than others. Therefore, in some cases, the sole fact that an IP address belongs to such a bad neighborhood may be enough for it to be suspicious, although the address itself has never been reported as malicious. This phenomenon cannot be covered by classic blacklists.

We envision a much richer source of information about misbehaving entities, which we call a *reputation database*. It will gather alerts from large number of detectors (via some of the existing alert sharing systems) and keep information about all network entities (not only IP addresses, but also network prefixes, domains, *etc.*) reported as sources of malicious behavior, including information on reasons why the entity was listed, when and by whom. It will further enhance this information by data from external sources, such as geolocation, information from DNS (*e. g.* hostnames assigned to IP addresses), other databases or black-lists. In general, it will gather as much security related information about the reported entities as possible. All this information will be provided to security teams to help them to protect their networks and investigate incidents.

An important part of the system should be an algorithm summarizing all the information known about an entity, *i.e.* its reputation, into a single num-ber representing a measure of threat the entity poses – its *reputation score*. For example, it should allow to easily differentiate between an address which sent a single spam email a week ago and an address which tries to break into pass-word protected services by dictionary attacks every day for last two months. It thus allows to quickly decide on which problems to focus first, or to easily cre-ate blocklists by getting a top-n list of IP addresses with the worst reputation score, for example. The goal of our research is to find a method to evaluate the reputation of an entity numerically by computing its reputation score.

2   Proposed Approach

The first thing that has to be done is to formally define the meaning of reputa-tion score. In common language, the word "reputation" expresses the common opinion people have about someone or something (an entity) [4,8]. It is based on shared experience with past behavior of the entity. But although it is based on the past, it is intended to describe the most likely state in the near future and thus to help with current decisions. Similarly, reputation score of a network entity should be based on the history of security incidents caused by the entity, but it should represent the level of threat the entity poses now and in the near future. Therefore, we formally define it as follows:

> *Reputation score* of a network entity (*e. g.* an IP address) represents the *probability* that the entity will perform a *malicious activity* in the *near future* (*e. g.* next 24 h), based on its past behavior and other information.[2]

---

[2] Ideally, the probability should be combined with anticipated severity of the malicious activity. Such variant is much more complex and is not covered by this short paper.

This definition means that evaluation of the reputation score must be based on prediction of future attacks. Our approach to build such a predictor is as follows.

The input of the prediction algorithm will be mainly a summary of all malicious events reported in some past time window. They can be supplemented by various other inputs related to the entity and the threat it potentially poses. For an IP address, it may be the country and the autonomous system it belongs to, whether it is listed on some of the public blacklists, whether its hostname can be resolved using a reverse DNS query, or whether the address is dynamically assigned or there is NAT (which can be sometimes guessed from the hostname).

All this information form the input of an algorithm, whose output should be the probability that the given entity will behave maliciously in a specified future time window. However, due to the number of inputs, their diversity and potential interdependencies, it is unfeasible to design such algorithm by hand. Our approach is to use some of the supervised machine learning methods to infer the algorithm from the data.

Indeed, this task is suitable for supervised learning, since it is easy to get a training set. For example, consider we have a week long sample of alerts. For each malicious IP address in the sample, we can get information about it from the first six days as an input and information whether it behaved maliciously in the last day as the expected output. By repeating this with data from several weeks it is possible to get very large labeled dataset. Moreover, the algorithm can constantly improve itself during operation by comparing its prediction with actually detected attacks.

2.1   Challenges

Besides issues connected to the machine learning itself, we foresee several other non-trivial problems that have to be solved. Some of them are briefly discussed here.

Reputation in a Context. The definition of reputation score above implies that there may not be a single score for a given entity. It depends on parameters, such as length of time window for prediction, and context, *i.e.* which kind of malicious activity we are interested in. It should be possible to compute an overall reputation score using some appropriate set of parameters and by combining probabilities of various kinds of predicted attacks. But in many cases a more specific score will be needed, *e.g.* focusing on a specific kind of attack. For example, an IP address may be known as a frequent source of SYN flood attacks, so it would have a bad reputation score in the context of (D)DoS attacks, but its score in other contexts, *e.g.* port scanning or sending spam, might be good.

Information Aging. If an IP address is reported to perform some kind of attack, it means it was probably part of a botnet or otherwise controlled by an attacker at the moment of the attack. It is likely that it holds true a minute, an hour or even several days later. However, with increasing time from the last report the probability the address is still malicious is getting lower and we can hardly infer anything from data older than a month. The host behind the address might get fixed or the address might be assigned to another host in the meantime. This adds a degree of uncertainty to all the data which changes over time. Moreover, it is hard to specify how exactly does it change, since it may depend on various aspects, *e.g.* whether the address is statically or dynamically assigned (more on this later).

Information Uncertainty. Many of the pieces of information entering the reputation scoring process may be imprecise, unreliable or otherwise uncertain. They may be, for example, deduced using some heuristic or approximate algorithm, or they may be obtained from an external data source we do not fully trust. Since most of that uncertainty can be described using probability, its incorporation into the reputation scoring process should not a problem in principle, but it will further increase its complexity.

IP to Host Mapping. The main purpose of having a reputation database is to gain knowledge about malicious *hosts*, but we work with IP addresses instead. And mapping of hosts to IP addresses is far from one-to-one due to dynamic address assignment and extensive use of NAT. However, tracking of individual hosts is practically impossible, especially with alert data only (and even if it would be possible, it would be probably considered very privacy intrusive). Therefore, we will at least try to recognize dynamic address ranges and NATs and adjust the scoring method for them. For example, information about dynamically assigned addresses should expire faster than that about static ones. We will draw from many existing works on this topic, *e.g.* [7,11,12].

3   Preliminary Results

We started with analysis of alert data from CESNET's alert sharing system Warden [5]. It currently receives data from 16 detectors, mostly in CESNET2 network. We took two month-long datasets gathered in 2015, containing over 70 million alerts in total, and analyzed them from various points of view.

For example, we confirmed that sources of malicious traffic are geographically distributed non-uniformly, but we found that this distribution is very different for different types of malicious traffic. Also, although most IP addresses were reported only once, there were some addresses that were reported repeatedly for a long time. And for example, while only 8.5 % of scanning addresses were reported in 5 or more days of a month, they were responsible for 65 % of all port scanning events reported in that month. Thus, even knowing only the most active attackers might be very useful. For more information we refer the reader to our technical report [1] which presents more results of the analysis.

Currently we are experimenting with various machine learning methods trying to create the best predictor of network attacks. Also, we continue to gather data from more and more sources, since to successfully capture the global threat landscape by the reputation database, we need to know about a significant portion of all attackers on the Internet. In order to achieve this, we are involved in one national and two international projects about alert sharing.

Acknowledgments. This research was supported by Security Research grant no. VI20162019029 in project Shaing and analysis of security events in Czech republic granted by Ministry of the Interior of the Czech republic. It was also partially supported from IT4Innovations excellence in science project (IT4I XS – LQ1602) and by Brno University of Technology grant no. FIT-S-14-2297.

References

1. Bartoš, V.: Analysis of alerts reported to Warden. Technical report 1/2016, CESNET, February 2016
2. Bartoš, V., Žádník, M.: An analysis of correlations of intrusion alerts in anNREN. In: 19th International Workshop on Computer-Aided Modeling Analysis and Design of Communication Links and Networks (CAMAD), pp. 305–309. IEEE, December 2014
3. Shue, C.A., et al.: Abnormally malicious autonomous systems and their internet connectivity. IEEE/ACM Trans. Netw. **20**(1), 220–230 (2012)
4. Cambridge English Dictionary: reputation. http://dictionary.cambridge.org/dictionary/english/reputation. Accessed January 14, 2016
5. CESNET: Warden – alert sharing system. https://wardenw.cesnet.cz/
6. ENISA: Standards and tools for exchange and processing of actionable information, November 2014
7. Gokcen, Y., Foroushani, V., Heywood, A.: Can we identify NAT behavior by analyzing traffic flows? In: Security and Privacy Workshops (SPW), pp. 132–139. IEEE, May 2014
8. Merriam-Webster Dictionary: Reputation. http://www.merriam-webster.com/dictionary/reputation. Accessed on January 14, 2016
9. Moreira Moura, G.C., Sadre, R., Pras, A.: Internet bad neighborhoods temporal behavior. In: Network Operations and Management Symposium (NOMS), pp. 1–9. IEEE, May 2014
10. Moreira Moura, G.C.: Internet bad neighborhoods. Ph.D. thesis, University of Twente, Enschede. http://doc.utwente.nl/84507/
11. Moreira Moura, G.C., et al.: How dynamic is the ISPs address space? Towards internet-wide DHCP churn estimation. In: 14th International Conference on Networking. IFIP, May 2015
12. Vu, L., Turaga, D., Parthasarathy, S.: Impact of DHCP churn on network characterization. SIGMETRICS Perform. Eval. Rev. **42**(1), 587–588 (2014)

Detecting Advanced Network Threats
Using a Similarity Search

Milan Čermák[✉] and Pavel Čeleda

Institute of Computer Science, Masaryk University, Brno, Czech Republic
{cermak,celeda}@ics.muni.cz

Abstract. In this paper, we propose a novel approach for the detection of advanced network threats. We combine knowledge-based detections with similarity search techniques commonly utilized for automated image annotation. This unique combination could provide effective detection of common network anomalies together with their unknown variants. In addition, it offers a similar approach to network data analysis as a security analyst does. Our research is focused on understanding the similarity of anomalies in network traffic and their representation within complex behaviour patterns. This will lead to a proposal of a system for the real-time analysis of network data based on similarity. This goal should be achieved within a period of three years as a part of a PhD thesis.

Keywords: Similarity search · Network data · Classification · Network threats

1 Introduction

A large number of attacks threaten computer networks. Although the basis of these attacks is similar, a lot of variants exist differing in the protocol used, behaviour, or methods used to avoid their detection. Every day a lot of new attack variants emerge, which represents a challenge for current Intrusion Detection Systems (IDS) [13]. Almost all of these variants require a fast reaction by the authors of these systems to suppress it in time to defend their systems.

Currently, several approaches exists for network anomaly detection [3]. These approaches utilize various techniques for network data analysis from statistical to machine learning methods. Each of these has its own advantages and disadvantages that affect its success in detecting network attacks. Nevertheless, most of the currently used detection tools are based on only statistical analysis and the exact matching of pre-known behavioural patterns, due to their simplicity and lower false positives rate. This approach, however, has a drawback in the inability to detect advanced network threats such as hidden or obfuscated attacks which try to hide their specific characteristics within normal network traffic.

Our research aims to overcome the constraints of these network data analysis approaches through similarity search techniques [15]. This will allow us to combine the advantages of both knowledge-based detection (capable of easily identifying network anomalies without high false positive rates) and cluster-based

© IFIP International Federation for Information Processing 2016
R. Badonnel et al. (Eds.): AIMS 2016, LNCS 9701, pp. 137–141, 2016.
DOI: 10.1007/978-3-319-39814-3_14

detection (which allows us to recognize unknown attack variants). We will focus on network traffic classification based on the same principle as automated images annotation using a similarity search [4]. We plan to classify the analysed network traffic by comparing its similarity with a collection of annotated patterns, reflecting pre-known characteristics of common network attacks. The network traffic will be classified as well as patterns that are closest to it. This approach allows us to take advantage of our knowledge of network anomalies' characteristics, while also revealing their unknown variants.

2 Research Questions

The aim of our research is *to use similarity search techniques for detecting advanced network threats based on similarity of traffic behaviour patterns*. Our intention is to analyse these behaviour patterns in a similar way as a security analyst would usually do, which is an investigation of known attack patterns and searching for their variants. We have identified the following three research questions that reflect the main topics of our research:

1. *How can we characterize similarity in network traffic?*

The majority of current methods for measuring network traffic collect only specific traffic information, which is not comprehensive enough to describe complex behaviour [3]. Thus, we need to explore methods of transforming these simple data into more complex data, and so providing a reasonable amount of information for comparing their similarity. This research question covers the research of a suitable representation of complex behaviour patterns and the selection of appropriate distance functions to measure their similarity.

2. *How can similarity search techniques be utilized for detecting network anomalies?*

Our second research question is focused on research into the transformation possibilities of fundamental methods for detecting network anomalies into the similarity search concept. We plan to utilize network traffic classification based on a similarity search of defined behaviour patterns and propose a proof-of-concept system for detecting anomalies. This research question, besides other factors, also includes the creation of a collection of anomalous behaviour patterns. Based on their similarity, analysed network traffic should also be classified.

3. *What possibilities do the similarity search techniques have for detecting advanced network threats?*

The main goal of the third research question is to explore the benefits of the proposed method for network anomaly detection in detecting advanced network threats, such as hidden or obfuscated network attacks. We will pay attention to the verification of different characteristics of similarity searches and to the various representations of network behaviour patterns. Specifically, we will focus on different functions to measure the patterns' distances and the identification of combinations of smaller behaviour patterns based on general models of network attacks.

3   Proposed Approach

We will focus on the interconnection of similarity search techniques and methods for detecting anomalies in network traffic. To achieve this aim, we will progressively work through the research questions.

3.1   Characterization of a Similarity in Network Traffic

To achieve the aim of our research, it is necessary to understand network traffic characteristics and their similarities, which should be used within anomaly detection. Weller-Fahy et al. [14] demonstrate that almost every method for detecting network anomalies utilizes some kind of a similarity measure. Thus, we plan to study publications focused on this area and extract all the presented network traffic characteristics and their similarity properties. These findings will be evaluated on publicly available datasets [1,5] and on live network traffic to verify their suitability for specifying network behaviour patterns.

Based on the identified traffic characteristics and their similarities, we will specify behaviour patterns which reflect all important events in network traffic. For their specification, we plan to utilize the Bro Network Security Monitor [11] and IP flow monitoring systems [7], which are suitable for collecting data quickly and analysing in large networks. We will consider two forms of network behaviour patterns: *aggregated*, represented by the aggregation of specific traffic features per unit of time and *sequential*, consisting of sequences of traffic features ordered in time. Each of these forms has its advantages and disadvantages, which we want to understand. Our goal is to associate the appropriate form of specific anomalies to correctly represents their characteristics and avoid behavioural aliasing [9], which occurs when anomaly behaviour looks like normal traffic.

During the definition of network traffic behaviour patterns, it is important to consider their characteristics' similarity. The selection of suitable distance functions and methods for their utilization plays a crucial role in our research since it directly affects the success of detecting network anomalies. For this purpose, we plan to analyse publications focused on the similarity measure, discuss our observations with specialists in the similarity search topic and verify our findings using simulated and live network traffic. For this verification, we plan to utilize the Metric Similarity Search Implementation Framework (MESSIF) [2], which provides a suitable environment for verifying the selected similarity measure techniques.

3.2   Utilizing Similarity Search Techniques for Detecting Network Traffic Anomalies

As we are focused on knowledge-based anomaly detection, the next necessary part of our research is the preparation of annotated behaviour patterns corresponding to network anomalies. To define these patterns we plan to analyse current network attacks and anomalies observed within live network traffic. These patterns will form the basis of a proof-of-concept framework. This framework will be based on the kNN-classification [15] of ongoing traffic using a similarity comparison of analysed traffic, with the annotated collection of anomaly behaviour patterns.

The anomaly detection capabilities of the proof-of-concept framework will be verified within real and simulated network traffic using simulated network attacks. To validate within simulated traffic, we plan to utilize the KYPO platform [10] that enables network attacks to be securely testing and provides extensive options for monitoring them. Thanks to this environment we will be able to properly compare our anomaly detection approach with other approaches specified in specialized publications or used within common anomaly detection tools, such as Snort [12], Bro [11] or Flowmon ADS [8].

3.3 Detection of Advanced Network Threats Based on a Similarity Search

After verifying our approach, we will focus on the optimization of similarity search attributes and test different distance functions. The aim of this effort is a complex study of impacts, the possibilities of similarity search techniques and advanced network threat detection. These attacks are characterized by their effort to bypass known detection techniques and by hiding their specific characteristics within normal network traffic, which makes them difficult to detect by current anomaly detection methods.

Apart from the complex behaviour patterns of network traffic anomalies, we will also focus on recognising their individual phases. We plan to extend Drašar's [6] research into network attack models and utilize these models as a basis for defining our anomaly behaviour patterns. The updated form of patterns will correspond to the attack phases instead of the whole attack. We believe that such behaviour patterns will make it possible to identify multiple forms of attacks, even those that are as yet unknown.

4 Conclusion

Since this is the first work of its kind, it is necessary to deal with several complications that come with the application of similarity search into the field of network data analysis. The most important part of such an application is the proper understanding of the similarity of network traffic and the specification of complex behaviour patterns reflecting this similarity. The correct specification of these patterns is crucial for achieving adequate results in the detection of common network threats and their unknown variants.

Acknowledgement. This research was supported by the Security Research Programme of the Czech Republic 2015 - 2020 (BV III/1 VS) granted by the Ministry of the Interior of the Czech Republic under No. VI20162019029 *The Sharing and analysis of security events in the Czech Republic.*

References

1. Barbosa, R.R.R., Sadre, R., Pras, A., van de Meent, R.: Simpleweb/University of twente traffic traces data repository. Technical report TR-CTIT-10-19, Centre for Telematics and Information Technology, University of Twente, April 2010. http://eprints.eemcs.utwente.nl/17829/
2. Batko, M., Novak, D., Zezula, P.: MESSIF: metric similarity search implementation framework. In: Thanos, C., Borri, F., Candela, L. (eds.) Digital Libraries: Research and Development. LNCS, vol. 4877, pp. 1–10. Springer, Heidelberg (2007)
3. Bhuyan, M.H., Bhattacharyya, D.K., Kalita, K.J.: Network anomaly detection: methods, systems and tools. IEEE Commun. Surv. Tutorials 16(1), 303–336 (2014)
4. Budikova, P., Batko, M., Botorek, J., Zezula, P.: Search-based image annotation: extracting semantics from similar images. In: Mothe, J., et al. (eds.) CLEF 2015. LNCS, vol. 9283, pp. 327–339. Springer, Heidelberg (2015). doi:10.1007/978-3-319-24027-5_36
5. CAIDA: The CAIDA UCSD Anonymized Internet Traces 2015-20150219-130000 (2015). http://www.caida.org/data/passive/passive_2015_dataset.xml
6. Drašar, M.: Behavioral detection of distributed dictionary attacks. Doctoral theses, dissertations, Masaryk University, Faculty of Informatics, Brno (2015)
7. Hofstede, R., Čeleda, P., Trammell, B., Drago, I., Sadre, R., Sperotto, A., Pras, A.: Flow monitoring explained: from packet capture to data analysis with NetFlow and IPFIX. IEEE Commun. Surv. Tutorials PP(99), 2037–2064 (2014)
8. INVEA-TECH a.s.: Flowmon ads. Web page (2015). https://www.invea.com/cs/produkty-sluzby/flowmon/flowmon-ads. Accessed 06 Jan 2016
9. Kompella, R.R., Singh, S., Varghese, G.: On scalable attack detection in the network. IEEE/ACM Trans. Netw. 15(1), 14–25 (2007)
10. Kouřil, D., Rebok, T., Jirsík, T., Čegan, J., Drašar, M., Vizváry, M., Vykopal, J.: Cloud-based testbed for simulation of cyber attacks. In: 2014 IEEE Network Operations and Management Symposium (NOMS), May 2014
11. Paxson, V.: Bro: a system for detecting network intruders in real-time. Comput. Netw. 31(23–24), 2435–2463 (1999). http://www.icir.org/vern/papers/bro-CN99.pdf
12. Roesch, M.: Snort - lightweight intrusion detection for networks. In: Proceedings of the 13th USENIX Conference on System Administration, LISA 1999, pp. 229–238. USENIX Association, Berkeley (1999)
13. Symantec Corporation: 2015 Internet Security Threat Report. Technical report 20, Symantec Corporation, April 2015. http://www.symantec.com/security_response/publications/threatreport.jsp
14. Weller-Fahy, D.J., Borghetti, B.J., Sodemann, A.A.: A survey of distance and similarity measures used within network intrusion anomaly detection. IEEE Commun. Surv. Tutorials 17(1), 70–91 (2015)
15. Zezula, P., Amato, G., Dohnal, V., Batko, M.: Similarity Search: The Metric Space Approach, Advances in Database Systems, vol. 32. Springer, New York (2006)

How to Achieve Early Botnet Detection at the Provider Level?

Christian Dietz[1,2]([⊠]), Anna Sperotto[2], Gabi Dreo[1], and Aiko Pras[2]

[1] Universität der Bundeswehr München, Neubiberg, Germany
{christian.dietz,gabi.dreo}@unibw.de
[2] University of Twente, Enschede, Netherlands
{c.dietz,a.sperotto,a.pras}@utwente.nl

Abstract. Botnets are an enabler for many cyber-criminal activities and often responsible for DDoS attacks, banking fraud, cyber-espionage and extortion. Botnets are controlled by a botmaster that uses various advanced techniques to create, maintain and hide their complex and distributed C&C infrastructures. First, they use P2P techniques and domain fast-flux to increase the resilience against take-down actions. Second, botnets encrypt their communication payload to prevent signature based detection. Both, the actions to increase the resilience and the prevention of signature based detection are counteractions against detection techniques. In contrast to existing approaches, our novel approach includes DNS registration behaviour, which we currently analyse for the .com, .net and .org domains, representing half of registered domains on the Internet. Hence, the goal of this PhD research is to enable early detection of the deployment and operation of botnets to facilitate proactive mitigation strategies, whereas current approaches usually detect botnets while these are already in active use. Consequently, this proactive approach prevents botnets to fully evolve their size and attack power. Moreover, as many end users are unable to detect and clean infected machines, our approach tackles the botnet phenomenon without requiring any end user involvement, by incorporating ISPs and domain name registrars. In addition, this will enable the discovery of similar behaviour of different connected systems, which allows detection in cases where bots are registered under domains that are not willing to cooperate.

Keywords: Botnet · Early detection · Provider network · DNS · IP flow monitoring · Coordinated cyber threats · Domain registration behaviour

1 Introduction

Botnets are an enabler for many cyber-criminal activities and often responsible for DDoS attacks, banking fraud and cyber-espionage. As reported in [9,10] such criminal activities cause substantial economic damage. Recent estimations [15] expect that cyber attacks could cost global economy $3 trillion by 2020. Botmasters use various techniques to create, maintain and hide their complex

© IFIP International Federation for Information Processing 2016
R. Badonnel et al. (Eds.): AIMS 2016, LNCS 9701, pp. 142–146, 2016.
DOI: 10.1007/978-3-319-39814-3_15

C&C infrastructures. First, they use P2P techniques [1] and domain fast-flux to increase the resilience against take-down actions. Second, botnets encrypt their communication payload to prevent signature based detection [12].

However, botnets often use the domain name system (DNS) [2,7,11], e.g., to find peers and register malicious domains. Since, botmasters manage a large distributed overlay network, but have limited personal resources, they tend to automate domain registration, e.g. using domain name generation algorithms (DGAs) [17]. Such automatically generated domains share similarities and possibly appear to be registered in close temporal distance. Such characteristics will be used for bot detection, while their deployment is still in preparation.

Hence, the goal of this PhD research is early detection of botnets to facilitate proactive mitigation strategies. Using such a proactive approach prevents botnets from evolving their full size and attack power. As many end users are unable to detect and clean infected machines, we favour a provider-based approach, involving ISPs and DNS registrars. This approach benefits from its overview of the network that allows to discover behavioural similarities of different connected systems. The benefit of tackling distributed large-scale attacks at provider level has been discussed in [13] and demonstrated by [4]. Further, initiatives to incentivize ISPs to mitigate botnets are already ongoing [8]. In addition, several studies discuss and high-light the role of ISPs in detection and mitigation of various cyber threats, e.g. DDoS, Botnets or SPAM [3,14,16].

The work done in [6] addresses the domain registration behaviour of spammers and [5] demonstrated DGA based malware detection by using flow-based techniques. In contrast, our approach includes the detection of malicious DNS registration behaviour, which we currently analyse for the .com, .net and .org domains. These domains represent half of the registered Internet domains. By combining DNS registration behaviour analysis with passive monitoring of DNS requests and IP flows, we are able to tackle botnets throughout their whole life-cycle. This research is still in its initial state and will result in a PhD thesis.

The remaining parts are structured as follows. Section 2, describes the research problem and questions. Section 3, describes our approach. Next, Sect. 4 provides early results and the current state of research. Finally, the paper is concluded in Sect. 5.

2   Research Problem and Questions

The goal of this research is to enable early botnet detection in provider environments. To achieve this goal, our approach is based on large-scale DNS registration behaviour analysis, as this will allow to discover botnet activity in the (pre-)deployment phase of its life-cycle (see Fig. 1). Thus, our novel approach could possibly prevent the botnet from becoming deployed and actively used. Furthermore, the proposed approach takes into account the dynamics of botnet malware and the Internet infrastructure, high data rates, incompleteness of data and encrypted bot communication. In order to tackle the early botnet detection problem, we ask the following questions:

RQ 1: How do botnets interact with the domain name system?
RQ 2: Can domain registration characteristics be used for botnet detection, and
       if yes, how?
RQ 3: (How) Does early detection work, if some registrars do not cooperate?

The approach used for answering these research questions will be described in the next Section. Figure 1 shows the bot life-cycle and relating research questions.

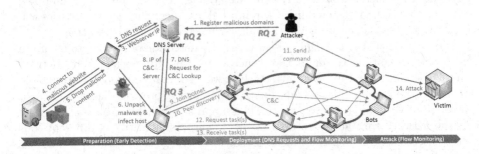

Fig. 1. Detailed overview of botnet operations with mapped research questions.

3   Approach

The goal of this research is to allow faster botnet detection and mitigation. Current approaches are usually limited to detect bots after they already became active or while they are used in attacks. Our approach targets botnet detection in the pre-deployment phase. Therefore, our approach is based on two components: (1) passive monitoring of communication characteristics and (2) DNS registration behaviour analysis. DNS registration analysis allows to detect the preparatory actions of deployment of the C&C infrastructure and the bots. Therefore, our approach allows botnet early detection and consequently facilitates proactive botnet mitigation. In addition, our approach allows botnet detection in the subsequent phases of the bot life-cycle (preparation, infection, peer discovery, malware update, command propagation and attack) by using passive DNS and flow monitoring solutions. This is important, since bots might also be registered at domain providers that are not sharing data.

Research question *1* aims to get insight into the deployment and management of botnets. Therefore, we collect DNS registration data on a daily basis for the *.com*, *.net* and *.net* domains, representing half of the domains registered on the Internet. Second, we query different botnet tracking services and use DGAs to find botnet related records in the domain registration dataset.

Research question *2* aims to extract characteristics of botnets in their deployment phase. Which might allow an early detection and mitigation. To answer this question, we use registration databases of top level domain registrars. Currently, our study involves the *.com, .net, and .org* top level domains.

Research question *3* extends our novel approach to make it applicable in case bots are registered under domains that do not share data. In such cases, our approach might derive flow-based behaviour characteristics based on the knowledge gained in RQ1 and RQ2 for flow-based detection of bots. Flow monitoring solutions provide an overview of large parts of the Internet, in which we expect to find similarities that can be used for detection of bot behaviour.

We will validate our novel approach based on simulations and real-live environments. Further, we compile different datasets. First, we crawl the registration database of multiple top level domains, different botnet domain and IP blocklists with time stamps. This allows us to measure the temporal difference between botnet deployment and detection. Second, we passively capture IP flow data and DNS requests in multiple provider networks to evaluate (a) how accurate our approach can detect the large-scale similarities between distributed bots and (b) determine the temporal delay between malicious domain registration and the first activity. This evaluation also uses IP and DNS blocklists.

4   Early Results

In a first step, we used data captured from Kelihos sinkholing operation, that allowed us to observe real bots in two different states of their life-cycle, peer discovery and job requests. We successfully used our insights gained to developed a concept for flow-based detection. Further, we use multiple DGAs and C&C domain lists to extract the botnet domains (e.g., Zeus, Kelihos.B, Palevo, Drye). Early results show that botnet domains are registered in close temporal distance (bulk registration) and often have structural similarities. Thus, we assume that our approach will be able to accurately detect malicious DNS registration activities and host behaviour of bots.

5   Final Considerations

When provider based solutions are used for bot detection, it is important that data should be accurate and be derived characteristics should be independent of the capture infrastructure. However, as botnets are globally spread, usually one provider can only detect a fraction of a botnet. Therefore, the detection system should run and cooperate across multiple provider networks, by means of providing infrastructure independent detection information and being able to use such data from different networks. ISPs often apply sampling to their flow monitoring to reduce memory consumption, which might be an additional challenge to our approach. Moreover, anti-detection techniques of malware become more sophisticated and often involve encryption and anonymisation techniques. Our approach will be resistant against many of these techniques, due to its high-level overview and independence of packet payloads. The main goal of this approach, should be achieved within a period of four years as part of a PhD thesis.

Acknowledgments. This work is partially funded by EU FP7 Flamingo Network of Excellence Project (ICT-318488).

References

1. Andriesse, D., Rossow, C., Stone-Gross, B., Plohmann, D., Bos, H.: Highly resilient peer-to-peer botnets are here: An Analysis of Gameover Zeus. In: 8th IEEE International Conference on Malicious and Unwanted Software (MALWARE) (2013)
2. Antonakakis, M., Perdisci, R., Nadji, Y., Vasiloglou II, N., Abu-Nimeh, S., Lee, W., Dagon, D.: From throw-away traffic to bots: detecting the rise of DGA-based malware. In: USENIX Security Symposium (2012)
3. Asghari, H., van Eeten, M.J., Bauer, J.M.: Economics of fighting botnets: Lessons from a decade of mitigation. IEEE Secur. Priv. **5**, 16–23 (2015)
4. François, J., Aib, I., Boutaba, R.: FireCol: a collaborative protection network for the detection of flooding DDoS attacks. IEEE/ACM Trans. Netw. (TON) **20**(6), 1828–1841 (2012)
5. Grill, M., Nikolaev, I., Valeros, V., Rehak, M.: Detecting DGA Malware using NetFlow. In: IFIP/IEEE International Symposium on Integrated Network Management (IM) (2015)
6. Hao, S., Thomas, M., Paxson, V., Feamster, N., Kreibich, C., Grier, C., Hollenbeck, S.: Understanding the domain registration behavior of spammers. In: Proceedings of the 2013 Conference on Internet Measurement. ACM (2013)
7. Kwon, J., Lee, J., Lee, H., Perrig, A.: PsyBoG: a scalable botnet detection method for large-scale DNS traffic. Comput. Netw. **97**, 48–73 (2016)
8. Lone, Q., Moura, G.C.M., Van Eeten, M.: Towards incentivizing ISPs to mitigate botnets. In: Sperotto, A., Doyen, G., Latré, S., Charalambides, M., Stiller, B. (eds.) AIMS 2014. LNCS, vol. 8508, pp. 57–62. Springer, Heidelberg (2014)
9. McAfee: The Economic Impact of Cyber-crime. http://www.mcafee.com/mx/resources/reports/rp-economic-impact-cybercrime.pdf. Accessed 05 Jan 2016
10. Mossburg, E.: A Deeper Look at the Financial Impact of Cyber Attacks. http://daily.financialexecutives.org/a-deeper-look-at-the-financial-impact-of-cyber-attacks. Accessed 05 Jan 2016
11. Nguyen, T.D., CAO, T.D., Nguyen, L.G: DGA botnet detection using collaborative filtering and density-based clustering. In: Proceedings of the Sixth International Symposium on Information and Communication Technology. ACM (2015)
12. Rossow, C., Dietrich, C.J.: PROVEX: detecting botnets with encrypted command and control channels. In: Rieck, K., Stewin, P., Seifert, J.-P. (eds.) DIMVA 2013. LNCS, vol. 7967, pp. 21–40. Springer, Heidelberg (2013)
13. Steinberger, J., Schehlmann, L., Abt, S., Baier, H.: Anomaly detection and mitigation at internet scale: a survey. In: Doyen, G., Waldburger, M., Čeleda, P., Sperotto, A., Stiller, B. (eds.) AIMS 2013. LNCS, vol. 7943, pp. 49–60. Springer, Heidelberg (2013)
14. Steinberger, J., Sperotto, A., Baier, H., Pras, A.: Collaborative attack mitigation and response: a survey. In: IFIP/IEEE International Symposium on Integrated Network Management (IM) (2015)
15. Taylor, B.: Cyber Attacks Fallout Could Cost the Global Economy 3 Trillion Dollar by 2020. http://www.techrepublic.com/article/cyberattacks-fallout-could-cost-the-global-economy-3-trillion-by-2020/ Accessed 05 Jan 2016
16. Van Eeten, M., Bauer, J.M., Asghari, H., Tabatabaie, S., Rand, D.: The role of internet service providers in botnet mitigation an empirical analysis based on spam data. TPRC (2010)
17. Yadav, S., Reddy, A.K.K., Ranjan, S., et al.: Detecting algorithmically generated domain-flux attacks with DNS traffic analysis. IEEE/ACM Trans. Netw. **20**(5), 1663–1677 (2012)

Anycast and Its Potential for DDoS Mitigation

Wouter B. de Vries[(✉)], Ricardo de O. Schmidt, and Aiko Pras

University of Twente, Enschede, The Netherlands
{w.b.devries,r.schmidt,a.pras}@utwente.nl

Abstract. IP anycast is widely being used to distribute essential Internet services, such as DNS, across the globe. One of the main reasons for doing so is to increase the redundancy of the service and reduce the impacts of the growing threat of DDoS attacks. IP anycast can be further used to mitigate DDoS attacks by confining the attack traffic to certain areas. This might cause the targeted service to become unavailable only to a fraction of its users. In this PhD research we aim at investigating how IP anycast can be optimized both statically and dynamically to support the mitigation of DDoS attacks.

1 Introduction

IP anycast is an addressing and routing strategy in which multiple physical servers in the Internet are configured with the same logical IP address. This strategy has been widely used to achieve high-availability and redundancy of services over the Internet, such as DNS and CDNs. IP anycast takes advantage of the robustness of BGP (Border Gateway Protocol) routing that defines the catchment of each anycast instance. BGP helps to define the catchment of each anycast instance by, for example, mapping users to the topologically nearest anycast instance. However, anycast catchment has proven to be more chaotic mainly due to routing policies that are defined within and between Autonomous Systems (ASes) [2,9].

There may be multiple motivations for deploying an anycast service. Nowadays, however, redundancy and resilience of Internet services against cyber attacks has gained importance. Particularly resilience against Distributed Denial-of-Service (DDoS) attacks since their occurence and intensity have significantly increased in the recent years [1], and essential Internet services are among their common targets [5]. This problem is exacerbated by the fact that today anyone can perform DDoS attacks [6].

When a service such as DNS is anycasted, there is no single point of failure. An anycasted service has the advantage that when being subject to a DDoS attack, the service might become unavailable to a fraction of the Internet only. That is, the service might be unreachable to the specific "catchment areas" of the affected anycast instances.

Although there are clear benefits to using IP anycast, and it generally works well [3], it alone does not solve the DDoS problem altogether. For example, on November 2015 [5] the DNS root servers received so many requests (caused by a

© IFIP International Federation for Information Processing 2016
R. Badonnel et al. (Eds.): AIMS 2016, LNCS 9701, pp. 147–151, 2016.
DOI: 10.1007/978-3-319-39814-3_16

DDoS) that it saturated the network connections to some of them. The impact of this particular attack was limited though, due to the sheer scale of the DNS root servers; 11 out of 13 root nameservers are anycasted. However, for other (non-) anycasted services the impact can be more severe. Examples of severe service degradation were recently reported by RIPE through their DNS-WG mailing-list[1]: unusual amount of incoming traffic on the authoritative servers for RIPE DNS services on 14-Dec-2015 and on 14-Jan-2016. Recently, also the ccTLD DNS infrastructure of Turkey was attacked, causing severe service degradation [8].

In this PhD research, we will investigate how IP anycast deployments can be optimally planned and used to support service resilience against DDoS attacks. In the following we describe our main research goal, research questions, and planned approaches (Sect. 2). We also describe our first steps on building a global IP anycast service for our research (Sect. 3).

2   Goal, Research Questions, and Approach

The goal of this PhD research is *to investigate methods to optimize anycast deployments in order to improve service resilience against DDoS attacks*. To meet our goal we define four research questions.

First, to gain a more complete understanding of how operators currently mitigate DDoS attacks we define (**RQ1**) as *what are the current DDoS mitigation strategies in use by operators of critical Internet infrastructure*. Our approach will be focused on talking with operators, mainly those involved in the research, to understand their procedures and to be able to tailor improvements to them. To gain insight into the routing changes that will affect the catchment of anycast network when instances are added or removed, we define our second research question as (**RQ2**): *what impact does the deployment of an anycast node in a given anycast network have on the overall catchment?*. To answer this question we will perform active and passive measurements on a real anycast deployment. We are deploying our own experimental anycast testbed, comparable to PEER-ING [7]. This testbed will allow us to announce and withdraw IP prefixes (both IPv4 and IPv6) from each anycast location. We will use the RIPE Atlas [4] framework to perform the active measurements This framework will allow us to closely monitor the effects of anycast node deployment from the perspective of thousands of vantage points worldwide. In addition, we will analyze the deployment from the BGP perspective using passive measurement data, provided by services such as BGPmon, and RIPE's Routing Information Service (RIS).

The knowledge obtained from RQ1 and RQ2 will be used to support anycast planning and instances placement targeting resilience against DDoS attacks. This leads us to our third question (**RQ3**): *in what ways can the catchment of an anycast network be influenced to increase resilience against DDoS attacks?*. By analyzing the data obtained from RQ2 we attempt to find ways of optimizing the placement of nodes, aiming at increasing resilient against DDoS attacks. The key challenge is the fact that BGP routing is influenced by many, both

---

[1] https://www.ripe.net/mailman/listinfo/dns-wg/.

technical and non-technical, factors. Potential methods will be verified in practice by implementing them using the anycast testbed and performing attacks on our own infrastructure. In addition, we will analyze the source of major DDoS attacks to determine if these are mostly located in certain areas. This will further assist in optimizing the anycast catchment for mitigation.

Finally, we determine if it is possible, and to what extent, the anycast catchment can be changed dynamically to further strengthen the DDoS mitigating property of an anycast network. For example by actively adding and/or removing instances during a DDoS attack near the source of attack traffic. Therefore, we define our fourth and final research question (**RQ4**) as: *how can service resilience be positively influenced by dynamically changing the composition of the anycast network?*. The results from RQ1, RQ2 and RQ3 as well as the operational experience gained using the anycast testbed will all contribute to answering RQ4. A potential solution is the deployment of inactive (i.e., sleeping) instances that are activated on demand in the case of an attack. This setup can potentially lead to reduced operational costs as compared to the static approach of RQ3. The challenge lies in the fact that setting up anycast instances is not trivial because it might depend on routing policies and peering agreements involved in the anycast IP prefix announcement.

3   Preliminary Steps

As described above, one of the key components of this research plan is the anycast testbed. There is an existing testbed called PEERING [7], which provides the sort of functionality that is required for the research that we intend to carry out. However, access is limited in duration and in functionality, in the sense that experiments are very bandwidth limited. Therefore, we have started the development of a new anycast testbed in collaboration with SURFnet (the Dutch NREN). Having access to this testbed will allow us to perform experiments without having to rely on models that may or may not be an accurate representation of reality. During the past months we have obtained a /24 IPv4 prefix and a /48 IPv6 prefix, which are of a sufficient size to be announcable through BGP. Furthermore, we have started development of an anycast management webinterface (TANGLER) that will allow for easy control of the IP prefixes announcement from our anycast instances. The intention is that it will also allow advanced experiments to be performed by scheduling route announcements and withdrawals.

Figure 1 shows the locations of the (planned) anycast instaces of our testbed. Nodes are configured using an orchestration tool (Ansible), which makes it trivial to add new instances. Management occurs through a single management node to which each of the anycast instances maintains a VPN-connection. The BGP announcements for each of the anycast instances can currently be controlled through a webinterface running on the management node. In the future we will also focus on creating a more local anycast network in Europe, constisting solely

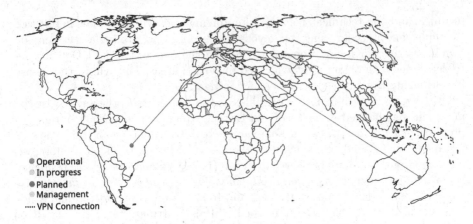

Fig. 1. Map of (planned) anycast nodes

of European nodes. This will allow for studies on local impacts of DDoS mitigation and routing policies. Once our anycast testbed is fully operational, we plan to open the access (restricted by request and nature of research) to other researchers.

4 Final Considerations

The PhD research outlined in this paper is planned to be carried out in a period of four years, which has started in late 2015 and will end in 2019. The preliminary steps (Sect. 3) have been carried out in the first six months.

Acknowledgements. This research is partially funded by SIDN and NLnet Labs through the projects DAS (http://www.das-project.nl) and SAND (http://www.sand-project.nl), by the EU FP7 FLAMINGO NoE (318488), and the SURFnet Research on Networks project.

References

1. Akamai: Q3 2015 state of the internet security report (2015). https://www.akamai.com/us/en/about/news/press/2015-press/akamai-releases-third-quarter-2015-state-of-the-internet-security-report.jsp
2. Anwar, R., Niaz, H., Choffnes, D., Cunha, I., Gill, P., Katz-Bassett, E.: Investigating interdomain routing policies in the wild. In: Proceedings of the 2015 ACM Conference on Internet Measurement Conference. IMC 2015, pp. 71–77. ACM, NewYork (2015). http://doi.acm.org/10.1145/2815675.2815712
3. Liu, Z., Huffaker, B., Fomenkov, M., Brownlee, N., claffy, K.: Two days in the life of the DNS anycast root servers. In: Uhlig, S., Papagiannaki, K., Bonaventure, O. (eds.) PAM 2007. LNCS, vol. 4427, pp. 125–134. Springer, Heidelberg (2007). http://dx.doi.org/10.1007/978-3-540-71617-4_13
4. NCC, R.: Ripe atlas (2016). https://ripe.atlas.net

5. Root Server Operators: Events of 2015-11-30 (2015). http://root-servers.org/news/events-of-20151130.txt
6. Santanna, J.J., Sperotto, A.: Characterizing and mitigating the DDoS-as-a-service phenomenon. In: Sperotto, A., Doyen, G., Latré, S., Charalambides, M., Stiller, B. (eds.) AIMS 2014. LNCS, vol. 8508, pp. 74–78. Springer, Heidelberg (2014)
7. Schlinker, B., Zarifis, K., Cunha, I., Feamster, N., Katz-Bassett, E.: Peering: an as for us. In: Proceedings of the 13th ACM Workshop on Hot Topics in Networks, p. 18. ACM (2014)
8. Sozeri, E.K.: Turkish internet hit with massive DDoS attack (2015). http://www.dailydot.com/politics/turkey-ddos-attack-tk-universities/
9. Teixeira, R., Shaikh, A., Griffin, T., Rexford, J.: Dynamics of hot-potato routing in IP networks. SIGMETRICS Perform. Eval. Rev. **32**(1), 307–319 (2004). http://doi.acm.org/10.1145/1012888.1005723

Short Papers — Methods for Management and Security

Context-Aware Location Management of Groups of Devices in 5G Networks

Konstantinos Chatzikokolakis[1](✉), Alexandros Kaloxylos[2],
Panagiotis Spapis[2], Chan Zhou[2], Ömer Bulakci[2],
and Nancy Alonistioti[1]

[1] Department of Informatics and Telecommunications,
National and Kapodistrian University of Athens, Athens, Greece
{kchatzi,nancy}@di.uoa.gr
[2] European Research Center, Huawei Technologies Duesseldorf GmbH,
Munich, Germany
{alexandros.kaloxylos,panagiotis.spapis,
chan.zhou,Oemer.Bulakci}@huawei.com

Abstract. Location Management (LM) is an important function of mobile cellular networks that enables network to locate the users. Mechanisms applicable in legacy systems are not able to cope with the vast increase of devices and the strict communication requirements expected in 5G networks. In this paper we propose a novel scheme for LM that exploits mobility context of User Equipments (UEs), keeps track of their location with high accuracy and pages small number of cells when incoming calls arrive. The analysis shows that Location Management is significantly benefitted from the proposed mechanisms.

Keywords: Location Management · Location update · Paging · 5G cellular networks · Cluster-based communication

1 Introduction

According to forecasts [1], by the year 2019, operators worldwide will have to support more than 8 billion of smart phones. This vast increase of wirelessly connected devices increases the control information that has to be exchanged thus stretching the networks' performance to the limits. Additionally, the deployment of small cells will also create additional overhead to the network components [2]. To efficiently support such communication needs, it is required to optimize control functions for avoiding bottlenecks of control channels. One specific area that calls for improvement is Location Management (LM) [3], which comprises two processes, one related to Location/Tracking Area Update (TAU) and one to location search/paging. The former is an occasional process during which UE regardless if it is in idle or connected state, sends information related to its current location to the network – the user location is linked to Tracking Areas (TA) which are sets of cells, and Tracking Area List (TAL) is a list of TAs assigned to a is a user. When a users moves out of the boundaries of his TAL he performs a TAU and the network assigns to him a new TAL. On the other hand, paging is a process initiated from the network so as to discover the UE when it is in idle state.

© IFIP International Federation for Information Processing 2016
R. Badonnel et al. (Eds.): AIMS 2016, LNCS 9701, pp. 155–159, 2016.
DOI: 10.1007/978-3-319-39814-3_17

Between TAU and Paging processes there is a signaling trade-off. In particular, large TAs and/or long TALs reduce the number of updates but increase drastically the number of paged cells and vice versa. Hence, it is important to use LM schemes that keep a concise set of location information for all UEs, while optimizing the signaling overhead for finding them.

Existing solutions for TAU can be roughly classified into two main categories; user-centric approaches that monitor the activity of each user [4, 5], and solutions dictating periodic network reconfiguration based on network traffic to alleviate the overall LM signaling [6, 7]. Paging schemes aim to improve the efficiency of the 3GPP standards (i.e. blanket-paging scheme [8]) that is used in legacy systems by minimizing the paging signaling. In [9, 10] sequential paging of subsets of TAL is proposed. These are further extended with Paging Area shuffling and concurrent users' serving [11], or hierarchical paging schemes [12, 13].

One promising solution for handling the location update and paging challenges in 5G networks relates to group communication. Group based TAU will enable performing updates more often thus significantly reducing the load in the paging channels. Towards this direction, in this paper we propose a Context Aware Location Management (CALM) mechanism in which only one device performs TAU on behalf of a group which is being formed for application specific purposes (e.g., car to car communication) based on context information. The intra cluster communication (for cluster formation and maintenance) takes place using secondary interfaces such as 802.11p.

The rest of the paper is organized as follows. In Sect. 2 we introduce our novel mechanism for efficient LM of UEs in wireless networks. The method can be applied to vehicular ad-hoc networks, and machine-type communication devices, but can also be applied to human-centric devices. Then, in Sect. 3 we provide the experimental results that compare our solution against the state of the art solutions and finally, Sect. 4 concludes the paper summarizing our work.

2 CALM - Context-Aware Location Management

The proposed solution solves the mentioned problems and achieves efficient LM for UEs in wireless networks. The mechanism takes advantage of existing clustering protocols (e.g., the one in [14]), where grouping is done based on time-stamp, speed, direction, etc. UEs form groups dynamically without network intervention and Cluster Members (CMs) have the possibility to communicate directly without the intervention of the cellular network.

The main goals of the mechanism are to allow a single device, namely Cluster Head (CH), to update the location of all the CMs, thus reducing the TAU overhead for all the members of the cluster, increase the granularity of TAUs and thus increase considerably the paging accuracy. During the initialization phase the CMs of a group will turn off periodic TAU timers and stop sending TAUs when crossing the borders of a TA. From that point on CMs will communicate only with the CH via a secondary interface (e.g. 802.11p). In the proposed scheme when the CH sends group's location performs an RRC connection request but instead of requesting the establishment of a signaling connection so as to perform a higher layer TAU, sends a modified RRC connection establishment request to signify that instead of establishing a signaling connection, the BS should reject this request and notify instead the Location Server about the current location of the group. Whenever the Location Server receives the CH's location from the BS it may proactively produce a new TAL based on this information and the Group ID. Then, since the network is aware of the location and the cluster information, it may accurately determine the Paging Area and there is no need to communicate the updated TAL to the CH or any CM, leading thus to further reduction of signaling. The proposed scheme, called RRC+ since it is based on enhancements of the RRC protocol, can be used on per cell basis or on any other granularity defined by the network, after CH performs cell selection/reselection procedure. Additionally, in order to avoid missing the track of any device when a UE becomes CM it may keep the standard LM functions active until the network has received the information regarding it being member of a group. During this time the UE is still reachable through paging, since the network is aware of the TAL of the device. When a CM leaves the group, based on its location, it determines whether location update is needed or not.

3 Performance Evaluation

In this section we present the evaluation outcomes of the assessment of the CALM solution that we propose against the Group Mobility Management (GMM) which has proven to be more efficient than 3GPP standards [5]. As described afore, CALM is triggered when the CH has selected to camp to a new eNB. Cell Reselection rate, cluster size and the Location Updates affect the performance of LM techniques and thus, in this section we measure the Location Update and Paging signaling overhead of the CALM solution for various scenarios with different cluster sizes, TAL sizes and Cell Reselection rates. Table 1 summarizes the assumptions of our analysis.

In Fig. 1(a) we present the way the cluster size affects the number of TAUs executed in the GMM mechanism and the messages sent in CALM. Since the traditional TAU does not have the same signaling messages as the Location update scheme we follow, the comparison was made based on signaling events triggered in each case, so as to have a common metric between our solution and the GMM mechanism. As shown in the figure our solution has fewer messages exchange for cluster size greater than 10 devices which is a rather small number taking into account the device density in 5G scenarios [18]. Such gains are achieved because in our solution when a device enters

Table 1. Parameter values for CALM assessment

Parameter	Assessment value
Cluster size	{1, 5, 10, 20, 30, 40, 50} nodes
TAL size	{15, 30, 45, 60, 75, 90, 105, 120} cells
Cell reselection rate	30 per UE/h [15]
Location update rate (for GMM [4])	1.2 per UE/h [16, 17]
Time window duration	3 h
Periodic location update timer T_{PLU}	56 min

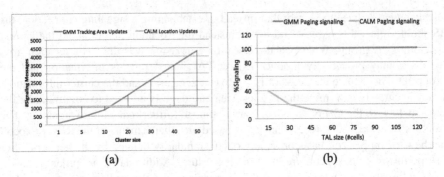

Fig. 1. (a) Location updates for various cluster sizes (b) Paging signaling

the group it deactivates all its Location Update procedures, while in the GMM mechanism the devices will still have their periodic TAU active. Thus, even for groups with rather small number of group members, our solution outperforms the GMM solution whereas for large numbers of group members, our algorithm achieves very significant gains.

Although, there are cases that our mechanism increases the signaling overhead for Location Update compared to the GMM solution (e.g., when having small clusters), in paging, the accuracy of our mechanism is always better, as the paging area is too restricted, while in GMM mechanism there is the need to page the whole TAL. Figure 1(b) below demonstrates the percentage of signaling reduction for paging procedure for various TAL sizes. The gains range from 60 % for small TAL size up to 95 % for very large TAL size. It is worth mentioning that our solution eliminates completely the possibility of page misses, due to the mobility context that is always up-to-date in the network. On the contrary, the GMM solution (as well as the other SOTA solutions) fails to avoid page misses, which may occur when a UE leaves a group, because the group maintenance is based on the periodic TAU of each device.

4   Conclusions

In this paper we have proposed a novel context-aware mechanism for efficient location management of groups of users/devices in wireless networks so as to reduce the overhead of the signaling channels. The method targets vehicular ad-hoc networks, machines, etc. but can also be applied to human-centric devices that move in groups (e.g., crowd movement). Our mechanism exploits already formed groups, for performing group based TAU. Thus, only one device (the cluster head) performs frequent TAUs on behalf of the overall group. This enables reduction on the TAU overhead and significantly precise paging compared to the state of the art solutions.

References

1. White Paper, Cisco Visual Networking Index: Global Mobile Data Traffic Forecast Update (2014–2019)
2. The Impact of small cells on MME signaling, Application Note, Alcatel Lucent. http://resources.alcatel-lucent.com/asset/169993
3. Chatzikokolakis, K., et al.: A survey of location management mechanisms and an evaluation of their applicability for 5G cellular networks. Recent Adv. Commun. Netw. Technol. **3**(2), 106–116 (2014)
4. Pollini, G.P., Chih-Lin, I.: A profile-based location strategy and its performance. IEEE J. Sel. Areas Commun. **14**(8), 1415–1424 (1997)
5. Fu, H., Lin, P., Yue, H., Huang, G., Lee, C.: Group mobility management for large-scale machine-to-machine mobile networking. IEEE Trans. Veh. Technol. **63**(3), 1296–1305 (2014)
6. Lei, Y, Zhang, Y.: Efficient location management mechanism for overlay LTE macro and femto cells. In: IEEE International Conference on Communications Technology and Applications, ICCTA 2009, pp. 420–424, 16–18 October 2009
7. Razavi, S.M., Yuan, D.: Performance improvement of LTE tracking area design: a re-optimization approach. In: Proceedings of the 6th ACM International Symposium on Mobility Management and Wireless Access (MobiWac 2008), pp. 77–84. ACM, New York, NY, USA (2008)
8. GPP TS 36.304: Evolved Universal Terrestrial Radio Access (E-UTRA); User Equipment (UE) procedures in idle mode
9. Xiao, Y., Chen, H., Guizani, M.: Performance evaluation of pipeline paging under paging delay constraint for wireless systems. IEEE Trans. Mob. Comput. **5**(1), 64–76 (2006)
10. Lin, Y.-B., Liou, R.-H., Chang, C.-T.: A dynamic paging scheme for long-term evolution mobility management. In: Wireless Communications and Mobile Computing. Wiley, New York (2013). http://dx.doi.org/10.1002/wcm.2371
11. Xiao, Y.: A parallel shuffled paging strategy under delay bounds in wireless systems. IEEE Comm. Lett. **7**(8), 367–369 (2003)
12. Xiao, Y., Chen, H., Guizani, M., Chen, H.-H.: Optimal pipeline paging load balancing for hierarchical cellular networks. IEEE Trans. Mob. Comput. **11**(9), 1532–1544 (2012)
13. Xiao, Y., Chen, H., Du, X., Zhang, Y., Chen, H.-H., Guizani, M.: On hierarchical pipeline paging in multi-tier overlaid hierarchical cellular networks. IEEE Trans. Wirel. Comm. **8**(9), 4406–4410 (2009)
14. Vodopivec, S., Bester, J., Kos, A.: A survey on clustering algoritms for vehicular ad-hoc networks. In: 35th International Conference on Telecommunications and Signal Processing (TSP) (2012)
15. Catovic, A., Narang, M., Taha, A.: Impact of SIB scheduling on the standby battery life of mobile devices in UMTS. In: 16th IST Mobile and Wireless Communications Summit, pp. 1–5, 1–5 July 2007
16. Widjaja, I., Nuzman, C.: Mitigating signaling overhead from multi-mode mobile terminals. In: 2011 23rd International Teletraffic Congress (ITC 2011), San Francisco, CA, pp. 55–62 (2011)
17. Managing the Signalling Traffic in Packet Core. Bell Labs, Alcatel Lucent. http://resources.alcatel-lucent.com/asset/155160
18. Fallgren, M., Timus, B. (eds.): Future radio access scenarios, requirements and KPIs. METIS deliverable D1.1, March 2013. https://www.metis2020.com/documents/deliverables/

Scalability and Information Exchange Among Autonomous Resource Management Agents

Siri Fagernes[1](✉) and Alva L. Couch[2]

[1] Department of Technology, Westerdals Oslo ACT, Oslo, Norway
siri.fagernes@westerdals.no
[2] Tufts University Medford, Medford, MA, USA
couch@cs.tufts.edu

Abstract. We study a scenario of autonomous resource management agents, aiming for fulfilling a management goal of balancing value of service with cost. We aim for a model of management based on fully distributed knowledge, avoiding traditional challenges associated with centralized approaches. Our results indicate that lack of information about the actions of other agents can be mitigated via direct observation of each agent's environment.

Keywords: Resource management · Autonomous agents · Cloud management · Reactive approaches · Decentralized knowledge

1 Introduction

We present a theoretical model of distributed resource management, which is analysed through simulations. The model involves autonomous agents that must collaborate, either directly or indirectly, to achieve a common management goal (balance cost and value). Our previous work has focused on studying the coordination of only two agents, whose primary task is to control resource usage in the system they operate, and try to estimate, based on varying information access, how to adjust their current resource level optimally.

In this paper, we study the coordination of a larger group of autonomous resource management agents, in the setting where they share a common resource pool. The main research objective is to determine whether the agents can achieve their common goal in an optimal manner without exchanging local information with each other. We see that individual observations of behaviour observed by each agent can replace information exchanged directly among the agents, which increases scalability.

2 Related Work

An automatic resource management process can be either *reactive* [1] or *predictive*, determined by how resources are automatically adjusted. The predictive

© IFIP International Federation for Information Processing 2016
R. Badonnel et al. (Eds.): AIMS 2016, LNCS 9701, pp. 160–164, 2016.
DOI: 10.1007/978-3-319-39814-3_18

approaches are typically based on having access to a complete model of the system, which (in theory) gives the ability to provide QoS guarantees and a more detailed view of the dynamics of the system. The major challenge of such approaches is getting access to such knowledge, if it is even possible. Examples of model-based approaches are [2–7].

Reactive approaches are designed to make appropriate decisions when one lacks complete knowledge of the system model, and are used in complex systems for decision making. A common challenge in reactive approaches is that the learning algorithm responsible for making decisions requires a *training period* for gathering data to make appropriate action decisions. Examples of reactive approaches are presented in [1,8–12].

Most of the existing approaches are based on *centralized knowledge*. This means they have the advantage of one component having complete system knowledge, which avoids the complexity of coordination and communication overhead in distributed approaches. However, centralized approaches in larger complex systems – cloud systems – have several drawbacks, including limited scalability, single point of failure issues, and potential bottlenecks.

3   Method and Approach

Our management scenario consists of ten autonomous resource management agents $Q_i, i \in [1, 10]$, where Q_i controls a separate resource variable R_i. Each resource variable (or component in the system) contributes to delivering a service S. The main objective of management is to achieve efficient management of all the different system resource variables, with the objective to achieve a balance between cost and produced value. To determine value of the delivered service, the performance metric P represents job throughput, i.e., the reciprocal of response time. The response time will depend on how the system is able to cope with current load, which is defined as an arrival rate of requests. The system performance is hence defined as the request completion rate, and is modeled approximately as

$$P = B - \frac{\gamma L}{R} \tag{1}$$

where B is the baseline performance (the performance when the system is not affected by load). γ is a constant representing resource-intensitivity, i.e. increased γ represents a service in which the service requests are more resource-intensive. Further, we define associated value of service to be proportional to throughput, so that

$$V = \alpha P = \alpha \sum_{i=1}^{10} P_i. \tag{2}$$

Similarly, cost C is proportional to resource use R, so that

$$C = \beta R. \tag{3}$$

The autonomous agents (resource controllers), which are responsible for making decisions on resource use and adjustments, do *not* have access to knowledge of this theoretical model of the system's performance. Each agent observes how system value V changes with changes in R_i, $\Delta V/\Delta R_i$, and based on the local knowledge of associated cost $C(R_i)$, the closure operator can make an estimate of how net value $N = V - C$ changes with R_i, by calculating $\Delta N/\Delta R_i$. If this value is positive, the controller will increase R_i, and if it is negative, decrease R_i. This *hill-climbing* strategy will converge to a global optimum whenever the objective function N is convex.

The agents have a perception of how system value depends on resource use. The theoretically correct global value is defined as

$$V = \alpha(B - \frac{\gamma L}{R_1} - \frac{\gamma L}{R_2} - \dots - \frac{\gamma L}{R_{10}}) \tag{4}$$

In our experiments, the agents assume that the value-resource relationship is modelled as

$$V = a\frac{L}{R} + b. \tag{5}$$

4   Results

When each operator receives individual value feedback, no external information about other operators is needed. When the operator has a semi-accurate model of the system dynamics and current system load, all operators perform very close to optimal, as seen in Fig. 1.

Providing less information (no load information) reduces the precision of the results (Fig. 2a), but the performance (achieved net value) is quite close to the theoretical optimum (Fig. 2b).

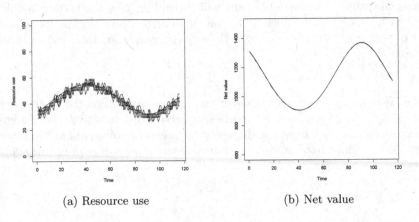

(a) Resource use   (b) Net value

Fig. 1. 10 operators, each controller has information about current load. $\gamma = 1$ for all agents.

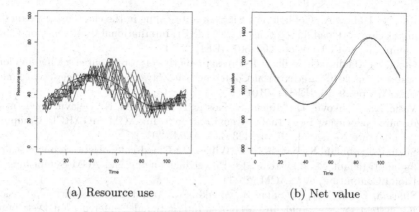

(a) Resource use   (b) Net value

Fig. 2. 10 operators, each controller lacks information about system load. $\gamma = 1$ for all agents.

5   Conclusion and Further Work

Although there has been significant research efforts aimed at achieving fully de-centralized management of larger complex systems, most proposed solutions so far has been based on either pure centralization or partly centralization based on delegation of responsibility. Our work has been an attempt to achieve pure de-centralized management. The goal of our approach is trying to come up with an intermediate approach between delegated management and agent based manage-ment, in which there is higher predictability and more accurate goal achievement.

This study indicates that to achieve self-optimising behaviour among autonomous agents working towards the same goal, without direct coordina-tion, excessive information exchange or centralized knowledge, is the ability to monitor their indvidual behaviour. This means that developing efficient feed-back mechanisms is a crucial factor to reduce the need for global information exchange.

One particular issue that we have not studied, is how the precision of our proposed model is affected by more heavily varying system load. Also, to test the robustness of the model, this needs to be implemented in a real scenario.

References

1. Lim, H.C., Babu, S., Chase, J.S., Parekh, S.S.: Automated control in cloud com-puting: challenges and opportunities. In: Proceedings of the 1st Workshop on Auto-mated Control for Datacenters and Clouds, pp. 13–18. ACM (2009)
2. Dawoud, W., Takouna, I., Meinel, C.: Elastic VM for cloud resources provisioning optimization. In: Abraham, A., Lloret Mauri, J., Buford, J.F., Suzuki, J., Thampi, S.M. (eds.) ACC 2011, Part I. CCIS, vol. 190, pp. 431–445. Springer, Heidelberg (2011)

3. Roy, N., Dubey, A., Gokhale, A.: Efficient autoscaling in the cloud using predictive models for workload forecasting. In: 2011 IEEE International Conference on Cloud Computing (CLOUD), pp. 500–507. IEEE (2011)

4. Gong, Z., Xiaohui, G., Wilkes, J.: Press: predictive elastic resource scaling for cloud systems. In: 2010 International Conference on Network and Service Management (CNSM), pp. 9–16. IEEE (2010)

5. Vasić, N., Novaković, D., Miučin, S., Kostić, D., Bianchini, R.: Dejavu: accelerating resource allocation in virtualized environments. In: ACM SIGARCH Computer Architecture News, vol. 40, pp. 423–436. ACM (2012)

6. Shen, Z., Subbiah, S., Xiaohui, G., Wilkes, J.: Cloudscale: elastic resource scaling for multi-tenant cloud systems. In: Proceedings of the 2nd ACM Symposium on Cloud Computing, p. 5. ACM (2011)

7. Sharma, U., Shenoy, P., Sahu, S., Shaikh, A.: A cost-aware elasticity provisioning system for the cloud. In: 2011 31st International Conference on Distributed Computing Systems (ICDCS), pp. 559–570. IEEE (2011)

8. Padala, P., Shin, K.G., Zhu, X., Uysal, M., Wang, Z., Singhal, S., Merchant, A., Salem, K.: Adaptive control of virtualized resources in utility computing environments. In: ACM SIGOPS Operating Systems Review, vol. 41, No. 3, pp. 289–302 (2007)

9. Demberel, A., Chase, J., Babu, S.: Reflective control for an elastic cloud application: an automated experiment workbench. In: Proceedings of the 2009 Conference on Hot Topics in Cloud Computing (HotCloud 2009) (2009)

10. Meng, S., Liu, L., Soundararajan, V.: Tide: achieving self-scaling in virtualized datacenter management middleware. In: Proceedings of the 11th International Middleware Conference Industrial Track, pp. 17–22. ACM (2010)

11. Calheiros, R.N., Vecchiola, C., Karunamoorthy, D., Buyya, R.: The Aneka platform and Qos-driven resource provisioning for elastic applications on hybrid clouds. Future Gener. Comput. Syst. **28**(6), 861–870 (2012)

12. Martinez, J.F., Ipek, E.: Dynamic multicore resource management: a machine learning approach. IEEE Micro **29**(5), 8–17 (2009)

Analysis of Vertical Scans Discovered by Naive Detection

Tomas Cejka[1]([⊠]) and Marek Svepes[2]

[1] CESNET, a.l.e., Zikova 4, 160 00 Prague 6, Czech Republic
cejkat@cesnet.cz
[2] FIT, CTU in Prague, Thakurova 9, 160 00 Prague 6, Czech Republic
svepemar@fit.cvut.cz

Abstract. Network scans are very common and frequent events that appear in almost every network. Generally, the scans are quite harmless. Scanning can be useful for network operators, who need to know state of their infrastructures. Contrary, scans can be used also for gathering sensitive information by attackers. This paper describes a simple detection method that was used to detect vertical scans. Our aim is to show results of long-term measurement on backbone network and to show that it is possible to detect scans efficiently even with a simple method. The paper presents several interesting statistics that characterize network behavior and scanning frequency in a large high-speed national academic network.

1 Introduction

Network scanning is a common and frequent activity that can be observed in almost every network infrastructure. It is a normal benign mechanism used by network operators or automatic tools for monitoring and management. A network scan is based on probing targets to recognize the active ones. That is a scan referred as *horizontal*. Scans can also probe ports of one target. Such scans are called *vertical*. A *block* scan is a combination of horizontal and vertical scans.

Scans are easily performed even by attackers. Attackers can use scanning to search for publicly available services and vulnerable devices in the internet. Even though network scanning is basically harmless, current researches show, that it can be dangerous in some ways. Bartos et al. in [2] show correlation between network scans and attacks (e.g. bruteforce guessing of passwords or DoS attacks) that follow scans. Similarly in [11], Raftopoulos et al. discuss their observation about high probability of malware infection of devices that had been scanned previously. Therefore, it is important not to underestimate a danger of scans.

Unfortunately, there is no universal detection method, that would be suitable for all sizes of networks. According to [13], large transit networks or National Research and Education Network (NREN) infrastructures require a special detection approach. The main issues related to such networks are: high speed, wider diversity of IP addresses, lack of knowledge about end-hosts' configuration, asymmetric routing, coexistence with other monitoring and detection tasks without interference. This paper presents observations from the perimeter

© IFIP International Federation for Information Processing 2016
R. Badonnel et al. (Eds.): AIMS 2016, LNCS 9701, pp. 165–169, 2016.
DOI: 10.1007/978-3-319-39814-3_19

of CESNET2. It is Czech NREN, a backbone and a transit network. Based on observations, we created a straightforward detection method.

2   Related Work

Bhuyan et al. presents a taxonomy of network scanning and a survey of some existing detection approaches in [3]. Using the taxonomy, we can classify the detection method presented in our paper as a threshold-based method.

One of the well-known methods is a Threshold Random Walk (TRW) proposed for scan detection by Jung et al. in [7]. The detection method was implemented as a part of Bro [10]. Sridharan et al. in [13] points out disadvantage of TRW that needs knowledge about the configuration of end-hosts. In backbone networks there are several issues that complicate scan detection. However, it is still useful to perform detection even on backbone level. The paper investigates effectiveness of existing methods and proposes a new method Time-based Access Pattern Sequential hypothesis testing (TAPS). Lee et al. is one of the most closely related works to this paper. Their paper presents a report about observed port scans. The authors analyzed two weeks of traffic at University of California, San Diego (UCSD) using Snort [12]. The paper was written in 2003 and the authors discovered 9,927 vertical scans. Whereas, we have been monitoring network traffic from CESNET2 more recently (2015) for longer time (two months) and average number of discovered vertical scans in two weeks was 203,000.

As it was shown, there are various approaches of scan detection. However, we used a simple flow-based method with thresholds and filtering flow records.

3   Detection Algorithm

The detection algorithm uses information from basic flow records (source and destination IP addresses and ports, protocol, #packets, #bytes). The principle of algorithm was inspired by characteristics of scans generated by nmap [8]. Analysis showed that scans are composed of plenty flow records with small number of packets (≤ 4) transferred between the source IP (potential attacker) and a destination IP (victim).

We have focused on a default scanning technique supported by nmap. It uses Transmission Control Protocol (TCP) packets with set SYN flag. This simulates establishment of a new TCP session and the target should reply with SYN+ACK if the probed port is opened. The detection results of SYN scans are verifiable manually even in unknown network traffic of backbone since TCP normal traffic from a host always contain not only SYN flag and should not imply plenty RST responses. Detection of other scan types is more complicated due to verification of false positives and missing ground truth in the real backbone traffic.

The detection algorithm is based on analysis of the number of destination ports per source IP and uses threshold for number of ports. It is important to remember all unique destination ports for each pair of addresses separately. The source IP is a potential source of scan, meanwhile, the destination IP is a victim.

The algorithm was implemented as a module of the NEMEA system [1,5] and is described in more detail in [4].

4   Evaluation and Measurements

Our measurement started on 31. 10. 2015 and stopped on 31. 12. 2015. In total, we observed over 388 billion flow records from all monitoring probes. That is on average 76,283 flows per second with over 144,506 flows per second in peak.

In order to find a reasonable threshold for the number of destination ports, we measured average number of destination ports used by a source IP. Moreover, we were interested in maximal number of destination ports per source. These observations were based only on TCP protocol without any consideration of TCP flags. Values were computed in hour intervals. The results are shown in Fig. 1. It is clear that intensive port scans probe a lot of destination ports. Therefore, the maximal number of ports is over fifty thousand. Most of source addresses use only a few destination ports and therefore total average number of destination ports per source IP lies around ten. From this point of view, with respect to memory consumption, the threshold was experimentally set to 50. Distribution function in Fig. 2 shows, that over 99 % addresses use less then 50 destination ports. Therefore, source IP address which has used 50 or more destination ports is considered as a potential attacker.

On average, network scans take about 1.2 % of observed flows. Alerts are aggregated in 10 min time windows. Using the aggregation, the number of alerts decreases by 94 %. Average length of the aggregated alerts is about 2 min 45 s and over 2,600 destination ports are being probed. On average, there are over 580 aggregated alerts per hour.

During the analysis of scans targeted to a single target, we found distributed scans as well. Scanning hosts were active for about 10 min and each scanner probed about 2,000 ports. Altogether, scanners probed disjoint sets of ports.

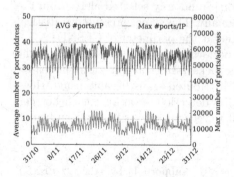

Fig. 1. Average and maximal number of destination ports per source IP.

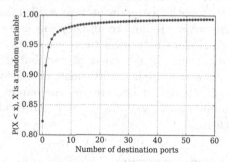

Fig. 2. Distribution function of number of destination ports per source IP.

According to the results, most of scans occur at 8:00 and 13:00 UTC. The rest of scans are spread over all hours. We expect that the distribution is caused by peaks of traffic that we normally see in these hours.

The deployed detector has discovered non-uniform intensity of some scans that was changing in time. For example, 47,156 addresses of Czech university of economics were scanned during 19 mins by one block scan. The highest intensity (over 10,000 alerts per minute) was in the middle of the scan. Over 50 ports were probed for each target.

Memory consumption of the module was analyzed by valgrind [9]. The measurement was performed for almost two days and the module consumed 576 MiB during the peak. The amount of required memory is decreased due to auto-regulation based on removing inactive addresses. It is set by module's threshold.

The used detection algorithm, from its nature, suffers from some limitation. The algorithm skips repeating SYN flows with the same destination port. Such traffic is assumed to be benign traffic. However, this fact can be easily exploited by scanners to avoid the detection. Distributed scans are generally difficult to detect. Large botnets can scan the whole internet using just a few packets generated by each bot [6]. A distributed scan can be detected by our algorithm if and only if at least some of the scanners fulfill conditions to be detected (e.g. number of destination ports threshold).

5   Conclusion

Vertical scans are frequent events that occur in almost every computer network. In this paper, we have proven this fact by observation of the vertical scans in the backbone network. The measurement showed that it is possible to detect scans with a simple straightforward detection algorithm using commodity hardware.

The proposed algorithm is limited to detection of TCP scans, however, it can be deployed in large network infrastructures and analyze huge volume of data. On average, there are about 580 aggregated alerts per hour that are detected by the implemented detection module. Some randomly selected alerts from the two-month measurement were verified manually. This paper presented statistical characteristics and results of scans detected at the perimeter of CESNET2.

Modern network attacks are mostly performed by botnets. Therefore, the importance of detection of distributed attacks (scans in our case) increases. According to our observations, intensive distributed scans became usual. However, the larger botnets are, the harder the detection is because each bot can probe just a few ports and so it is difficult to recognize bot's traffic from benign clients.

Acknowledgments. This work was partially supported by the "CESNET E-Infrastructure" (LM2015042) and CTU grant No. SGS16/124/OHK3/1T/18 both funded by the Ministry of Education, Youth and Sports of the Czech Republic.

References

1. Bartoš, V., et. al.: Nemea: framework for stream-wise analysis of network traffic. Technical report, CESNET, a.l.e. (2013). http://www.cesnet.cz/wp-content/uploads/2014/02/trapnemea.pdf

2. Bartos, V., Zadnik, M.: An analysis of correlations of intrusion alerts in an NREN. In: 2014 IEEE 19th International Workshop on Computer Aided Modeling and Design of Communication Links and Networks (CAMAD), pp. 305–309. IEEE (2014)

3. Bhuyan, M.H., et al.: Surveying port scans and their detection methodologies. Comput. J. **54**, 1565 (2011)

4. Cejka, T., Svepes, M.: Vertical Scan Detector README. https://github.com/CESNET/Nemea-Detectors/tree/master/vportscan_detector

5. CESNET, a. l. e.: NEMEA: Network Measurements Analysis Framework. https://github.com/CESNET/Nemea

6. Dainotti, A., et al.: Analysis of a /0 stealth scan from a botnet. In: Proceedings of the 2012 ACM Conference on Internet Measurement Conference, pp. 1–14. ACM (2012)

7. Jung, J., et al.: Fast portscan detection using sequential hypothesis testing. In: Proceedings 2004 IEEE Symposium on Security and Privacy, pp. 211–225. IEEE (2004)

8. Lyon, G.F.: Nmap network scanning: the official Nmap project guide to network discovery and security scanning. In: Insecure (2009)

9. Nethercote, N., Seward, J.: Valgrind: a framework for heavyweight dynamic binary instrumentation. In: ACM SIGPLAN Notices, vol. 42, pp. 89–100. ACM (2007)

10. Paxson, V.: Bro: a system for detecting network intruders in real-time. Comput. Netw. **31**(23), 2435–2463 (1999)

11. Raftopoulos, E., Glatz, E., Dimitropoulos, X., Dainotti, A.: How dangerous is internet scanning? In: Steiner, M., Barlet-Ros, P., Bonaventure, O. (eds.) TMA 2015. LNCS, vol. 9053, pp. 158–172. Springer, Heidelberg (2015)

12. Roesch, M., et al.: Snort: Lightweight intrusion detection for networks. In: LISA, vol. 99, pp. 229–238 (1999)

13. Sridharan, A., Ye, T., Bhattacharyya, S.: Connectionless port scan detection on the backbone. In: 25th IEEE International Performance, Computing, and Communications Conference. IPCCC 2006, p. 10. IEEE (2006)

Author Index

Printed in the United States
By Bookmasters